United States Department of Agriculture

I0411815

Climate Change Effects on Vegetation in the Pacific Northwest: A Review and Synthesis of the Scientific Literature and Simulation Model Projections

David W. Peterson, Becky K. Kerns, and Erich K. Dodson

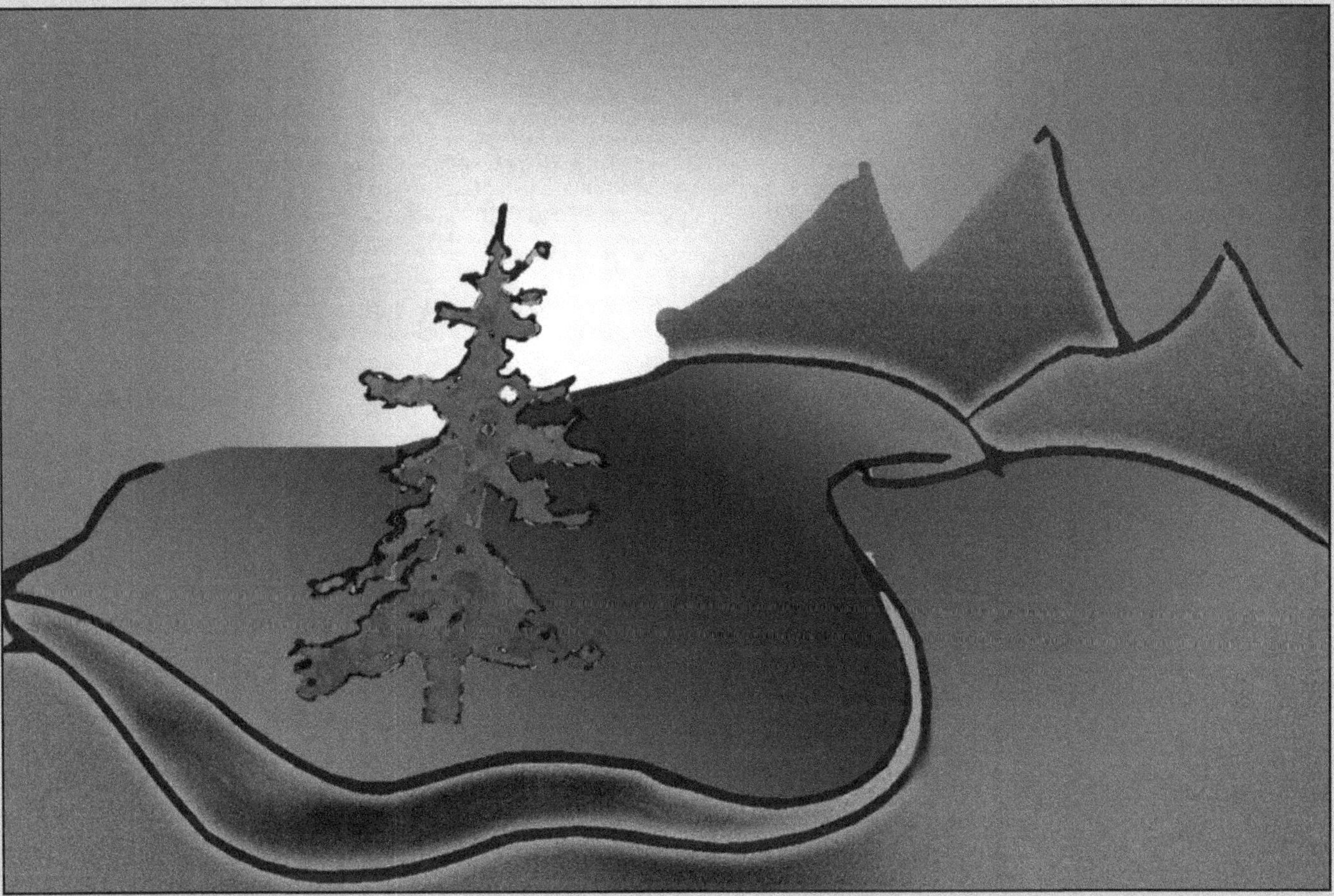

Forest
Service

Pacific Northwest
Research Station

General Technical Report
PNW-GTR-900

September 2014

Authors

David W. Peterson is a research forester, U.S. Department of Agriculture, Forest Service, Pacific Northwest Research Station, Forestry Sciences Laboratory, 1133 N Western Avenue, Wenatchee, WA 98801; **Becky K. Kerns** is a research ecologist, U.S. Department of Agriculture, Forest Service, Pacific Northwest Research Station, Forestry Sciences Laboratory, 3200 SW Jefferson Way, Corvallis, OR 97331; and **Erich K. Dodson** is a faculty research assistant, Oregon State University, Forest Ecosystems and Society Department, 321 Richardson Hall, Corvallis, OR 97331-5752.

Cover art by Mari L. Schramm, USDA Forest Service.

Climate Change Effects on Vegetation in the Pacific Northwest: A Review and Synthesis of the Scientific Literature and Simulation Model Projections

David W. Peterson, Becky K. Kerns, and Erich K. Dodson

U.S. Department of Agriculture, Forest Service

Pacific Northwest Research Station

Portland, Oregon

General Technical Report, PNW-GTR-900

Published in cooperation with:

U.S. Department of the Interior

Bureau of Land Management

Abstract

Peterson, David W.; Kerns, Becky K.; Dodson, Erich K. 2014. Climate change effects on vegetation in the Pacific Northwest: a review and synthesis of the scientific literature and simulation model projections. Gen. Tech. Rep. PNW-GTR-900. Portland, OR: U.S. Department of Agriculture, Forest Service, Pacific Northwest Research Station. 183 p.

The purpose of this study was to review scientific knowledge and model projections on vegetation vulnerability to climatic and other environmental changes in the Pacific Northwest, with emphasis on five major biome types: subalpine forests and alpine meadows, maritime coniferous forests, dry coniferous forests, savannas and woodlands (oak and juniper), and interior shrub-steppe. We started by reviewing and synthesizing the scientific literature on past and projected changes in atmospheric carbon dioxide concentrations and climate for the Pacific Northwest (and globally), and how these changes are likely to influence snowpack dynamics, soil water availability, and selected disturbance regimes. We also reviewed and synthesized the scientific literature on plant growth, reproduction, and mortality in response to changing climate and disturbance regimes, and on the ability of plants to adapt to these changes through phenotypic plasticity, local adaptation, and migration. We then reviewed the strengths and weaknesses of several types of simulation models commonly used to project vegetation responses to climate change and discussed recent model projections of vegetation responses to future climate change scenarios in the Pacific Northwest, as well as how these projections might best be used in developing management plans for forests and rangelands. We next reviewed the existing scientific literature on plant sensitivity and adaptation to changing climate and disturbance regimes for five major vegetation biomes in the Pacific Northwest. We concluded with a discussion of current approaches and resources for developing climate change adaptation strategies, including restoring historical vegetation structure and composition, promoting resistance to change, promoting resilience to change, and facilitating anticipated responses to change.

Keywords: Climate change, Pacific Northwest, forests, rangelands, vulnerability.

Summary

Climate change is expected to profoundly alter vegetation structure and composition, terrestrial ecosystem processes, and the delivery of important ecosystem services over the next century. Since 1750, atmospheric carbon dioxide (CO_2) concentrations have increased from 280 to over 390 parts per million (ppm) and are expected to continue rising, reaching 450 to 875 ppm by 2100. Global mean temperatures have increased by about 0.74 °C over the past century and could increase by another 2 to 4 °C by 2100 as a result of increasing atmospheric concentrations of CO_2 and other greenhouse gases. Globally, mean annual precipitation is expected to increase somewhat, but there is great uncertainty about precipitation changes for any particular region, including the Pacific Northwest. Temperature and precipitation changes are expected to alter soil water availability by altering amounts and timing of precipitation, snowpack dynamics, and evapotranspiration rates.

Climatic variability and change can affect plant physiological processes, including altering growth and reproductive phenology, rates of photosynthesis and respiration, root and shoot growth, and seed production. Elevated CO_2 can influence many of these same processes, either enhancing or offsetting climatic influences. Biotic interactions, population and community dynamics, and ecosystem processes can further modify vegetation responses to elevated CO_2 and changing climate. Changing climate can also alter disturbance processes—including stress-related mortality, fire, and insect outbreaks—and their impacts on vegetation.

Vegetation adapts to changing climate in various ways. Individual plants adjust to climatic changes through phenotypic plasticity via traits like growth phenology and biomass allocation. Populations adapt through natural selection of traits based on genetic variability within the population and through long-distance pollen or seed dispersal. Species also adapt to changing climate through migration, resulting in establishment of new populations in favorable habitats and the extirpation of populations from unfavorable habitats.

Computer simulation models offer a way to project vegetation responses to various scenarios of future atmospheric CO_2 concentrations and climate based on current knowledge about species biogeography, physiological requirements, biotic interactions, and ecosystem processes. Unfortunately, we rarely know enough to fully inform model functions, and no single model can address all vegetation processes at all spatial scales, so judgment must be used in selecting models and interpreting their outputs.

The Pacific Northwest supports a diverse flora, ranging from grasslands to forests and from deserts to rain forests. Environmental controls differ considerably among the major biomes but mostly involve winter temperatures, snowpack duration, summer vapor pressure deficits, and soil water deficits. Climate can also influence vegetation structure and function indirectly through the effects of fire and other climate-influenced disturbance agents. Climate change and elevated CO_2 can increase or reduce the importance of these environmental controls, alter disturbance processes, and alter the importance of biotic interactions like facilitation and competition, with uncertain impacts on vegetation communities and ecosystem functioning. Experimental studies give insights into potential vegetation responses but cannot represent the range of complexity found in most ecosystems.

Modeling results suggest that subalpine forests may be the Pacific Northwest biome most vulnerable to climatic changes, but there are no projections for alpine meadows. Models suggest that maritime coniferous forests may be somewhat vulnerable to future climate change in the southern portion of the region. There is little model agreement about projected changes for dry coniferous forests, and only limited model output for the shrub-steppe biome. Models remain critical for alerting us to the potential magnitude of the effects of climate and, although they are imperfect, model projections complement projections made based on empirical studies and expert opinion. The role of models in this context is not to predict the future but rather to help (1) identify the more plausible future conditions, (2) highlight vulnerabilities with respect to specific resources and management objectives, (3) provide insight into the range and variability of potential climate change effects, (4) examine general ecological principles rather than predict the behavior of a specific ecosystem, and (5) inform strategic decisionmaking processes and policy development.

Although climate change clearly could have profound effects on global and regional vegetation, it is less clear what those effects will be and what activities land managers could or should undertake to preserve values at risk and continue to achieve a variety of management objectives. Previous publications have endorsed a "toolbox approach" to managing ecosystem responses to climate change that features three basic adaptive strategies: (1) promote resistance to change, (2) promote resilience to change, and (3) facilitate response to change. We note that the "historic range of variability" concept has a limited application and that future conditions will strongly differ from those of the past. Applying our knowledge and understanding of processes, interactions, and conditions to the current biophysical, social, and economic environment may be the best way to manage for uncertainty and change.

Contents

Chapter 1: Introduction

Climate change is expected to profoundly alter vegetation structure and composition, terrestrial ecosystem processes, and the delivery of important ecosystem services over the next century. Climate influences the spatial distribution of major vegetation biomes, the abundance of species and communities within biomes, biotic interactions, and the geographic ranges of individual species. Climate influences the rates at which terrestrial ecosystems process water, carbon, and nutrients and deliver ecosystem services like fresh water, food, and biomass. Climate also influences the disturbance processes that shape vegetation structure and composition and are often the catalysts for vegetation change. Climate-induced vegetation changes have important implications for wildlife habitat, biodiversity, hydrology, future disturbance regimes, ecosystem services, and the ability of ecosystems to absorb and sequester carbon from the atmosphere.

Land managers are currently seeking scientific information about the potential effects of climate change on terrestrial vegetation and practical approaches to managing forests and rangelands to sustain key ecosystem functions, ecosystem services, and critical habitats, despite considerable uncertainty about the nature and magnitude of future climatic change. Scientists have learned much about historical rates and patterns of vegetation change during glacial and interglacial epochs; forest growth responses to past climatic variability; plant physiological responses to higher temperature and carbon dioxide levels; and how phenotypic plasticity, local adaptation, and migration can help individual plants, plant populations, and species adapt to changing environments. However, this information has not been adequately reviewed, synthesized, and compiled into a form that managers can use to establish short- and long-term management objectives and adopt appropriate management strategies. Research-management partnerships are needed to develop science-based management approaches, fill knowledge gaps in critical areas, and resolve apparent conflicts in the scientific record.

Federal land management agencies recognize the potential for climate change to disrupt terrestrial ecosystems and alter delivery of vital ecosystem services and are working to develop appropriate and effective approaches for facilitating ecosystem adaptations to climate change. For example, the 2010–2015 U.S. Department of Agriculture Strategic Plan established a strategic goal to "ensure our national forests and private working lands are conserved, restored, and made more resilient to climate change, while enhancing our water resources," and set the "restoration of watershed and forest health as a core management objective of the National Forests and Grasslands" (USDA 2010). Building upon this and the Strategic Framework, the Forest Service then developed a National Roadmap for Responding to Climate Change (USDA FS 2010) that called for the Forest Service to respond to projected

Climate-induced vegetation changes have important implications for wildlife habitat, biodiversity, hydrology, future disturbance regimes, ecosystem services, and the ability of ecosystems to absorb and sequester carbon from the atmosphere.

Vegetation vulnerability to environmental changes depends on three factors: exposure, sensitivity, and adaptability.

climatic changes by (1) assessing risks and vulnerability for ecosystems, (2) identifying knowledge gaps and policy shortcomings that limit our ability to respond appropriately, (3) establishing and supporting monitoring programs to detect ecosystem responses to climate change and assess the effectiveness of management activities, (4) educating the public and federal land managers about climate change science and its implications for natural resources, and (5) encouraging the development and use of research-management partnerships to address climate change issues. The U.S. Department of the Interior (USDI) developed a comparable climate-change-response strategy in 2009 (USDI 2009) and has created two national networks to provide an integrated approach to climate change science and adaptation. Eight regional USDI Climate Science Centers provide scientific information, tools, and techniques that land managers can apply to anticipate, monitor, and adapt to climatic changes at regional to local scales. The USDI Landscape Conservation Cooperatives represent a network of public-private partnerships that seek to address broad-scale conservation and adaptation issues (USDI 2009).

This study reviews scientific knowledge and model projections regarding vegetation vulnerability to climatic and other environmental changes in the Pacific Northwest, with emphasis on five major biome types: subalpine forests and alpine meadows, maritime coniferous forests, dry coniferous forests, juniper savannas and woodlands, and interior shrub-steppe. We adopt the approach that vegetation vulnerability to environmental changes depends on three factors: exposure, sensitivity, and adaptability (Glick et al. 2011, IPCC 2007c).

- **Exposure** depends on the type, magnitude, rate, and variability of observed (or projected) changes in climate; climatic interactions with site factors like topographic position and vegetation structure that alter plant biophysical environments; and climate-induced changes in disturbance regimes.

- **Sensitivity** refers to the degree to which the environmental changes alter plant growth, reproduction, and mortality; plant population dynamics; biotic interactions; plant community dynamics, and ecosystem functioning.

- **Species adaptability** refers to physiological, evolutionary, and biogeographical changes that can occur at the individual, population, and species levels to mitigate negative impacts of environmental changes or allow a species to better take advantage of environmental changes.

This report reviews knowledge about observed and projected environmental changes and how vegetation might respond, providing a foundation for the development of vulnerability assessments related to vegetation. We draw on experimental, observational, and modeling studies to summarize current scientific knowledge about vegetation responses to climate change in a broad sense, and specifically in the context of major vegetation types in the Pacific Northwest. Material in this document overlaps somewhat with other recent reviews of potential vegetation responses to climate change in the Pacific Northwest (Aubry et al. 2011, Bachelet et al. 2011, Chmura et al. 2011, Halofsky et al. 2011, Littell et al. 2010) but is intended to be more general and cover a wider range of vegetation types. We provide minimal guidance on developing adaptation plans or other management strategies related to climate change, as these topics are well covered in other recent publications (e.g., Glick et al. 2011, Halofsky et al. 2011, Littell et al. 2012, Peterson et al. 2011, Stephens et al. 2010, Swanston and Janowiak 2012).

Chapter 2: Observed and Projected Environmental Changes

Earth's atmosphere and climate system are changing. Long-term climate records show that global mean temperatures have increased over the past century, and scientists are now convinced that this warming is partly due to human activities (IPCC 2007a). Atmospheric concentrations of greenhouse gases have risen significantly over the past century or more and will continue to rise over the next century, likely causing further increases in mean global temperatures (IPCC 2007a). Climatic changes have, in turn, altered the seasonal timing and magnitude of snowpack accumulation and melt, stream peak and base flows, soil water recharge, evapotranspiration, and soil water deficits (IPCC 2007b). Changing climatic conditions may also be driving changes in disturbance processes such as wildfires and insect outbreaks. All of these environmental changes have the potential to affect Pacific Northwest vegetation, although the relative exposure of vegetation to these different environmental changes may vary through time and among biomes.

In this chapter, we describe historical observations and model projections of environmental changes at the global and regional (Pacific Northwest) scales. Environmental changes of interest include atmospheric carbon dioxide (CO_2) concentrations, mean temperature and precipitation, snowpack hydrology, and soil water dynamics. Some observations of environmental changes are limited to the past century or so (the period of instrumental records), while others extend back in time for millennia or longer (e.g., CO_2 concentrations in air bubbles from ice cores).

Historically, climatic changes have been driven primarily by changes in the Earth's radiation balance.

Mechanisms for Changes in Temperature and Precipitation

Historically, climatic changes have been driven primarily by changes in the Earth's radiation balance. This radiation balance is a function of the amount of incoming solar radiation (insolation), the fraction of incoming solar radiation that is reflected, and the amount of longwave radiation (heat) that is radiated back to space (fig. 2.1). Each of these elements has changed over time, either directly as a result of physical processes (e.g., variations in the Earth's orbit) or indirectly through feedbacks in the system (e.g., reflectance of incoming solar radiation by surface snow and ice).

Evidence strongly suggests that Ice Age cycles are driven, in large part, by variations in Earth's orbital characteristics (often called Milankovich cycles) that alter the tilt of the Earth on its rotational axis and the eccentricity of the Earth's orbit (fig. 2.2). The tilt angle influences the seasonality of incoming solar radiation and the amount of summer solar radiation reaching the higher latitudes. Eccentricity in the Earth's orbit controls variation in the distance of the Earth from the sun throughout the year, and the season in which the Earth is closest to the sun.

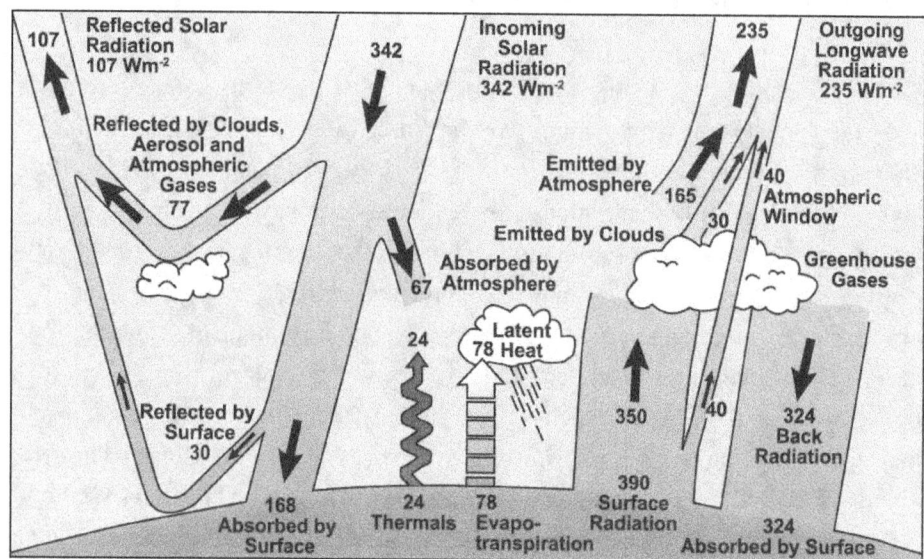

Figure 2.1—Estimate of the Earth's annual and global mean energy balance. Over the long term, the amount of incoming solar radiation absorbed by the Earth and its atmosphere is balanced by the Earth and atmosphere releasing the same amount of outgoing longwave radiation. About half of the incoming solar radiation is absorbed by the Earth's surface. This energy is transferred to the atmosphere by warming the air in contact with the surface (thermals), by evapotranspiration, and by longwave radiation that is absorbed by clouds and greenhouse gases. The atmosphere in turn radiates longwave energy back to Earth as well as out to space. (Source: Kiehl and Trenberth 1997. From LeTreut et al. 2007, FAQ 1.1, fig. 1.)

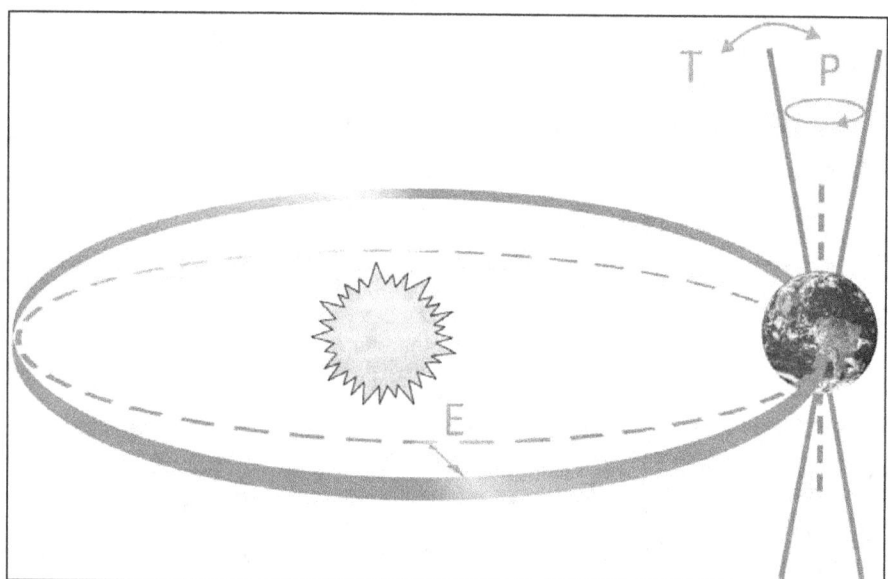

Figure 2.2—Schematic of the Earth's orbital changes (Milankovitch cycles) that drive ice age cycles. "T" denotes change in the tilt (or obliquity) of the Earth's axis, "E" denotes changes in the eccentricity of the orbit (owing to variations in the minor axis of the ellipse), and "P" denotes precession, that is, changes in the direction of the axis tilt at a given point in the orbit. (Source: Rahmstorf and Schellnhuber 2006. From Jansen et al. 2007, FAQ 6.1, fig. 1.)

Although these variations in the Earth's orbit have little effect on total incoming solar radiation, they do influence the amount of solar radiation reaching different latitudes in different seasons. These seasonal variations in incoming solar radiation help drive glacial and interglacial cycles by interacting with seasonal variations in the amount of incoming radiation that is reflected by the atmosphere (e.g., cloud cover) and land surface (e.g., snow cover), and by strengthening or weakening feedback between climate and the radiative properties of the Earth. Milankovitch cycles function over time periods of 23,000 to 100,000 years (Hays et al. 1976) but are not expected to trigger global cooling and another Ice Age for about 30,000 years (Jansen et al. 2007).

There are additional factors that influence incoming solar radiation and operate on much shorter time scales. The best known is the 11-year solar cycle associated with sunspot activity, which creates small, systematic variations in incoming solar radiation (Gray et al. 2010). None of these factors produce large effects (the solar cycle produces changes of 0.1 percent), but they may still influence the climate system.

Incoming solar radiation is reduced by the amount of radiation that is reflected back into space, either by the Earth's atmosphere or the land surface (fig. 2.1). Cloud cover reduces net incoming radiation as water droplets reflect incoming radiation. Because cloud cover frequency and extent varies seasonally and between oceans and land masses, variability in incoming solar radiation is believed to be most important for summer months in the Northern Hemisphere, when cloud cover is relatively low and where large land masses can absorb the incoming radiation. Volcanic activity is another major source of aerosols (small suspended particles in the atmosphere) that can reflect incoming radiation and reduce net absorbed radiation at the Earth's surface. A single volcanic eruption can alter global climate, but only for a short time as the residence time of ash particles in the atmosphere is limited to one to several years. However, periods of elevated volcanic activity (multiple events) can reduce global mean temperatures significantly, as appears to have happened in the middle of the 19th century.

Surface albedo influences the fraction of net incoming solar radiation that is absorbed at the Earth's surface (fig. 2.1). Ice, snow, and concrete reflect large fractions of incoming solar radiation, while green vegetation, wet soil, and water bodies absorb most of incoming solar radiation. Therefore, incoming solar radiation during summer in the Northern Hemisphere is most likely to contribute to global warming (or cooling) because the large land masses with large areas of green vegetation and little snow or ice tend to absorb a large fraction of incoming solar radiation.

Land surface albedo changes seasonally with vegetation and snow cover and can change over time owing to human land use changes and natural disturbances. Climate can also produce long-term changes in surface albedo via feedback mechanisms. A cooling climate allows snow cover to persist longer and allows glaciers to expand, thereby increasing reflectance and reducing absorption of incoming solar radiation, which can lead to further cooling of the climate. Similarly, a warming climate can reduce the duration of snow cover and shrink glaciers while potentially increasing plant cover, thereby increasing absorption of solar radiation and promoting further warming.

Transmission of longwave (heat) radiation from the Earth back into space is the third major factor influencing the Earth's radiation balance and global mean temperatures (fig. 2.1). Incoming solar radiation that is absorbed at the Earth's surface heats the Earth's surface and that heat is radiated back to the atmosphere. Some longwave radiation is reflected back toward the Earth's surface by atmospheric "greenhouse" gases, which act as a blanket of sorts, warming the lower atmosphere and allowing it to support a wide variety of biological organisms. This process forms the basis of the "greenhouse effect" and the atmospheric gases that contribute most to retention of long-wave radiation are called "greenhouse gases" (fig. 2.3). Water vapor is by far the most common greenhouse gas (about 80 percent

> **Some longwave radiation is reflected back toward the Earth's surface by atmospheric "greenhouse" gases, which act as a blanket of sorts, warming the lower atmosphere and allowing it to support a wide variety of biological organisms.**

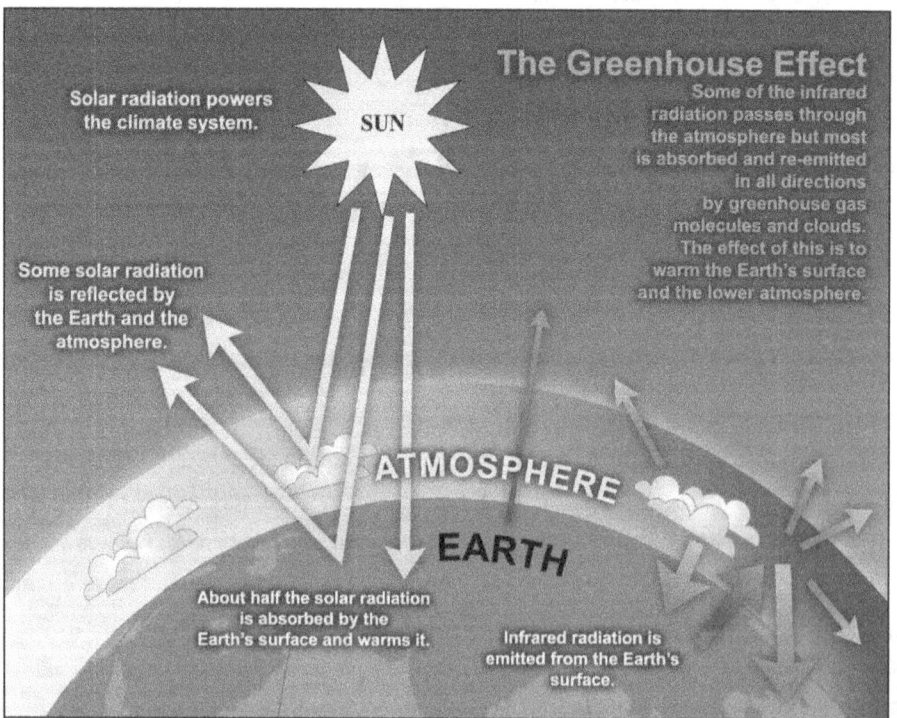

Figure 2.3—An idealized model of the natural greenhouse effect. (From Le Treut et al. 2007, FAQ 1.3, fig. 1.)

of greenhouse gases by mass, 90 percent by volume) and produces 66 to 85 percent of greenhouse warming. Effects of water vapor on air temperatures become clear if one compares summer day-night temperature differences in humid versus non-humid climates. High humidity traps heat, reducing night-time cooling (e.g., a hot, muggy night).

In addition to water vapor, major natural greenhouse gases include CO_2, nitrous oxide (N_2O), and methane (CH_4). These gases also produce a warming of the lower atmosphere but differ from water vapor in two important ways. First, they persist in the atmosphere much longer, on average, than water vapor. The mean atmospheric residence time for a molecule of water is estimated at about 10 days, while mean residence times are estimated at 12 years for CH_4, 100 years for CO_2, and over 100 years for N_2O. Second, humans have directly and indirectly contributed to increased atmospheric concentrations of CO_2, N_2O, and CH_4 (fig. 2.4).

Models strongly suggest that increasing concentrations of greenhouse gases in the atmosphere are producing ("forcing") much of the warming that has been observed in the past century (IPCC 2007b). Increasing concentrations of these greenhouse gases may produce additional warming by increasing evaporation

Models strongly suggest that increasing concentrations of greenhouse gases in the atmosphere are producing ("forcing") much of the warming that has been observed in the past century.

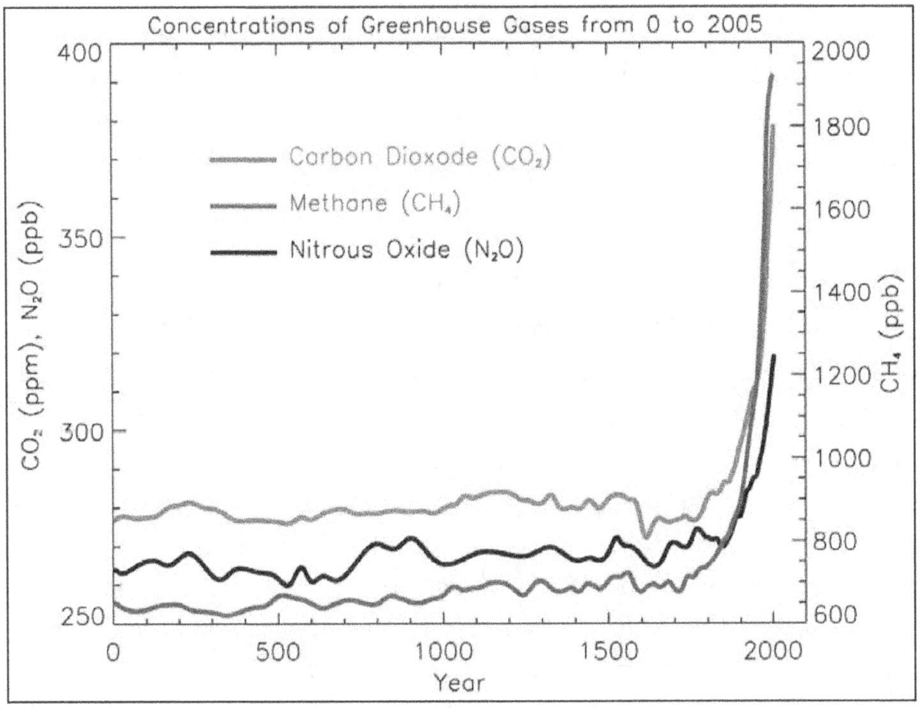

Figure 2.4—Atmospheric concentrations of important long-lived greenhouse gases over the past 2,000 years. Increases since about 1750 are attributed to human activities in the industrial era. Concentration units are parts per million (ppm) or parts per billion (ppb), indicating the number of molecules of the greenhouse gas per million or billion air molecules, respectively, in an atmospheric sample. (From Forster et al. 2007, FAQ 2.1, fig. 1.)

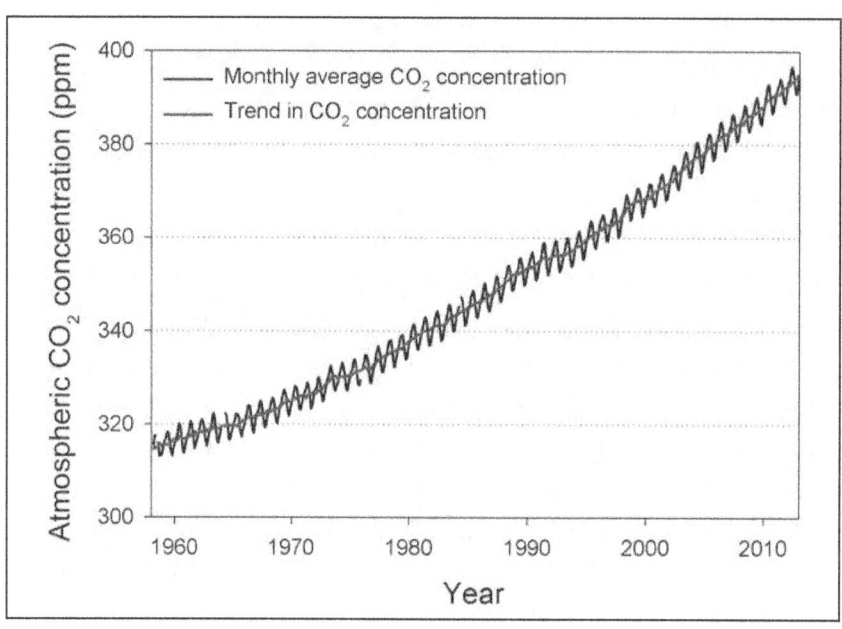

Figure 2.5—Observed changes in atmospheric carbon dioxide (CO_2) concentration (ppm [parts per million]), 1958–2012, at Mauna Loa Observatory in Hawaii. (Data from Tans and Keeling 2013).

Atmospheric CO_2 concentrations have been steadily increasing since the start of modern industrialization.

of water and atmospheric water vapor concentrations. In addition, atmospheric warming forced by increasing concentrations of greenhouse gases may lead to further increases in greenhouse gases owing to release of CO_2 from warming oceans and release of CO_2 and CH_4 from boreal soils following the melting of permafrost layers.

Atmospheric CO_2 Concentrations

Observed Changes in Atmospheric CO_2 Concentrations

Atmospheric CO_2 concentrations have been steadily increasing since the start of modern industrialization, from about 280 parts per million (ppm) in 1750 (as measured from air bubbles in dated ice cores) to about 394 ppm in 2012 (Hofmann et al. 2009, Keeling et al. 1976, Tans and Keeling 2013) (fig. 2.4). Much of this increase (about 68 percent) has occurred in the last 50 years, with atmospheric CO_2 concentrations rising by about 79 ppm (315 to 394 ppm) since 1960 (fig. 2.5). Hofmann et al. (2009) analyzed atmospheric CO_2 data from Mauna Loa in Hawaii and noted that (1) CO_2 concentrations have been increasing exponentially since measurements began in 1958, (2) the doubling period for both anthropogenic CO_2 concentrations and the rate of change in CO_2 concentrations is about 31 years, and (3) changes in atmospheric CO_2 concentrations have closely tracked human population growth over the past 50 years.

Over geological time scales, atmospheric CO_2 concentrations have fluctuated considerably between glacial and interglacial periods. Atmospheric CO_2 concentrations have generally been low during cold glacial periods (Ice Ages), with values as low as 180 ppm being observed in ice core records from the past 650,000 years (Jansen et al. 2007). Atmospheric CO_2 concentrations were higher during warm, interglacial periods. Although CO_2 concentrations in the ice core records were limited to 300 ppm prior to the increases of the past century, proxy evidence suggests that CO_2 concentrations exceeded current levels for extended periods over the past 400 million years, particularly during warm periods of the Pliocene (3 to 5 million years ago) and the Paleocene-Eocene Thermal Maximum (about 55 million years ago) (Jansen et al. 2007). Historical records also indicate that, in the past, changes in global mean temperatures have preceded changes in atmospheric CO_2 concentrations, suggesting that high CO_2 concentrations were the result of, rather than the cause of, warming temperatures in the past (Jansen et al. 2007).

In the past, changes in global mean temperatures have preceded changes in atmospheric CO_2 concentrations.

High CO_2 concentrations were the result of, rather than the cause of, warming temperatures.

Projected Changes in Atmospheric CO_2 Concentrations

Projecting future anthropogenic climatic changes first requires projections or scenarios about future emissions and atmospheric concentrations of greenhouse gases. Projections of future greenhouse gas emissions require many assumptions about the future course of human events—including human population growth, economic development, technological innovation, energy systems, and political cooperation—that are often packaged as scenarios or "stories" (Nakićenović 2000). These scenarios not only consider conditions at some point in the distant future, but also intermediate (transient) conditions. Many scenarios have been developed by a variety of research groups, but the Intergovernmental Panel on Climate Change (IPCC) has organized the scenarios into four groups, in which scenarios share a common storyline (Nakićenović 2000).

The IPCC generated four storylines of the future, which included potential future variability in major socioeconomic factors that would influence greenhouse gas emissions (Nakićenović 2000, Nakićenović et al. 2000). The A1 storyline describes a future world with very rapid economic growth, low population growth, and rapid technological advancement, with convergence among regions, increased cultural and social interactions, and a substantial reduction in regional differences in per capita income. The A1 scenario family subdivides into four scenario groups that describe alternative directions of technological change in the energy system.

The A2 storyline describes a very heterogeneous world in which self-reliance and preservation of local identities is a key theme, population growth is high, economic development is regionally oriented, and per capita economic growth and technological change are more fragmented and slower than in other storylines.

The B1 storyline describes a convergent world with the same low population growth as in the A1 storyline, but with rapid economic changes toward a service and information economy, with reductions in material intensity, and the introduction of clean and resource-efficient technologies. The emphasis is on global solutions to economic, social, and environmental sustainability, including improved equity.

The B2 storyline describes a world of moderate population growth, intermediate economic development, and slower technological change (relative to A1 and B1), in which the emphasis is on local solutions to economic, social, and environmental sustainability.

For each storyline of the future, research groups developed (modeled) specific future emissions scenarios, which include a quantitative interpretation of the future storyline and the resulting greenhouse gas emissions. A set of 40 future emissions scenarios were developed for the IPCC fourth assessment, and more have been developed in recent years. Taken as a group, these scenarios encompass a wide range of possible futures, each one representing a pertinent, plausible, alternative future. Unfortunately, there is no way to know which one will be the most accurate, and even assigning probabilities to scenarios would be a highly subjective process. Thus, in evaluating future risks and developing adaptation strategies, it is important to consider the whole range of possible emissions outcomes and the associated ranges of climatic changes and ecosystem impacts (Beaumont et al. 2008).

Biogeochemical models are used to convert projected emissions from the scenarios described above into the atmospheric greenhouse gas concentration used in climate models. Biogeochemical models simulate the uptake and release of CO_2 through photosynthesis and respiration, and the storage of carbon in plant biomass, soils, and ocean sediments. As with any model, biogeochemical models generate additional sources of potential error and uncertainty owing to errors or biases in input datasets, imperfect understanding of biogeochemical processes, and potential errors in model representation of those processes (Beaumont et al. 2008).

Scenarios developed for the IPCC Special Report on Emission Scenarios (SRES) (Nakićenović et al. 2000) all project increasing greenhouse gas emissions between 2000 and 2030, with individual scenarios projecting increases of 25 to 90 percent over baseline (IPCC 2007a). Carbon dioxide emissions from energy use (mostly fossil fuels) are expected to increase by 40 to 110 percent over that period. Extending scenario projections to 2100 produces a wide range of possible changes in greenhouse gas emissions, from slight reductions to tenfold increases, relative to 1990 baseline emissions, with corresponding variability in resulting atmospheric greenhouse gas concentrations and radiative forcing (fig. 2.6). The lowest emission SRES scenario produces global mean CO_2 concentrations of 450 ppm by 2100,

Commonly used SRES emission scenarios project increases of 25 to 90 percent in greenhouse gas emissions between 2000 and 2030.

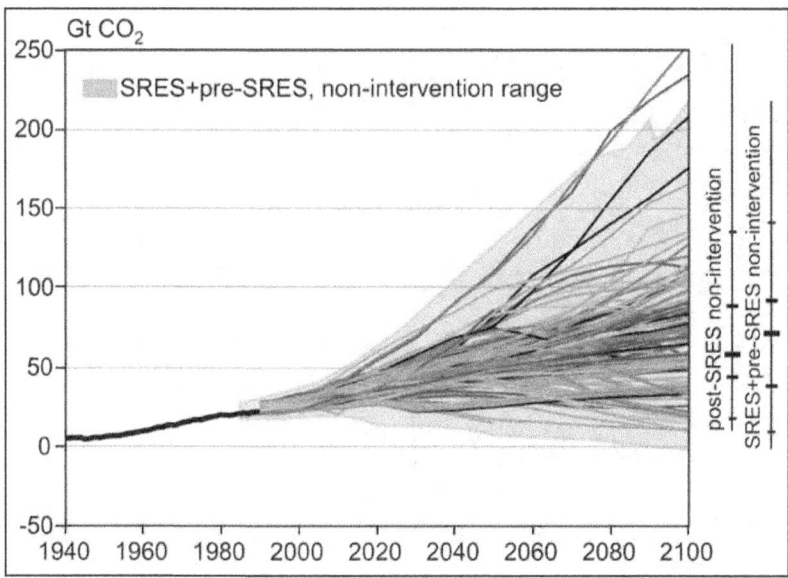

Figure 2.6—Comparison of the Special Report on Emission Scenarios (SRES) and pre-SRES energy-related and industrial carbon dioxide (CO_2) emissions scenarios in the literature with the post-SRES scenarios. (Source: After Nakićenović et al. 2006. From Fisher et al. 2007, fig. 3.8.)
Note: The two vertical bars on the right extend from the minimum to maximum of the distribution of scenarios and indicate the 5th, 25th, 50th, 75th, and the 95th percentiles of the distributions by 2100.

while scenarios with higher emissions produce mean CO_2 concentrations of 875 ppm (or more) by 2100 (Clarke et al. 2007).

Although the SRES (Nakićenović et al. 2000) states that the emission scenarios are pertinent, plausible, alternative futures that are equally possible, this claim has been disputed. Moreover, rates of increase in CO_2 emissions have recently exceeded those in the highest of the SRES scenarios (Raupach et al. 2007). Because of this, Beaumont et al. (2008) suggested that the use of more conservative emission scenarios (B1 and B2) be replaced by the more extreme A1 and A2 scenarios. The A1FI scenario is even more extreme in terms of emissions but has not been widely used for making future climate projections. Scenarios developed since the SRES have projected an even wider range (higher and lower) of estimates of future emissions and atmospheric CO_2 concentrations (IPCC 2007b) (fig. 2.7).

The SRES scenarios are limited in some ways, which has led to further scenario development and in changes to the scenario development process. The SRES scenarios assume no effective mitigation policies for greenhouse gas emissions over the next century, so they may be biased toward higher emissions. Several new "intervention" scenarios have now been developed that include future mitigation efforts and generally produce lower future greenhouse gas concentrations and associated climatic effects. More recently, the IPCC developed a new parallel

Rates of increase in CO_2 emissions have recently exceeded those in the highest of the SRES scenarios.

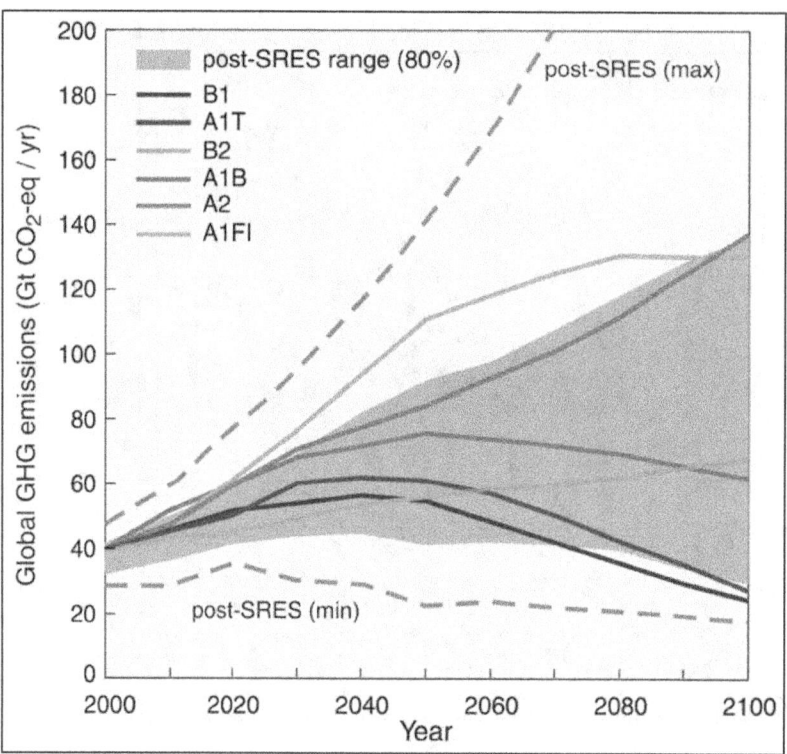

Figure 2.7—Global greenhouse gas (GHG) emissions (in gigatons of carbon dioxide $(GtCO_2)$-eq per year) in the absence of additional climate policies: six illustrative SRES marker scenarios (coloured lines) and 80th percentile range of recent scenarios published since SRES (post-SRES) (gray shaded area). Dashed lines show the full range of post-SRES scenarios. The emissions include carbon dioxide, methane, nitrous oxide and fluorinated or F-gases. (From IPCC 2007a, fig. 3.1.)

process for scenario development that starts with four scenarios of future changes in atmospheric forcing levels. The process allows climate modelers to assess a range of potential future climate scenarios for each forcing scenario at the same time as researchers explore suites of future social, economic, and policy scenarios under which each of the forcing scenarios could occur (Moss et al. 2010).

Temperature and Precipitation

Observed Changes in Temperature and Precipitation

Global mean temperatures have been gradually increasing over the past 150 years.

Global mean temperatures have been gradually increasing over the past 150 years, the period for which we have fairly reliable measurements with global coverage (fig. 2.8). Global mean temperatures have increased by about 0.65 °C (± 0.2 °C) over the past century (1900 to 2005), with much of the warming occurring in the last 50 years (Trenberth et al. 2007) (figs. 2.8 and 2.9). Warming has been greater in the Northern than in the Southern Hemisphere, greater at high latitudes than near the equator, and greater over large land masses than over the oceans (Trenberth et al.

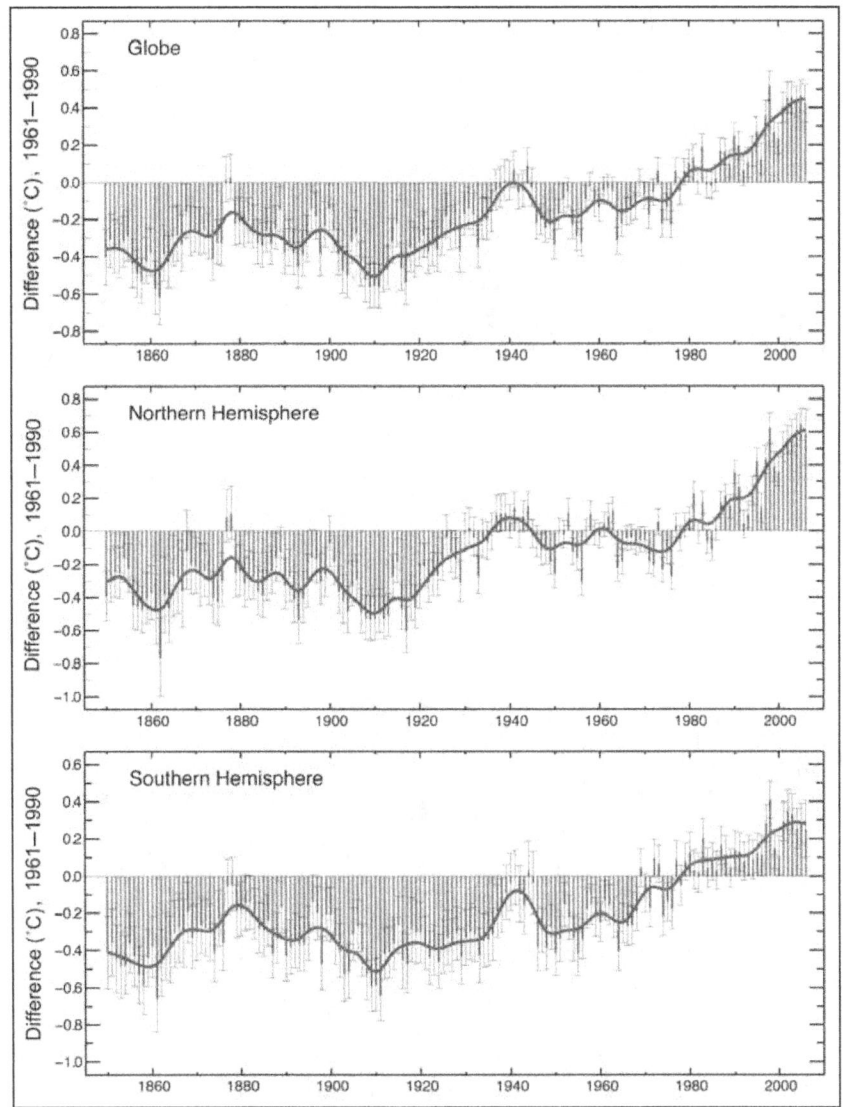

Figure 2.8—Global and hemispheric annual combined land-surface air temperature and sea surface temperature (SST) anomalies (°C) (red) for 1850 to 2006 relative to the 1961 to 1990 mean, along with 5 to 95 percent error bar ranges, from HadCRUT3 (adapted from Brohan et al. [2006]). The smooth blue curves show decadal variations (see app. 3.A). From Trenberth et al. 2007, fig. 3.6.)

2007) (fig. 2.8). Nighttime low temperatures have increased more than daytime high temperatures, thereby reducing diurnal temperature fluctuations somewhat (Trenberth et al. 2007).

Comparing current global mean temperatures and trends with historical climates prior to 150 years ago is difficult owing to a lack of global coverage by instrumental records and uncertainty in reconstructions from proxy data, such as tree rings. However, current global temperatures are probably warmer than any previous period in the last 2,000 years, being slightly warmer than the so-called

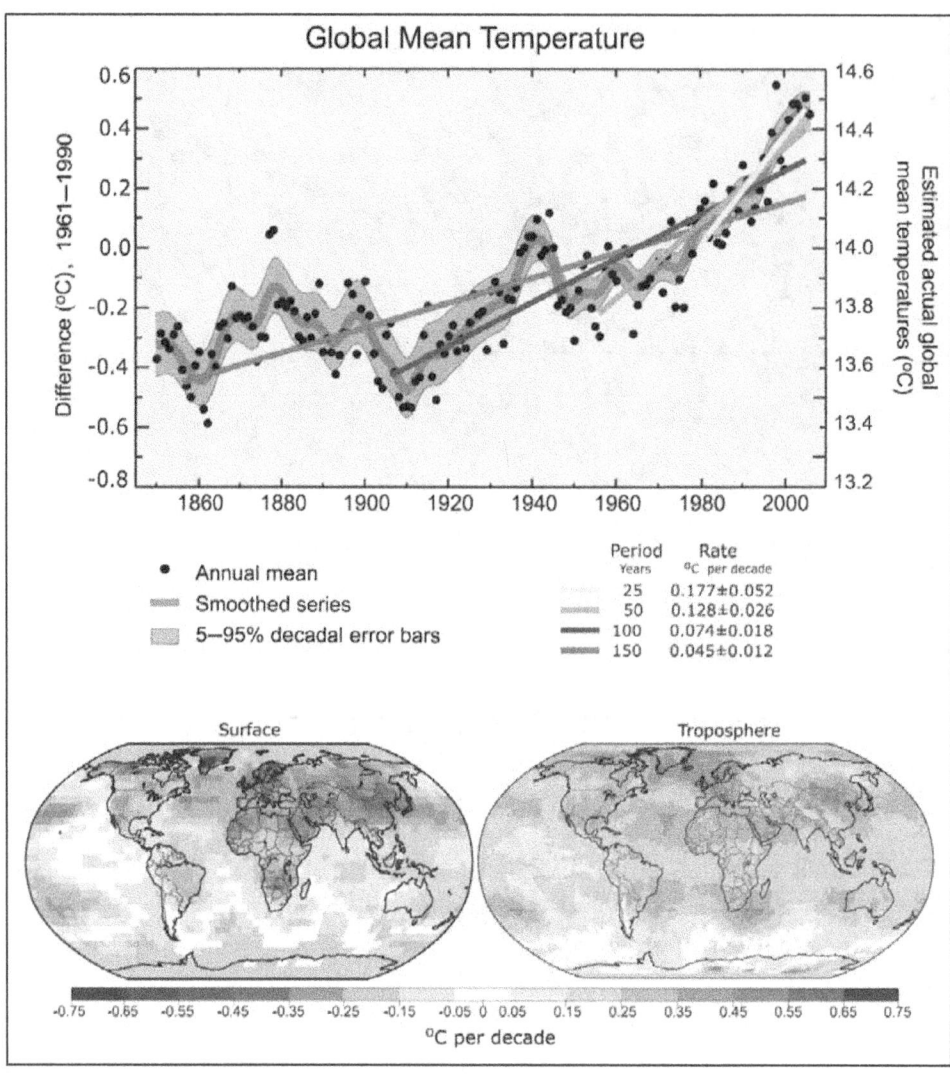

Figure 2.9—(Top) Annual global mean observed temperatures (black dots) along with simple fits to the data. The left hand axis shows anomalies relative to the 1961 to 1990 average, and the right hand axis shows the estimated actual temperature (°C). Linear trend fits to the last 25 (yellow), 50 (orange), 100 (purple), and 150 (red) years are shown, and correspond to 1981 to 2005, 1956 to 2005, 1906 to 2005, and 1856 to 2005, respectively. Note that for shorter recent periods, the slope is greater, indicating accelerated warming. The blue curve is a smoothed depiction to capture the decadal variations. To give an idea of whether the fluctuations are meaningful, decadal 5 percent to 95 percent (light grey) error ranges about that line are given (accordingly, annual values do exceed those limits). Results from climate models driven by estimated radiative forcings for the 20th century suggest that there was little change prior to about 1915, and that a substantial fraction of the early 20th-century change was contributed by naturally occurring influences including solar radiation changes, volcanism, and natural variability. From about 1940 to 1970, the increasing industrialization following World War II increased pollution in the Northern Hemisphere, contributing to cooling, and increases in carbon dioxide (CO_2) and other greenhouse gases dominate the observed warming after the mid-1970s. (Bottom) Patterns of linear global temperature trends from 1979 to 2005 estimated at the surface (left), and for the troposphere (right) from the surface to about 10 km altitude, from satellite records. Grey areas indicate incomplete data. Note the more spatially uniform warming in the satellite tropospheric record, whereas the surface temperature changes more clearly relate to land and ocean. (From Trenberth et al. 2007, FAQ 3.1, fig. 1.)

"Medieval Warm Period" (950–1200 CE) (Jansen et al. 2007). Global temperatures have probably been higher than today in the distant past, however, most recently in the last interglacial period, roughly 116,000 to 130,000 years ago.

Climate change is not always a global phenomenon, however, and there are several examples of persistent temperature changes at regional to continental scales that have persisted long enough to produce vegetation responses. Analysis of pollen records suggests that temperatures in northern Europe and parts of North America were warmer than today between 5,000 and 7,000 years ago. Parts of Europe may have also been warmer than today during the Medieval Warm Period, based on reconstructions from tree rings and other climate proxies (Jansen et al. 2007).

Climate reconstructions for the Pacific Northwest indicate that climate has varied considerably over the past 20,000 years, altering both the mean and seasonal variability in temperature and precipitation. Whitlock (1992) reviewed the vegetation and climatic history of the Pacific Northwest based on studies of fossil pollen and charcoal from different regions and climatic zones. She found evidence for both warmer and cooler temperatures and higher and lower levels of summer seasonal water deficits, compared to modern climate. Summers appear to have been warmer and drier for extended periods between 5,000 and 10,000 years ago, although winter temperatures may have been colder than at present. Likewise, Pacific Northwest climate appears to have been cooler and wetter than at present during a period roughly 2,500 to 3,500 years ago. The modern regional climate (and associated vegetation) developed only recently, within the past 2,500 years (Whitlock 1992).

During the 20th century, temperatures in the Pacific Northwest have risen by an average of 0.7 to 0.9 °C.

During the 20th century, temperatures in the Pacific Northwest have risen by an average of 0.7 to 0.9 °C, but rates of warming have varied spatially and among seasons (Mote 2003). Warming rates have been highest in winter, at low elevations, and in the maritime climate zones, and lowest in autumn, at high elevations, and in the interior climate zones (Mote 2003). Similarly, significant warming of winter temperatures was observed throughout the mountainous regions of the Western United States during the period 1950–1999 in excess of that which could be caused by cyclical variations in climate associated with the El Niño-Southern Oscillation and Pacific Decadal Oscillation (Bonfils et al. 2008).

Global annual precipitation over land has varied over the past century, but that variability displays no significant long-term linear trends. Rather, global annual precipitation over land has been cyclical with precipitation increasing and decreasing at decadal time scales. For example, precipitation was above average during much of the period 1950–1979 and below average for much of the period 1980–1995 (Trenberth et al. 2007). Although there is no significant linear trend in annual precipitation at the global scale, many regions experienced significant increases

In the Pacific Northwest, precipitation increases during the 20th century have averaged 13 to 38 percent.

and decreases in annual precipitation over the period 1900–2005 (Trenberth et al. 2007). There is a positive trend in precipitation for much of North America during this period, including the Pacific Northwest, but excluding the desert southwest (Trenberth et al. 2007).

In the Pacific Northwest, precipitation increases during the 20th century have averaged 13 to 38 percent, exceeding the global averages (Mote 2003). As with temperature, however, observed increases in precipitation have been spatially and seasonally variable. Proportional increases in precipitation were highest for spring and early summer and for dry areas of eastern Washington and northeastern Oregon (Mote 2003). Proportional increases in precipitation were smaller, though absolute increases in precipitation were generally highest, in the maritime region with the highest mean annual precipitation (Mote 2003).

Projections of Future Temperature and Precipitation

Climate models—

Climate models are the primary tools available for projecting future climatic changes in response to varying emissions scenarios. Climate models are mathematical representations of the Earth's climate system that are based on equations of physical laws describing the Earth's radiation budget and ocean and atmospheric dynamics (Beaumont et al. 2008, Randall et al. 2007). Climate is influenced by a

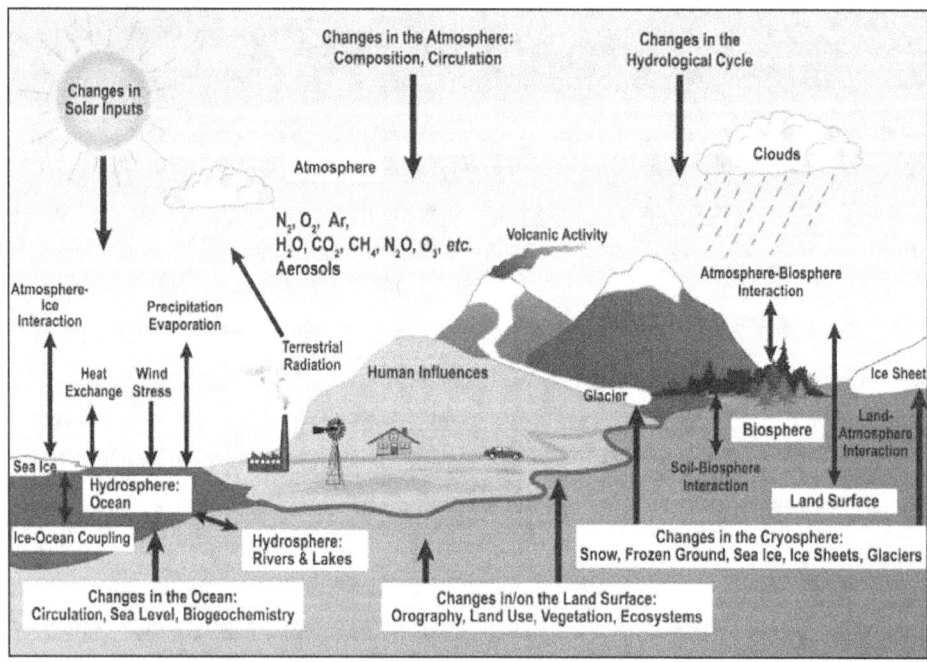

Figure 2.10—Schematic view of the components of the climate system, their processes and interactions. (From Le Treut et al. 2007, FAQ 1.2, fig. 1.) N_2 = nitrogen gas, O_2 = oxygen, Ar = argon, H_2O = water, CO_2 = carbon dioxide, CH_4 = methane, N_2O = nitrous oxide, O_3 = ozone.

wide range of factors (fig. 2.10); consequently, climate models vary in complexity as model developers incorporate different numbers and types of processes into the models, depending on data availability, available computing power, and model application objectives. Climate models used for climate change projections range from complex atmosphere-ocean general circulation models—which explicitly represent a wide range of interacting entities and processes that influence climate (e.g., atmosphere, oceans, land surfaces, sea ice, and seasonal snow cover)—to simple climate models that are more typically used in weather forecasting (Meehl et al. 2007).

Individual projections of future climate can be highly variable owing to differences in future emission scenarios, climate model structure and parameterization (Lynn et al. 2009), and data used. Currently, climate projections can be derived from over 20 available global climate models (GCMs). Global climate models differ in the physical processes represented, interactions among physical processes, initialization procedures, and assumptions about climate system sensitivity to changes in CO_2 concentration. They can therefore produce different climate projections when given the same emission scenario and initial conditions. Similarly, climate projections produced by a single GCM can differ in response to varying emission scenarios and initial conditions. This combined variability owing to model selection, emissions scenarios, and initial conditions provides a measure of the uncertainty in climate projections. Beaumont et al. (2008) asserted that end users of climate model projections (and associated impact model projections) should be aware of how well the climate models simulate components of the climate that are applicable to the questions being asked at the scale of interest.

When communicating future climate projections, the IPCC and others often present mean projected changes for each of a small group of emission scenarios. Emission scenarios are typically chosen to represent a wide range of future emissions, often using high, low, and intermediate CO_2 conditions (fig. 2.7). Each of these representative CO_2 scenarios is given as input to a suite of climate models, and the resulting climate projections are averaged together to produce a mean projected response for the scenario. This multimodel ensemble approach has been useful in that it produces a small number of future climate scenarios that represent much of the range of possible future conditions. These scenarios are easily communicated to the public and can be used to develop ensembles of potential climate and ecosystem responses. Unfortunately, the multimodel ensemble approach also obscures much of the model-based variability and uncertainty in future climate projections and focuses attention on mean projected conditions rather than the extremes. Some have also begun to question the current convention of giving equal weight to each model ("one model, one vote") in developing multimodel ensembles. Such a convention ignores potential differences in model skill; gives extra weight to projections from sibling models (whose projections may be similar because they share common assumptions and subroutines); and may obscure important spatial or temporal variability in model projections, including extreme behavior (Knutti 2010, Knutti et al. 2010).

> **Spatial downscaling methods are used to translate the climate projections from the coarse spatial resolution produced by GCMs to the finer resolutions deemed more useful for assessing impacts.**

Often the spatial scale of climate and other projections desired for management purposes is much finer than the scale at which most projections are available. Climate models produce projections at a spatial resolution (grain size) of 100 to 300 km, while regional studies require a resolution of 10 to 50 km or finer (Salathé et al. 2007). Spatial downscaling methods are used to translate the climate projections from the coarse spatial resolution produced by GCMs to the finer resolutions deemed more useful for assessing impacts. Two methods are commonly used— statistical downscaling and regional climate models—each of which has its strengths and weaknesses (Salathé et al. 2007).

Climate model projections are currently being downscaled to relatively fine spatial scales (e.g., 800-m^2 grain size) (Rogers 2011), but the accuracy and benefits of such downscaling are not entirely clear. The creation of fine-scaled projections does not necessarily mean that the projections are more accurate or better represent underlying mechanisms (Littell et al. 2011, Maslin and Austin 2012). Weather station data are sparse throughout much of the world, limiting the degree to which spatial interpolation methods can capture climate anomalies at finer spatial scales. Indeed, downscaling can overresolve the information in both the observational record and global models and create a false sense of confidence. There can also be significant topographic influences on local climate that may require analysis at an even finer spatial scale (e.g., 100 to 200 m^2 grain size) to describe adequately (Daly et al. 2010). Similarly, GCMs typically produce climate projections at a monthly temporal resolution, while ecosystem process models typically require weather inputs at a daily (or even hourly) time step, thereby requiring temporal downscaling (disaggregation) using estimates of monthly variability drawn from historical datasets (Salathé et al. 2007). Spatial and temporal downscaling are therefore important for local projections of climate change impacts, but add potential sources of error and uncertainty.

> **All climate models used in the 2007 IPPC fourth assessment project future increases in global mean surface air temperatures over the next century.**

Projected temperature changes—

All climate models used in the 2007 IPPC fourth assessment project future increases in global mean surface air temperatures over the next century, driven in large part by increased radiative forcing owing to anthropogenic CO_2 emissions and resulting higher atmospheric CO_2 concentrations (Meehl et al. 2007). The amount of warming projected differs considerably, however, depending on the climate model and CO_2 emission scenario used to make the projection and the time horizon being used (fig. 2.11). During the first part of the 21st century (2011–2030), models project a model-averaged increase in mean surface air temperature of 0.64 to 0.68 °C regardless of the emission scenario used, and much of this increase is considered a lagged response to past greenhouse gas emissions. By the middle of the 21st century (2046–2065), models project a model-averaged increase in surface air temperatures of 1.3 to 1.8 °C, depending on the emission scenario used. By the end of the 21st century (2090–2099), models project a model-averaged increase in surface air temperatures of 1.8 to 4.0 °C, depending on the emission scenario used.

For any given CO_2 emission scenario, there is considerable model-based uncertainty in projections of future warming, particularly by the end of the 21st century (Meehl et al. 2007). For example, the low-emissions B1 scenario produces the lowest model-averaged projected mean temperature increase of 1.8 °C by the end of the 21st century (fig. 2.11); however, the uncertainty range is 1.1 to 2.9 °C. Similarly, the high-emissions A1F1 scenario produces the highest model-averaged projected mean temperature increase of 4.0 °C by the end of the 21st century; however, the uncertainty range is 2.6 to 6.4 °C. Therefore, although all model projections indicate significant increases in global mean surface air temperatures over the next

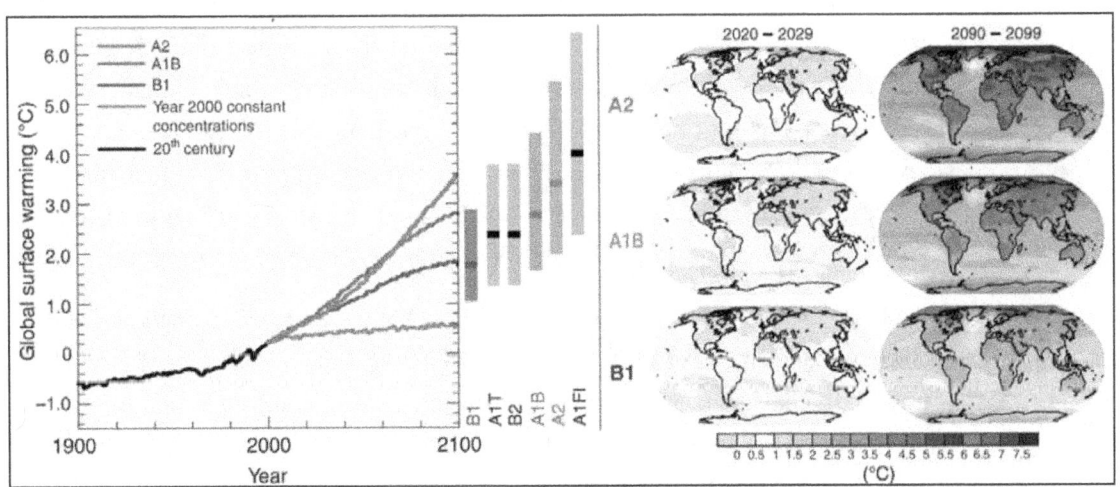

Figure 2.11—Left panel: Solid lines are multimodel global averages of surface warming relative to 1980–1999 for the Special Repost on Emission Scenarios (SRES) scenarios A2, A1B, and B1, shown as continuations of the 20th century simulations. The orange line is for the experiment where concentrations were held constant at year 2000 values. The bars in the middle of the figure indicate the best estimate (solid line within each bar) and the likely range assessed for the six SRES marker scenarios at 2090–2099 relative to 1980–1999. The assessment of the best estimate and likely ranges in the bars includes the Atmosphere-Ocean General Circulation Models (AOGCMs) in the left part of the figure, as well as results from a hierarchy of independent models and observational constraints. Right panels: Projected surface temperature changes for the early and late 21st century relative to the period 1980–1999. The panels show the multi-AOGCM average projections for the A2 (top), A1B (middle), and B1 (bottom) SRES scenarios averaged over decades 2020–2029 (left) and 2090–2099 (right). (From IPCC [2007a], fig. 3.2.)

The amount of warming expected remains uncertain, ranging from a little more warming than in the past century to almost eight times as much.

century, the amount of warming expected remains uncertain, ranging from a little more warming than in the past century to almost eight times as much.

Warming is not expected to be uniform (spatially) or even (temporally). Warming is expected to be greatest over land areas and at higher latitudes, and least over oceans (Meehl et al. 2007) (fig. 2.11). Heat waves (extreme temperatures) are expected to be more frequent and intense (Meehl and Tebaldi 2004, Meehl et al. 2007), but periods of extreme cold may continue to occur in response to spatial and temporal variability in climate. Daily minimum temperatures are expected to rise faster than daily maximum temperatures, reducing diurnal temperature fluctuations (Meehl et al. 2007). Drivers of interdecadal climatic variability (e.g., Pacific Decadal Oscillation) also will continue to operate, potentially creating extended periods of stable or cooling mean temperatures followed by periods of rapidly increasing mean temperatures (along with associated changes in precipitation). For the Pacific Northwest, Mote and Salathé (2010) analyzed climate projections from 21 GCMs to summarize the projected changes in climate during the 21st century under two emissions scenarios (B1 and A1B). They reported an average projected increase in mean surface air temperature by the late 21st century of 2.5 °C for the low-emission B1 scenario and 3.4 °C for the high-emission A1B scenario (total range of 1.5 to 5.8 °C for both scenarios across all models). This is slightly higher than the projected increases in global mean temperatures when controlling for emission scenario. Some of the difference may be attributed to the weighted mean used by Mote and Salathé (2010), which gives higher weight to models with high skill in reproducing climatic conditions and changes in the 20th century. Model projections suggest that the greatest warming will occur in summer (June through August), increasing seasonal temperature fluctuations (Mote and Salathé 2010).

Projected precipitation changes—

Globally, mean annual precipitation is expected to increase in conjunction with warming temperatures (Meehl et al. 2007). Although the model-averaged projections for global mean annual precipitation increases are relatively small (3 to 5 percent), the models project considerable regional and seasonal variability in precipitation changes (fig. 2.12), projected precipitation changes vary somewhat by emission scenario, and there is considerable variability among individual model projections for the same emission scenario (Meehl et al. 2007). Decadal variability in sea surface temperatures (e.g., the Pacific Decadal Oscillation) is likely to interact with changing climate to influence precipitation patterns at a regional scale, but models suggest that climate change resulting from increasing greenhouse gases will become dominant within two to three decades (Meehl et al. 2010).

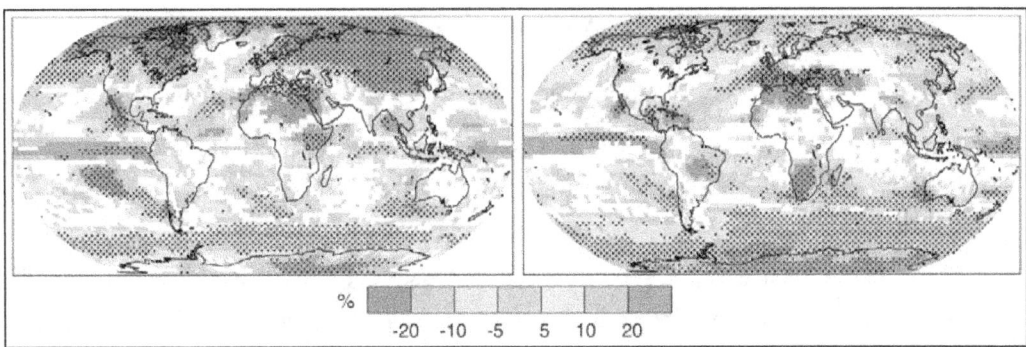

Figure 2.12—Relative changes in precipitation (in percent) for the period 2090–2099, relative to 1980–1999. Values are multimodel averages based on the Special Report on Emissions Scenarios A1B scenario for December to February (left) and June to August (right). White areas are where less than 66 percent of the models agree in the sign of the change and stippled areas are where more than 90 percent of the models agree in the sign of the change. (From IPCC [2007a], fig. 3.3.)

For the Pacific Northwest, GCM projections for changes in mean annual precipitation are equivocal, with model-averaged projections for changes in mean annual precipitation of less than 5 percent through the end of the 21st century, but also with individual model projections of change ranging from -10 percent to +20 percent by the end of the century (Mote and Salathé 2010). Most of the models reviewed by Mote and Salathé (2010) project reductions in summer precipitation in the Pacific Northwest, with the model-averaged mean reaching -14 percent by the end of the 21st century. Most of models also project increases in mean winter precipitation (December through February), with the model-averaged projection reaching as high as +8 percent by the end of the 21st century (Mote and Salathé 2010).

Water Availability

One of the most important mechanisms by which climate change can influence vegetation composition and dynamics is through its effects on soil water availability, water uptake by plants, and evapotranspiration. Soil water availability depends on precipitation inputs (form, amount, intensity, and seasonality), surface and subsurface water movement, evaporative demand, and vegetation structure and composition. Evapotranspiration is driven primarily by temperature and humidity but can be constrained by reductions in stomatal conductance or reduced water uptake owing to low soil water availability. In this section, we briefly review the likely effects of projected changes in annual and seasonal mean temperature and precipitation on important components of the hydrologic cycle, including the fraction of winter precipitation received as snowfall, snowpack water storage, snowmelt rates, evapotranspiration, and soil water availability.

One of the most important mechanisms by which climate change can influence vegetation composition and dynamics is through its effects on soil water availability, water uptake by plants, and evapotranspiration.

Snowfall and Snowpack Water Storage

Winter snowpack is an important regulator of vegetation structure and productivity in the Pacific Northwest and many other regions of the world. One of the most important functions of snowpack in western North America is storing winter precipitation for use in spring and summer months when demand for water by humans, fish and wildlife, and vegetation often exceeds supply.

The effectiveness of snowpack as a water storage mechanism depends on the total amount of winter precipitation, the proportion of winter precipitation that falls as snow, and rates at which snow melts during the winter and spring. In regions with reliably cold winter temperatures, like high-elevation mountainous areas of the interior West, snowpack accumulation is typically limited by the amount of winter precipitation, as most winter precipitation falls as snow (Cayan 1996, Hamlet et al. 2005). In warmer, maritime climates (e.g., lower elevation maritime mountains of Washington and Oregon), snowpack accumulation depends more on winter temperatures, as winter precipitation is often abundant, but much of it can fall as rain during warmer periods (Cayan 1996, Hamlet et al. 2005, Mote 2006). Spring snowpack melt rates depend largely on spring temperatures, winds, and the occurrence of warm rainfall events. Given the importance of climate in accumulating and melting snowpack, it is no surprise that snowpack dynamics are sensitive to climatic variability and change. For the Pacific Northwest, changes in snowpack in the colder interior mountains will largely be driven by changes in precipitation, while changes in snowpack in the warmer maritime mountains (e.g., Olympics and western Cascades) will be driven largely by changes in temperature (Hamlet et al. 2005).

Despite high interannual variability, several studies have reported long-term negative trends in snowpack accumulation, spring snowpack water storage, snowpack duration over the past 50 to 100 years that are attributable to warming winter and spring temperatures. Knowles et al. (2006) found significant reductions throughout the Western United States in the proportion of winter precipitation (November to March) that fell as snow from 1949 to 2004. Mote et al. (2005) found a corresponding reduction in spring (April 1) snowpack water equivalent for a similar region and time period. Finally, Stewart et al. (2004) analyzed streamflow patterns and found a trend toward earlier snowmelt in the Western United States from 1948 to 2000, with streams and rivers reaching the midway point in their annual water discharge up to 20 days earlier in the water year. Glacial ice has also declined dramatically in the Pacific Northwest over the past century (Pelto 2006).

Analysis of spring snowpack sensitivity to winter temperatures suggests that spring snowpack water storage (April 1 snowpack water equivalent) should decline

Changes in snowpack in the cedar interior mountains will largely be driven by changes in precipitation, while changes in snowpack in the warmer maritime mountains (e.g., Olympics and western Cascades) will largely be driven by changes in temperature.

by about 16 percent for every 1 °C of warming, assuming that warming is accompanied by increased precipitation (Casola et al. 2009). If this analysis is correct, mean spring snowpack water equivalent would have already declined by 8 to 16 percent over the past 30 years, and would be expected to decline by an additional 11 to 21 percent by 2050, based on projected temperature increases (Casola et al. 2009).

Projected future increases in winter temperatures and precipitation are likely to reduce snowpack accumulation and duration in much of the Pacific Northwest by increasing the proportion of winter precipitation that falls as rain and causing the snowpack to melt earlier (Barnett et al. 2005, Brown and Mote 2009). Changes in snowpack water content and duration will be most obvious at middle elevations in the mountains, where warming will cause the transitory snow zone and permanent snowline to move upward (Elsner et al. 2010, Stewart 2009). High-elevation sites that maintain freezing winter temperatures may accumulate additional snowpack as additional winter precipitation falls as snow; however, snowpack water storage is still likely to decline at the regional scale as high-elevation sites comprise a low fraction of total land area (Stewart 2009).

Evapotranspiration

Warmer winter and spring temperatures may also increase evaporative demand and alter the timing of evaporative water losses and plant water use. Evapotranspiration is the sum of water returned to the atmosphere through evaporation from the soil and other surfaces and through transpiration from plants. Potential evapotranspiration is driven largely by temperature and solar radiation, so it is expected to increase as mean temperatures increase unless cloud cover also increases and reduces solar radiation inputs. Actual evapotranspiration also depends on water availability, so increases in actual evapotranspiration are likely only if precipitation increases along with temperatures. In some areas, however, the seasonality of evapotranspiration may be altered with projected climatic changes, as warming temperatures cause water to be evaporated earlier in the spring, leaving less available in the summer and fall months.

Hamlet et al. (2007) used gridded historical climate records for the Pacific Northwest along with a hydrological model to examine possible trends in evapotranspiration over the past century. Based on model output, they reported a positive trend in spring evapotranspiration over the past century, as earlier snowmelt promoted earlier soil water recharge, plant activity, and evaporative losses (Hamlet et al. 2007). Summer evapotranspiration became more dependent on summer rainfall, as soil water from melting snowpack became less available for use in summer months (Hamlet et al. 2007).

Soil Water Balance

The frequency and intensity of summer drought depends on winter recharge of soil water, snowpack water storage, and spring/summer temperature and precipitation.

Summer water deficits occur annually in most regions and vegetation types of the Pacific Northwest, though the duration and intensity of water deficits vary considerably throughout the region and along elevational gradients. Precipitation falls primarily during the cooler months (October through March), while potential evapotranspiration is highest in the warmer and drier months (April through September). This temporal separation between precipitation inputs and evaporative demand creates high potential for summer water deficits where evaporative demand exceeds water storage capacity. At higher elevations, winter snowpack can store a significant portion of winter precipitation and release it to the soil during spring and early summer, thereby reducing the duration and magnitude of summer soil water deficits. The frequency and intensity of summer drought therefore depends on winter recharge of soil water, snowpack water storage, and spring/summer temperature and precipitation. The relative importance of these elements, and the mean summer drought duration and intensity, varies considerably within the Pacific Northwest and is an important factor determining the distribution of vegetation types, ecosystem productivity, and dominant disturbance regimes.

Summer soil water availability is likely to decline modestly in much of the Pacific Northwest under future projected climatic changes, but the magnitude and mechanisms of projected changes differ within the region (Elsner et al. 2010). In the western mountains and coastal lowlands, reduced snowpack, earlier snowmelt, and higher evapotranspiration rates are likely to enhance summer soil drying and reduce soil water availability (Elsner et al. 2010). In the interior regions, increased winter precipitation could enhance deep soil water recharge, thereby increasing deep soil water availability in the summer (Elsner et al. 2010). A continuation of the recent trend toward increasing spring precipitation in the dry interior could also enhance spring and summer soil water availability if amounts are sufficient to promote deep soil recharge; if not, it is likely to simply enhance spring evapotranspiration rates.

Chapter 3: Vegetation Sensitivity and Acclimation to Changing Climate and CO_2

Assessing vegetation sensitivity to climate change requires assessing the degree to which climatic variability and change alter vegetation performance and survival. Individual plants are immobile, so their sensitivity to climate can be assessed primarily in terms of their growth (productivity), reproduction, and survival. Plant population responses integrate climatic effects on reproduction and survival at the individual plant level and can be measured as rates of population increase (or decline), including local extirpation. Plant community responses integrate climatic effects on constituent plant populations, as well as effects on biotic interactions, and are commonly measured as the number and relative abundances of interacting species. Finally, assessing vegetation sensitivity to climate at the ecosystem level typically involves measuring responses—such as net primary productivity, total carbon stocks, and nutrient cycling rates—that integrate individual plant performance across populations and communities.

In this chapter, we review common vegetation responses that represent sensitivity to climate and elevated carbon dioxide (CO_2) at each of these levels, with emphasis on processes and responses commonly found in Pacific Northwest vegetation. We first examine climate and CO_2 effects on plant growth and reproduction, as these are basic measures of vegetation performance at the individual and population levels. We also examine the potential for changing climate to alter the intensity of and outcomes from biotic interactions and the implications for plant community responses to climate change. Finally, we examine ecosystem responses to changing climate and CO_2, including potential changes in net primary productivity, ecosystem carbon storage, and nutrient cycling. Plant mortality responses to climate-related stressors and disturbances are discussed in chapter 4, while plant adaptive responses are discussed in chapter 5.

Physiological Processes, Plant Growth, and Ecosystem Productivity

Climate influences plant growth through its effects on temperature, soil water, light, and nutrients. These factors are important for regulating rates of photosynthesis and respiration, water and nutrient uptake from soils, and biomass production. Temperature and soil water also influence soil biota and their contributions to organic matter decomposition, nutrient cycling, and exchange of resources with plants. Plant growth is also influenced by atmospheric CO_2 concentrations, which can directly alter rates of photosynthesis, respiration, and transpiration, and can indirectly influence soil water and nutrient availability.

Plant growth in temperate zones occurs within the context of a constantly changing climate. As sessile organisms, plants must have the ability to adjust to daily, seasonal, interannual, and longer term changes in solar radiation, temperature, and precipitation, and associated changes in soil temperature, soil water availability, and soil nutrient availability. In addition to these relatively predictable cycles in environmental conditions and resource availability, plants must also have mechanisms for coping with periodic episodes of extreme environmental conditions, such as heat waves, extreme cold temperatures, and drought.

Increasing atmospheric concentrations of CO_2 and associated changes in climate are expected to influence plant growth by altering the ranges of environmental conditions and resource availability plants experience throughout their annual growth cycle. In this section, we highlight some key experimental and observational research that provides insights to the likely effects of changing climate and atmospheric CO_2 on plant carbon uptake (photosynthesis and respiration), plant growth, and allocation of carbon to mycorrhizae, plant defense compounds, and other nonstructural purposes. We also describe ways in which plants acclimate to seasonal and longer term climatic variability and to elevated CO_2 concentrations. Experimental studies are particularly important sources for this information, as they provide information about potential responses of existing vegetation to future climate and CO_2, in the absence of genetic adaptation in populations or species migrations (which are addressed in chapter 5).

Increasing mean annual temperatures are likely to increase photosynthetic rates for many temperate plant species, given sufficient light and water.

Photosynthesis and Respiration

Photosynthesis and respiration regulate net uptake and fixation of carbon. Photosynthesis allows plants to convert CO_2 and water into organic compounds that store energy and can be used for plant growth and maintenance, seed production, conversion to plant defense compounds, or export to soil biota (among other things). Respiration allows plants to use stored energy for plant growth and maintenance. Both processes are sensitive to changing environmental conditions and resource availability, but they differ in both their initial responses and ability to acclimate.

Increasing mean annual temperatures are likely to increase photosynthetic rates for many temperate plant species, given sufficient light and water (Saxe et al. 2001). Photosynthetic rates in temperate-zone plants generally increase with short-term increases in temperature up to a maximum at about 25 to 40 °C, while acclimation to persistent temperature increases can raise photosynthetic maxima by up to 10 °C (Berry and Björkman 1980, Saxe et al. 2001). Warming nighttime temperatures can also increase photosynthetic rates by reducing the frequency of low-temperature photoinhibition (Germino and Smith 1999). Warming temperatures can increase plant photosynthetic rates indirectly by changing leaf nitrogen content and photosynthetic capacity (Lewis et al. 2004). In Douglas-fir (*Pseudotsuga menziesii* (Mirb.) Franco) seedlings, for example, experimental warming increased chlorophyll and carotenoid concentrations (Ormrod et al. 1999) and increased seedling needle nitrogen (N) concentrations by 26 percent and light-saturated photosynthetic rates by 17 percent (Lewis et al. 2004). Warming temperatures are not uniformly beneficial for photosynthesis, however, as temperatures in excess of the photosynthetic optimum can rapidly reduce photosynthesis by impairing protein functioning (Saxe et al. 2001) and high daytime temperatures can reduce net photosynthesis by increasing rates of photorespiration (Long et al. 1994).

Soil water availability is another major control on photosynthetic rates of Pacific Northwest plants. Summer soil water deficits occur annually in most vegetation types of the Pacific Northwest, producing some level of drought stress in plants. Plants typically respond to short-term drought stress by reducing stomatal apertures, which can reduce water loss through transpiration, but also reduces photosynthetic rates by reducing CO_2 concentrations within plant leaves. By increasing evaporative demands, warmer temperatures can increase the frequency and severity of summer drought and associated effects on photosynthesis.

Autotrophic respiration can consume 30 to 80 percent of net photosynthesis in plants, as respiration generates the energy needed for plants to do work (Atkin and Tjoelker 2003, Saxe at al. 2001). Although growth respiration is relatively insensitive to temperature, maintenance respiration is quite sensitive to short-term temperature changes. Respiration rates typically rise by a factor of 1.8 to 2.5 (roughly double) in response to a 10 °C increase in temperature (Atkin and Tjoelker 2003, Saxe et al. 2001). Over longer periods, however, respiration can acclimate to elevated ambient temperatures (Atkin and Tjoelker 2003). There is evidence that respiration may become substrate-limited at higher temperatures, so that respiration rates become more tightly coupled to photosynthetic rates over longer time scales (Atkin and Tjoelker 2003, Atkin et al. 2005, Saxe et al. 2001).

Elevated CO_2 may help to offset the effects of higher temperatures and reduced soil water availability on photosynthesis and net carbon uptake. Carbon dioxide is a critical resource for photosynthesis but is available at relatively low atmospheric concentrations. In acquiring CO_2 from the atmosphere through stomatal diffusion, plants lose water to the atmosphere through transpiration, requiring mechanisms like stomatal aperture control to balance the effects of low water, CO_2, and light availability on productivity (Hetherington and Woodward 2003, Lambers et al. 1998). Theory suggests that increasing atmospheric concentrations of CO_2 could increase individual plant growth and ecosystem productivity (Long et al. 2004),

Elevated CO_2 may help to offset the effects of higher temperatures and reduced soil water availability on photosynthesis and net carbon uptake.

and there has been considerable research in recent decades to detect and better understand this potential CO_2 "fertilization effect."

Experimental studies have shown that the primary effect of elevated CO_2 on plants is to increase resource-use efficiency—the amount of carbon fixed per unit of resource obtained or used (Drake et al. 1997). Elevated CO_2 allows plants to reduce stomatal conductance and leaf-level transpiration while maintaining adequate CO_2 concentrations for photosynthesis within leaves, thereby increasing water-use efficiency (Ainsworth and Long 2005, Drake et al. 1997, Leakey et al. 2009, Long et al. 2004, Medlyn et al. 2001). Improved water-use efficiency under elevated CO_2 is most prevalent in plants with the C_3 photosynthetic pathway, which includes the majority of forest plants in the Pacific Northwest as well as many rangeland species. Elevated CO_2 also stimulates photosynthesis and increases light-use efficiency by increasing the carboxylation rate of Rubisco and competitively inhibiting oxygenation of Ribulose-1, 5-bisphosphate (RubP) (Ainsworth and Long 2005, Drake et al. 1997). Plants appear to acclimate to prolonged exposure to elevated CO_2 by reducing Rubisco concentrations and mass-based leaf nitrogen content while maintaining elevated photosynthetic rates, thereby increasing nitrogen-use efficiency (Ainsworth and Long 2005, Drake et al. 1997, Leakey et al. 2009, Long et al. 2004).

Greater resource-use efficiencies can facilitate greater total carbon acquisition by plants, if plant demand for carbon (the "sink strength") is sufficiently high. Increased carbon acquisition rates, in turn, can produce a wide range of ecological impacts on plants and ecosystems, including increased plant growth and ecosystem productivity (Leakey et al. 2009), increased shade tolerance (Drake et al. 1997), reduced drought stress, increased soil water availability (Holtum and Winter 2010), reduced plant nutrient quality for insect and animal herbivores (Lincoln et al. 1993, Robinson et al. 2012, Zvereva and Kozlov 2006), and reduced rates of litter decomposition and soil nutrient cycling.

In general, warmer temperatures produce a positive effect on photosynthesis, except where ambient temperatures are already close to (or beyond) the photosynthetic optimum or where soil water availability strongly limits stomatal conductance and photosynthesis (Saxe et al. 2001). Warmer temperatures significantly increase respiration rates over short time periods, but respiration rates can acclimate to changes in mean temperatures over time. Elevated CO_2 can help reduce the frequency and severity of drought-induced reductions in photosynthesis by helping plants maintain adequate internal concentrations of CO_2 while reducing water losses by reducing stomatal aperture.

Phenology

Warmer mean temperatures may also influence vegetation growth and productivity through their effects on plant phenology (the timing and duration of growth stages) and growing season length. Plant phenology in temperate woody plants is largely controlled by winter and spring temperatures and by photoperiod (Polgar and Primack 2011). Processes influenced by temperatures include the initiation of flowering (Dunne et al. 2003), budburst (Guak et al. 1998, Harrington et al. 2010, Worrall 1983), root growth (Lopushinsky and Max 1990), and cold hardening (Guak et al. 1998, Saxe et al. 2001). For example, Worrall (1993) reported that budburst in subalpine larch (*Larix lyallii* Parl.) varied by up to 6 weeks and leaf-fall varied by up to 4 weeks from year to year and that both were correlated with spring and summer temperatures. Similarly, Lopushinsky and Max (1990) used a greenhouse study to show that root growth began when soil temperatures exceeded 5 °C.

Winter temperatures can also influence spring budburst timing. Some species delay budburst if they have not experienced a sufficiently long or intense period of cold temperatures, which is often referred to as a "chilling requirement" (Campbell and Sogano 1979, Cannell and Smith 1983, Harrington et al. 2010, Kozlowski and Pallardy 2002). In areas with mild winters, warmer winter temperatures could fail to satisfy the chilling requirements for some species (e.g., Douglas-fir), thereby delaying the onset of spring budburst and shoot growth and offsetting some of the potential benefits of warmer spring temperatures (Harrington et al. 2010). However, early initiation of budburst or flowering can also expose plants to increased risk of frost damage (Cannell and Smith 1986, Inouye 2008), so delays in budburst owing to unmet chilling requirements may also provide some benefits.

Temperature triggers on growth phenology, if well-adapted, can help plants synchronize their growth activity with periods of favorable resource availability, including favorable temperatures. In subalpine zones, low heat requirements allow trees to initiate and complete their annual growth cycle (including seed production and cold hardening) before the return of cold temperatures in the fall (Tranquillini 1979; Worrall 1983, 1993), thereby maximizing growing season length. In water-limited systems, early growth initiation may also be advantageous, allowing plants to capture and use soil water that would not be available later in the summer and perhaps gaining a competitive advantage over species with later growth initiation (resource preemption).

Plant phenological responses to warming of global temperatures in recent decades have been well documented by direct observation of plant species—some extending back hundreds of years—and, more recently, by satellite imagery and analysis of seasonal changes in atmospheric CO_2 concentrations (Badeck et al.

A recent meta-analysis of phenological studies from multiple sources indicated that spring growth phenology has been advancing at an average rate of 2.8 days per decade.

2004, Cleland et al. 2007, Parmesan 2006, Polgar and Primack 2011). A recent meta-analysis of phenological studies from multiple sources indicated that spring growth phenology has been advancing at an average rate of 2.8 days per decade (Parmesan 2007). Although phenological responses can differ considerably by species, a study of more than 500 European plant species found significant advances in 30 percent of leafing, flowering, and fruiting records, compared to significant delays in only 3 percent of records, in response to warming during 1971–2000 (Menzel et al. 2006). Unfortunately, records on the cessation of growth are less common, so it is difficult to conclusively link spring advancement of growth phenology with longer growing season lengths, except through remote sensing approaches.

Plant Growth and Ecosystem Productivity

Plant growth and biomass production are important measures of plant responses to changing climate and elevated CO_2. Plant growth allows plants to forage for and capture critical resources (e.g., root growth and water uptake; height growth and light interception), compete for resources and growing space with other plants, replace tissues lost to disturbances (e.g., herbivory or wind damage), and increase resistance to disturbances (e.g., thicker bark to resist fire; greater height to avoid herbivory). Plant growth is also a major sink for carbon fixed through photosynthesis, so high growth rates can promote higher levels of carbon uptake (and vice versa). Finally, biomass production is a required precursor for long-term ecosystem carbon storage and serves as an important feedback of ecosystem productivity on disturbance processes such as fire.

Plant growth and biomass production can be limited by one or more climatic limiting factors, including air and soil temperatures, soil water availability, and solar radiation. Ecosystem model simulations of global terrestrial biomes suggest that temperature and water availability are the dominant climatic factors limiting net primary productivity globally, with solar radiation being the dominant limiting factor for only about 5 percent of the biomes (Churkina and Running 1998). Given the diverse range of environments and biomes in the Pacific Northwest, all three climatic limiting factors are likely to operate in some regions and seasons, but winter temperatures and water limitations are considered the dominant controls on leaf area and net primary productivity in Pacific Northwest ecosystems (Gholz 1982, Grier and Running 1977). Soil nutrients (especially nitrogen) are another important factor limiting vegetation growth and productivity throughout much of the Pacific Northwest, which, though not directly climate-related, may modify vegetation structure and productivity (Gholz 1982).

Tree ring analyses have demonstrated the effects of climatic limiting factors on growth and biomass production in a number of forest types and biophysical settings. Tree growth in low-elevation juniper woodlands and ponderosa pine (*Pinus ponderosa* Lawson and C. Lawson) forests is positively correlated with precipitation, particularly outside the growing season, but relatively insensitive to temperature fluctuations (Knutson 2006, Kusnierczyk and Ettl 2002), suggesting a strong water limitation on net primary production. In contrast, tree growth in subalpine forests can be negatively correlated with winter precipitation and spring snowpack depth and positively correlated with summer temperatures, suggesting that temperature and growing season length limit production (Peterson and Peterson 1994, 2001; Peterson et al. 2002). Within the continuous forest zone, tree growth is often positively correlated with soil water availability to varying degrees (Case and Peterson 2005, 2007; Littell et al. 2008; Nakawatase and Peterson 2006). In general, tree ring studies support ecosystem model projections regarding the dominant environmental factors limiting net primary productivity (NPP) in forests; however, recent work suggests that site and individual tree characteristics may generate significant variability in growth responses to climatic variability and change (Carnwath et al. 2012; Ettl and Peterson 1995a,1995b; Knutson 2006).

Overall, research suggests that warming air and soil temperatures will enhance plant growth and ecosystem production, given sufficient water availability (Boisvenue and Running 2006, 2010). Warmer temperatures are expected to increase net carbon gain as respiration acclimates to warmer temperatures more than photosynthesis, allowing plants to adjust and maintain carbon-use efficiency (Maseyk et al. 2008). Temperature effects on phenology will tend to extend the growing season and, potentially, plant growth. Increased availability of soil N could also increase growth and productivity. All of these potential gains, however, depend on adequate availability of soil water, which is likely to decline with increasing temperatures.

Temperature and moisture effects on vegetation growth and productivity are likely to be highly variable within and among biomes. Positive responses to warming temperatures are more likely to be observed in subalpine and alpine ecosystems (where temperature is limiting) than in deserts, shrublands, and savannas (where water is the dominant limiting factor) (Latta et al. 2010). Warming temperatures appear to increase growth and productivity in deciduous species more than in evergreen trees (Way and Oren 2010), suggesting that warming temperatures may benefit early-seral and understory species (e.g., alders [*Alnus* spp.] and maples [*Acer* spp.]) more than evergreen conifers in the Pacific Northwest.

Plant growth responses to elevated CO_2 differ spatially and temporally with climate, soil water availability, and soil nutrient availability (Housman et al. 2006, McCarthy et al. 2010, McMurtrie et al. 2008, Norby et al. 2010, Reich et al. 2001) and also among species. In an experimental study with loblolly pine (*Pinus taeda* L.)

Overall, research suggests that warming air and soil temperatures will enhance plant growth and ecosystem production, given sufficient water availability.

at Duke Forest, 10 years of exposure to elevated CO_2 produced sustained increases in plant biomass production; however, positive responses to elevated CO_2 were greater on sites with high N availability than on sites with low N availability and were greater (on a relative basis) in dry years than in wet years (McCarthy et al. 2010). Similarly, experimental N additions have produced increased plant biomass production responses to elevated CO_2 on nutrient-limited sites (Oren et al. 2001, Reich et al. 2001). In the Mojave Desert, positive effects of elevated CO_2 on photosynthesis and productivity in three desert shrub species–creosote bush (*Larrea tridentatea* (DC.) Coville), littleleaf ratany (*Krameria erecta* Willd. Ex Schult.), and burrobush (*Ambrosia dumosa* (A. Gray) Payne)—were largely limited to seasons and years of higher relative water availability, suggesting that future responses of desert vegetation to elevated CO_2 may be dependent on concomitant changes in precipitation patterns and growing season length (Housman et al. 2006, Naumburg et al. 2003).

Species responses to elevated CO_2 have been shown to differ among plant functional groups (grasses, forbs, shrubs, and trees), among photosynthetic pathways (C_3 or C_4), between N_2-fixing and non-N_2-fixing species, and with leaf structure and longevity. A meta-analysis of experimental studies showed that trees were more responsive to elevated CO_2 than C_3 grasses, with greater percentage increases in leaf area index, height, and aboveground dry matter production (Ainsworth and Long 2005). Similarly, in studies of four crop species, only the woody crop, cotton, showed a significant yield enhancement under elevated CO_2 (Ainsworth and Long 2005). Species employing the C_3 photosynthetic pathway were more responsive than species employing the C_4 pathway, with C_3 grasses demonstrating greater mean increases in dry matter production than C_4 grasses (Ainsworth and Long 2005). Lee et al. (2003) found that elevated CO_2 increased production by 57 percent in a leguminous forb with symbiotic N_2 fixation (sundial lupine, *Lupinus perennis*), while the response of a nonleguminous forb (yarrow, *Achillea millefolium* L.) was less (0 to 25 percent increase), with positive growth responses dependent on nitrogen additions. Niinemets et al. (2011) have also proposed that evergreen plants that feature leaves with more robust structures will experience more gains in water use efficiency and productivity under elevated CO_2 than deciduous plants, as their "tougher" leaves inhibit internal diffusion of CO_2 and increase sensitivity to atmospheric CO_2 concentrations.

Plant responses to elevated CO_2 levels also differ considerably among species within functional groups. Housman et al. (2006) reported differences in growth enhancement under elevated CO_2 for three desert shrub species. Dawes et al. (2011) found that continued exposure (9 years) to elevated CO_2 in a subalpine forest increased leaf canopy cover, stem basal area, and new shoot production in European larch (*Larix decidua* Mill.), but found no significant growth response in mountain pine (*Pinus mugo* ssp. *uncinata* (Raymond) Domin. Biomass responses to elevated CO_2 also differed considerably among tallgrass prairie species within four plant functional groups: C_3 grasses, C_4 grasses, forbs, and legumes (Craine et al. 2003, Reich et al. 2001).

Interactions among elevated CO_2, water and nutrient availability, and altered climate make it difficult to predict the net productivity response of plants (Angert et al. 2005, Huang et al. 2007). Although elevated CO_2 has been shown to improve resource use efficiency and increase productivity for some species and sites under current climate, warmer temperatures or increased drought intensity projected under future climate scenarios could more than offset those benefits, leading to no net gains or reduced productivity for some species. Similarly, the potential benefits of elevated CO_2 on plant growth and productivity differ considerably with site conditions.

Future responses of Pacific Northwest vegetation to elevated CO_2 are highly uncertain owing to limited experimental studies with elevated CO_2 in the Pacific Northwest (or with Pacific Northwest species) and the wide range of biophysical settings and vegetation types. However, we can make a few projections based on general findings from studies in other ecosystems. First, increases in water-use efficiency produced by elevated atmospheric CO_2 levels could partially offset temperature-induced increases in evapotranspiration and drought stress, particularly in ecosystems with mild to moderate seasonal drought. However, Reich et al. (2006b) hypothesized that elevated CO_2 would provide little positive benefit in ecosystems where water is the dominant limiting factor (e.g., rangelands and dry forests of the interior Pacific Northwest), as appears to be the case for desert shrubs (Naumburg et al. 2003). Second, low nitrogen availability (and low atmospheric N deposition rates) in many Pacific Northwest forests and rangelands could limit the benefits of elevated CO_2 over time as progressive nitrogen limitation offsets increased nitrogen-use efficiency.

Plant Reproduction

Plant reproduction is another measure of vegetation sensitivity to changing climate and atmospheric CO_2 concentrations and is critical for population growth and species colonization. Plant reproduction influences the ability of species to migrate to new areas, persist in or colonize disturbed sites, and compete with established vegetation to influence plant community composition and successional dynamics. In this section, we provide a brief review of the sensitivity of plant reproductive

Future responses of Pacific Northwest vegetation to elevated CO_2 are highly uncertain owing to limited experimental studies with elevated CO_2 in the Pacific Northwest (or with Pacific Northwest species) and the wide range of biophysical settings and vegetation types.

processes—including flowering and pollen production, fertilization, seed production, dispersal, germination, and establishment—to climatic variability and elevated CO_2.

Seed Production

Seed production in plants can be influenced by climate and elevated atmospheric CO_2 (Jablonski et al. 2002, LaDeau and Clark 2006). Warmer air and soil temperatures can advance flowering phenology in plants (Beaubien and Hamann 2011, Dunne et al. 2003, Parmesan 2006). Although earlier flowering can promote increased seed production and viability (Richardson et al. 2005, Walck et al. 2011), it can also expose plants to frost damage and reduced seed production, particularly at high elevations and latitudes (Beaubien and Hamann 2011, Inouye 2008). Climate-induced shifts in reproductive phenology can also alter plant reproductive capacity by altering phenological synchrony between plants and insect pollinators or herbivores (Hegland et al. 2009, Liu et al. 2011). Studies of seed masting in trees suggest that temperature and precipitation (water availability) may act at different stages of flowering and fruiting to influence seed production (Selås et al. 2002, Woodward et al. 1994). In general, however, the climatic and other environmental factors influencing seed production and viability are still poorly understood for most species, making it difficult to project responses to future climatic changes.

Elevated CO_2 can stimulate seed production and mass in both crop and wild species.

Elevated CO_2 can stimulate seed production and mass in both crop and wild species (Jablonski et al. 2002), as seed production provides a sink for surplus carbon. For example, loblolly pines growing under elevated CO_2 matured earlier and produced more seeds and cones (adjusted for tree size) than those growing at ambient CO_2 levels (LaDeau and Clark 2001, 2006), but there was no CO_2 effect on seed mass, viability, or nutrient content (Way et al. 2010). However, CO_2 effects on seed production differ among plant species and functional groups (Hikosaka et al. 2011, Jablonski et al. 2002), and plant allocation to seed production can also decline under elevated CO_2 for some species (HilleRisLambers et al. 2009).

Dispersal (Including Long Distance)

Seed dispersal is an important process by which populations can expand into neighboring sites (e.g., colonizing disturbed sites) and by which species can expand their geographic ranges. Wind is the dominant seed dispersal agent in forests and rangelands of the Pacific Northwest, but animals (including humans) and water also transport seeds. Seed (and pollen) dispersal distances are typically skewed, with most seed falling close to the source and a very small number of seeds being transported great distances (Nathan et al. 2008). The mechanisms, frequency, and impacts of long-distance seed transport have received considerable research attention, as pollen studies have suggested that long-distance dispersal played an important role in species migrations following the last glacial period and may be the only way by which species migrations can track future climate change in some regions (Loarie et al. 2009, Nathan et al. 2008). However, recent studies have indicated that some populations once believed to have established via long-distance dispersal actually derived from remnant populations that persisted through the glacial period in refugia (McLachlan et al. 2005, Petit et al. 2008). These latter studies suggest that estimates of historical migration rates for some species will have to be reduced significantly and that true potential migration rates are substantially lower than what would be needed to track future climate changes (McLachlan et al. 2005).

Whether future climate changes will have a significant influence on long-distance seed dispersal is unclear. Increased fecundity in populations on the leading edges of species ranges could increase chances for long-distance dispersal simply by providing more seed (Hampe 2011). Changing climate could alter dispersal pathways at landscape to regional scales by altering arrival site suitability for seed germination and establishment (Hampe 2011). Kuparinen et al. (2009) also suggested that warmer air temperatures in the future could increase atmospheric instability and increase distances for wind dispersal (including extreme events). It is also unclear if other mechanisms for long-distance dispersal (e.g., transport by humans, rivers, or migratory animals) would be significantly influenced by a changing climate.

Seed Dormancy and Germination

Plant seeds often have some mechanism for maintaining dormancy and inhibiting germination until some external condition is met (Kozlowski and Pallardy 2002, Walck et al. 2011). Endodormancy is common in many woody species of the Pacific Northwest (e.g., Douglas-fir), in which moist seeds must be chilled to some degree prior to germination (Kozlowski and Pallardy 2002). Other species produce seeds with hard coats or waxes that must be broken (or melted) prior to germination (Kozlowski and Pallardy 2002); common examples from the Pacific Northwest include lodgepole pine (*Pinus contorta;* some populations feature serotinous cones that require heating to open and release seeds) and snowbrush ceanothus (*Ceanothus velutinus* Douglas ex Hook.; seeds with hard coats remain dormant in soil until heated).

Climate change has the potential to alter seed dormancy period and subsequent germination rates through its effects on fire regimes and winter temperatures. Changes in fire-return intervals would alter restocking of canopy and soil seed banks between fires, residence times for seeds in canopy and soil seed banks (potentially influencing viability), depths of seeds buried in soils (influencing responses to soil heating), and heights of canopy seed banks.

Warming winter temperatures in areas with mild winters could delay or prevent germination if they fail to meet the chilling requirements for releasing seeds from dormancy (Walck et al. 2011). On the other hand, warming winter temperatures could produce premature germination in cold environments, leading to seedling death (Walck et al. 2011). Chilling requirements are generally well studied for commercially important plant species in the Pacific Northwest, as they are important for processing seed for nursery stock. However, little is known about the potential for acclimation or adaptation of chilling requirements in altered climates.

Establishment

Successful establishment is crucial for maintaining the viability of existing populations, population expansion into new sites, and species migrations. Establishment is also the stage in the life cycle of plants that best exemplifies the influence of historical, physiological, and biotic filters on plant species presence and plant community composition (Lambers et al. 1998). Successful plant establishment requires the arrival of seed (historical filter) to a microsite with suitable environmental conditions and resource availability (physiological filter), where it can coexist with other biotic organisms (the biotic filter). Plants cannot become established and persist on a site unless each of these elements is in place.

Because most seed falls within relatively short distances of the parent plant, establishment tends to be dominated by species with established, reproducing populations at or near the site (Donato et al. 2009, Larson and Franklin 2005, Zald et al. 2008). Some local populations may be remnant or sink populations that are incapable of producing viable seed, whereas others may require favorable climatic conditions to produce seed. In the absence of an abundant local seed source, establishment becomes dependent on long-distance dispersal mechanisms, providing stability in established plant communities, but lengthening recovery times following severe disturbances.

> **Plants are usually the most sensitive to environmental stressors (the physiological filter) during the establishment phase when plants are small.**

Plants are usually the most sensitive to environmental stressors (the physiological filter) during the establishment phase when plants are small. Establishing plants initially have small root systems, making them dependent on soil water and nutrients from shallow soil depths in their immediate vicinity. Some species require or prefer specific types of seedbeds, like bare mineral soil. Carbohydrate and nutrient reserves needed for initial growth can also be very limiting early in the establishment process, depending on seed size and resource storage and local shading. High surface to volume ratios also make plant tissues more sensitive to extreme temperatures.

Because of these limitations, successful plant establishment often depends on favorable microsite conditions or beneficial biotic interactions (Gray and Spies 1997). Regeneration after wildfires and other large disturbances may be facilitated by shading from snags, large rocks, or topographic features (e.g., on north-facing slopes) that limits radiation inputs and potential evapotranspiration. Similarly, shading from neighboring trees and shrubs can help reduce heat and water stress for some species at the expense of lower light levels. Other species require high light levels, while tolerating low water availability. Downed logs can help tree seedlings become established by reducing competition from understory plants (Harmon and Franklin 1989). Recent studies have suggested the importance of soil biota— particularly ectomycorrhizal networks—for facilitating tree seedling establishment (Bingham and Simard 2012).

Changes in atmospheric CO_2 concentrations and climate are expected to have a wide range of impacts on tree seedling establishment. Higher CO_2 concentrations can increase light- and water-use efficiency in seedlings, potentially increasing shade tolerance, reducing drought stress, and increasing survival. However, Mohan et al. (2007) reported that the benefits of elevated CO_2 on understory seedling growth was largely limited to shade-tolerant species.

Changes in temperature and precipitation (and associated changes in drought stress) could reduce establishment rates by long-lived tree and shrub populations by creating establishment conditions that differ considerably from those under which the original population became established. These altered environmental conditions could exert selective pressure on future generations, leading to in situ adaptation of populations to changing climate. If changes exceed the adaptive capacity of the population, local regeneration could cease or be restricted to multiyear periods of favorable climate.

Biotic Interactions

Biotic interactions significantly influence species distributions and community composition at local to regional scales (Araújo and Luoto 2007). Competition has long been recognized as an important process in structuring plant communities and vegetation dynamics (Connell and Slatyer 1977, Grime 1979, Tilman 1982), while the importance of facilitation (positive interactions) in community structure has received increasing recognition in recent decades (Brooker et al. 2008, Callaway 1995, Callaway and Walker 1997). There is also a rich literature on herbivory and its effects on vegetation structure and dynamics (e.g., Bakker et al. 2006, Ritchie et al. 1998, Schreiner et al. 1996). Plants often rely on beneficial biotic interactions for initial establishment (e.g., nurse plants or logs, mycorrhizal infection), pollination, seed dispersal, and protection from herbivores. They must also respond to or defend against detrimental biotic interactions such as competition for limiting resources, herbivory, and seed predation.

Projecting the potential effects of elevated CO_2 and changing climate on biotic interactions and resulting plant community dynamics has become a topic of great interest in recent years, but much work remains to be done in this area. Rising CO_2 and changing climate could alter the outcomes of biotic interactions if competing individuals or species respond differently to environmental changes, thereby increasing or reducing relative rates of growth and reproduction. Changing climate and CO_2 could also alter the intensity of biotic interactions by increasing or reducing overall resource availability (physiological stress). In this section, we review some examples of biotic interactions that are important for structuring vegetation communities and how they might be influenced by elevated CO_2 and changing climate. We also describe potential ways that biotic interactions may mediate vegetation responses to changing climate and CO_2.

Mutualisms—Pollination and Mycorrhizal Associations

Phenological synchrony between plants and their pollinators could be disrupted if plants and pollinators respond differently to changing environmental cues.

Although many tree and shrub species in the Pacific Northwest are wind pollinated, other plants rely on insects or birds for pollination, exchanging nectar or pollen for pollen transport. This mutually beneficial arrangement requires close synchronization of phenology between plants and pollinators, so that pollinators are present and actively seeking rewards while the plants are flowering (Hegland et al. 2009, Rathcke and Lacey 1985). It can also promote synchrony or asynchrony in flowering among plant species; synchronous flowering can be beneficial for attracting pollinators, while asynchronous flowering can reduce competition for pollinator service and cross-pollination problems (Hegland et al. 2009, Rathcke and Lacey 1985).

Phenological synchrony between plants and their pollinators could be disrupted if plants and pollinators respond differently to changing environmental cues (Hegland et al. 2009, Memmott et al. 2007, Parmesan 2007). This could alter plant species fitness by increasing or reducing coflowering and competition for pollinators (Forrest et al. 2010, Forrest and Thomson 2011). Pollination mutualisms could also be altered by species migrations, either the arrival of a new potential pollinator, or the loss of a current pollinator. On the other hand, pollinators may be sufficiently flexible in their responses to environmental cues that they could modify their behavior to track changes in plant phenology; if so, the plant-pollinator mutualism would be modifying species responses to climate change.

Many plants also rely on mutualistic relationships with insects, birds, and animals for seed dispersal. As with flowering phenology, the success and timing of seed and fruit ripening is often related to climate (Rathcke and Lacey 1985). Synchrony of seed and fruit ripening could benefit co-occurring species by attracting animal dispersers, while competition for animal dispersers could promote asynchrony in seed and fruit ripening (Rathcke and Lacey 1985). Elevated CO_2 and changing climate could alter plant resource allocation to fruit and seed production, the timing of ripening and dispersal, and levels of synchrony in fruit and seed production within plant communities. As with pollination, potential dispersers might be sufficiently dependent on fruit rewards to track changes in the timing of fruit availability, thereby reducing climate change impacts on vegetation.

Mycorrhizal associations are another common and important mutualism that could be influenced by elevated CO_2 and changing climate in ways that alter plant performance and ecosystem functioning. Plants provide carbon compounds to mycorrhizal fungi in return for enhanced water and nutrient uptake (McCormack et al. 2010). Soil fungi provide a sink for carbon fixed through photosynthesis and could therefore be important for helping plants maintain high carbon uptake rates under elevated CO_2 (McCormack et al. 2010). Stimulation of plant carbon uptake and productivity could also be enhanced if the additional carbon provided to mycorrhizal fungi increases nutrient and water uptake and delivery to the plant.

Facilitation

Positive interactions (facilitation) among plant species have received increased attention in recent years (Callaway 1995, Brooker et al. 2008). Positive interactions are particularly important for initial plant establishment, after which competition for limiting resources often (but not always) becomes more dominant among mature plants. Positive interactions can occur in all vegetation types but appear to be most important in stressful environments, like alpine, semiarid, and arid ecosystems (Callaway 1995, Callaway et al. 2002). Elevated CO_2 and changing climate are likely to alter positive interactions among plants primarily by increasing or reducing their importance (making them more or less beneficial). In some cases, however, disturbances, species migrations, or local extinctions, could add or remove benefactor or beneficiary species, with potentially large impacts on vegetation structure and ecosystem functioning.

Large trees and shrubs can facilitate establishment and persistence of understory plants (and tree seedlings) by modifying understory microclimate and soil resource availability (McPherson 1997, Scholes and Archer 1997). Shading from overstory trees can reduce temperatures and evaporative demand in understory plants (McPherson 1997), while soils under tree canopies can accumulate nutrients and provide greater nutrient availability to plants through more rapid litter decomposition and nutrient cycling (Reich et al. 2001, Scholes and Archer 1997). Subalpine conifers can reduce snowpack duration and increase growing season length, thereby facilitating establishment of understory plants and tree seedlings (Brooke et al. 1970), or can increase local soil moisture by altering windflow patterns and enhancing local snow deposition (Holtmeier and Broll 1992).

In the Great Basin of North America, sagebrush (*Artemisia tridentatea* (Nutt.) can increase near-surface soil water availability by transporting water from deeper, moister soils at night via "hydraulic lift," thereby increasing water (and perhaps nutrient) availability to neighboring plants (Caldwell and Richards 1989, Caldwell et al. 1998, Richards and Caldwell 1987). Griffith (2010) found that higher soil fertility and less extreme microclimates under two Great Basin shrubs, big sagebrush (*A. tridentatea*) and bitterbrush (*Purshia tridentatea* (Pursh) DC.), promoted higher densities and growth rates of an invasive annual grass, cheatgrass (*Bromus tectorum* L.).

Trees and shrubs can also facilitate woody plant invasions of grasslands indirectly by suppressing or eliminating potential competitors (Rice et al. 2012). Although overstory tree and shrub canopies can facilitate initial understory establishment, relationships between understory and overstory plants can turn competitive if light becomes the dominant factor limiting growth and survival. In a changing climate, however, overstory modification of understory microclimate could become increasingly important for facilitating establishment and maintaining populations.

Plants can also facilitate establishment and persistence of other plants through their effects on soil nutrient availability and acquisition (Callaway 1995). Nitrogen fixation by legumes and nonleguminous shrubs can increase soil nutrient availability, which can facilitate establishment and persistence of species that might otherwise be excluded by low nutrient availability. Because nitrogen-fixing species benefit from elevated CO_2, such interactions could become more important in the future. Plants may facilitate the establishment of new individuals of the same species or of other species by maintaining local populations of compatible mycorrhizal fungi, thereby promoting rapid colonization of seedling roots and associated benefits for water and nutrient uptake (Amaranthus and Perry 1989, Dickie et al. 2005).

Competition

Competition for light, water, and nutrients is an important process driving vegetation structure and composition (Connell and Slatyer 1977, Tilman 1982). Competition occurs within and among species and is often density dependent. Plants can avoid direct competition for limiting resources by partitioning resource usage in time (e.g., different growth phenologies) or space ("first come, first served"). Theory suggests that many different species can coexist, despite competition, by varying their relative resource usage or if disturbances are frequent enough to prevent competitive exclusion (Grubb 1977, Tilman 1982).

Changing climate and atmospheric CO_2 concentrations could alter the intensity of competitive interactions among plants and the relative advantage of competing species by altering plant resource availability, rates of resource consumption, or relative demand for resources. Increasing atmospheric CO_2 levels make CO_2 more available to plants, alter demand for soil water resources, and potentially alter soil nutrient availability (see "Ecosystem Responses" section below); such changes could be more beneficial for some species than for others, thereby altering the competitive balance. Changes in temperature and precipitation alter soil water availability and potential evapotranspiration (demand for soil water), thereby altering water-related stress and potentially altering competition intensity (Maestre et al. 2009, and references therein). Changes in plant density could also alter competition intensity, while climate-mediated invasions of new species or extirpation of existing species could alter plant community composition and the relative demand for different resources (similar to changes in resource availability).

Demonstrating the effects of changing climate and CO_2 on vegetation composition and structure via competitive interactions is difficult. Many factors contribute to changes in vegetation structure and composition in natural vegetation (e.g., disturbances and factors regulating successful regeneration), making it difficult to determine proximate causes for change. Experimental approaches are better able to isolate causes but typically require limiting the number of species and environmental conditions. In a synthesis study of recent vegetation changes in arctic and alpine tundra, Elmendorf et al. (2012) reported increases in plant height, litter abundance, and evergreen shrub abundance, and reductions in bare soil, apparently in response to recent warming. Such changes are expected to increase the future importance of competition in these systems, particularly during plant establishment (Klanderud 2010). In experimental studies, Suttle et al. (2007) found that supplementing natural precipitation in winter and spring in California grasslands produced significant changes in plant community composition, while Niu and Wan (2008) found that warming temperatures altered the competitive hierarchies of grasses and forbs in temperate steppe vegetation of northern China. A comparison of warming and CO_2 enrichment effects on short-grass steppe vegetation found that warming favored C_4 grasses while elevated CO_2 favored C_3 grasses (Morgan et al. 2011); elevated CO_2 had little effect on total species richness but increased shrub cover 20-fold (Morgan et al. 2007).

Herbivory

Elevated CO_2 and changing climate could affect herbivore interactions and their impacts on vegetation by increasing or reducing synchrony in herbivore activity and plant availability, altering herbivore abundance or feeding behavior, and altering plant nutritional value. Plants and insect herbivores can both alter the timing of their growth stages based on environmental cues, but the cues used are not necessarily identical (Rathcke and Lacey 1985). Differing phenological responses to changing temperature and precipitation patterns could therefore alter plant-herbivore and insect-host interactions by increasing or reducing synchrony in life stage development (Harrington et al. 1999, Liu et al. 2011, Parmesan 2007). Inouye et al. (2000) observed a changing relationship over 25 years between snowmelt and flowering in alpine meadows (which was variable, but stable) and progressively earlier emergence of yellow-bellied marmots (*Marmota flaviventris*), apparently caused by warming air temperatures, which produced progressively longer periods of food shortages for the marmots prior to snowmelt.

Changing climatic conditions could alter herbivore communities through migrations or changes in predator activity (Tylianakis et al. 2008). Organisms at higher trophic levels are expected to respond more readily than vegetation to changing environmental conditions (mobility being the key), so migration responses could alter the species composition and abundance of herbivores and their predators, with uncertain effects on herbivory. Changes in winter snowpack depth and duration could alter migration patterns and winter feeding behavior by deer and other large herbivores, with potential impacts on vegetation structure and composition and herbivore performance.

Elevated CO_2 could also alter herbivore communities and herbivore performance through its effects on plant productivity and tissue chemistry (Robinson et al. 2012, Zvereva and Kozlov 2006). Numerous studies have reported effects of elevated CO_2 on plant tissue chemistry that could reduce palatability for herbivores, including increased concentrations of nonstructural carbohydrates and phenolics, reduced nitrogen concentrations, higher carbon/nitrogen ratios, and increased tissue toughness (Lincoln et al. 1993, Lindroth 2010, Robinson et al. 2012, Zvereva and Kozlov 2006). These changes in plant tissue chemistry under elevated CO_2 can reduce insect herbivore performance (Peñuelas and Estiarte 1998, Stiling and Cornelissen 2007, Zvereva and Kozlov 2006) and alter arthropod community composition (Hamilton et al. 2012). However, the detrimental effects of elevated CO_2 on herbivores via changes in plant tissue chemistry may be partially or fully offset when combined with warming temperatures, as warmer temperatures may alter net plant production of and demand for carbohydrates (Zvereva and Kozlov 2006).

Numerous studies have reported effects of elevated CO_2 on plant tissue chemistry that could reduce palatability for herbivores.

Community Responses

Plant community responses to elevated CO_2 and climate change reflect the sum of individual species responses, including changes in seed production and dispersal, establishment success, physiological tolerances of altered environmental conditions, and biotic interactions. Paleoecological studies suggest that species will respond individually to changing environmental conditions (Davis 1981, Jackson and Overpeck 2000). Some common plant associations may persist, whereas others disappear and are replaced by novel associations (Jackson and Overpeck 2000). As previous sections in this chapter have shown, interactions among plant physiological responses to changing CO_2 and temperature and biotic interactions can create a wide range of outcomes for plant communities.

Most examples of plant community responses to changing climate involve invasion of communities by new species and associated changes owing to altered resource availability and biotic interactions (Breshears et al. 2008, Elmendorf et al. 2012, Kelly and Goulden 2008, Walther et al. 2005). Community changes have also been documented in response to increased dominance of woody species in response to elevated CO_2 (Morgan et al. 2007) or changing disturbance regimes (Briggs et al. 2005). Extirpation of a dominant species can also produce significant community changes (Allen and Breshears 1998, Mueller et al. 2005), though stabilizing processes within communities may limit long-term community responses to extreme events (Kreyling et al. 2008, Lloret et al. 2012).

Community responses will also reflect responses of organisms at higher trophic levels (Walther 2010). These organisms may respond directly to changing climate and associated environmental stressors, or they may respond to climate- or CO_2-mediated changes in plant communities. Changes in pollinator, herbivore, and predator communities can also produce changes in plant communities through changes in reproduction, establishment, biomass loss, and mortality.

Ecosystem Responses

Changing climate and increasing CO_2 concentrations have important implications for ecosystem structure and function. Climate change and elevated CO_2 have the potential to alter ecosystem carbon uptake and storage, nutrient cycling rates, and feedbacks among carbon uptake, nutrient cycling, and vegetation structure and composition. In this section, we highlight some key findings regarding ecosystem responses to elevated CO_2 and changing climate.

Carbon uptake and storage is an important issue, as terrestrial ecosystems may be able to partially mitigate anthropogenic carbon emissions and their effects on

Paleoecological studies suggest that species will respond individually to changing environmental conditions.

climate by fixing atmospheric carbon and storing it in aboveground or belowground biomass, in coarse woody debris, or in soil organic matter. These different carbon pools provide different mean residence times for carbon and interact differently with environmental changes and disturbances (Norby and Zak 2011). Carbon uptake also provides energy for biological processes, including decomposition of organic matter and release of mineral nutrients, which leads to feedbacks between carbon uptake and nutrient availability.

Productivity and Nutrient Cycling

Experimental studies have shown that elevated CO_2, warming temperatures, and increasing precipitation can all increase plant growth and net primary production across a wide range of terrestrial ecosystems (Dieleman et al. 2012, Hyvönen et al. 2007, Norby and Zak 2011, Wu et al. 2011, Zak et al. 2011), although combined effects are not always additive (Dieleman et al. 2012, Wu et al. 2011). On average, elevated CO_2 and warming temperatures increase biomass production alone and in combination, but elevated CO_2 stimulated fine root biomass production more than aboveground biomass production (Dieleman et al. 2012, Norby and Zak 2011, Wu et al. 2011). In a young aspen (*Populus tremuloides* Michx.) forest, elevated CO_2 increased net primary productivity by 26 percent (Zak et al. 2011). The mechanisms by which productivity is enhanced (and sustained) are still unclear, however, and appear to involve not only the direct effects of CO_2, temperature, and water availability (and their interactions) on photosynthesis, respiration, and growth, but also indirect effects on nutrient cycling and nitrogen availability (Felzer et al. 2011).

Productivity gains under elevated CO_2 can decline over time on nutrient-limited sites as sequestration of nitrogen in long-lived plant biomass and soil organic matter progressively limits nitrogen availability (de Graaff et al. 2006, Luo et al. 2004, Reich et al. 2006a). Evidence for this progressive nitrogen limitation comes from long-term free-air CO_2 enrichment (FACE) studies with fertilization treatments in tallgrass prairie (Reich et al. 2006a) and sweetgum (*Liquidambar styraciflua* L.) forest (Norby et al. 2010), but not loblolly pine forest (McCarthy et al. 2010). Norby et al. (2010) noted that reduced forest productivity over time owing to progressive nitrogen limitation is common as forest biomass increases with stand age, but that elevated CO_2 appears to accelerate the process. Progressive nitrogen limitation on productivity can be delayed or avoided only if nitrogen inputs through fixation or atmospheric deposition equal or exceed rates of nitrogen sequestration in biomass, litter, and soils.

Recent results from long-term FACE studies suggest that several feedback processes may work to reduce or reverse the effects of progressive nitrogen limitation on productivity. Schleppi et al. (2012) attributed elevated nitrification rates and high levels of soil nitrate availability under trees subjected to elevated CO_2 to higher soil moisture levels produced by reduced evapotranspiration. Recent studies have concluded that observed reductions in soil carbon and increased nitrogen availability could be the result of root "priming," in which trees export carbon to soil biota through the root system, thereby stimulating soil organic matter decomposition by fungi and bacteria, and subsequent release of mineral nutrients bound up in that organic matter (Drake et al. 2011, Phillips et al. 2012, Schleppi et al. 2012, Zak et al. 2011).

Soil temperatures influence organic matter decomposition processes and the cycling of nitrogen and other important nutrients, which can feed back on plant growth and productivity (Berbeco et al. 2012, Felzer et al. 2011, Harmon et al. 1986, Melillo et al. 2011, Rustad et al. 2001). Warming temperatures typically stimulate biological activity and may significantly increase rates of soil organic matter decomposition in temperate forests (Berbeco et al. 2012, Saxe et al. 2001). Warming soils can also increase rates of nitrogen mineralization and nitrification, making more nitrogen available for uptake by plants (Butler et al. 2012, Melillo et al. 2011, Rustad et al. 2001, Van Cleve et al. 1990). Understanding the potential for increased nitrogen availability is important, as nitrogen is an important plant nutrient that often limits growth in forested ecosystems (Vitousek et al. 1997). Temperature effects on soil organic matter decomposition and nutrient cycling are likely to vary considerably, however, with soil fertility and vegetation composition, as these influence litter quality and the potential for immobilization of nutrients in microbial biomass.

The stimulatory effect of warming temperatures on organic matter decomposition and nutrient cycling is likely to be limited by precipitation and soil water availability, however (Felzer et al. 2011, Harmon et al. 1986, Saxe et al. 2001). Decomposition of coarse woody debris varies with wood moisture content, as water becomes unavailable to microbes below 30 percent water content, while very high moisture contents create anaerobic conditions (Harmon et al. 1986). Similarly, spatial and temporal variability in precipitation and soil moisture influence soil respiration rates in seasonally dry biomes like savannas and shrublands (Norton et al. 2011, Raich et al. 2002). Low soil moisture can also limit nitrogen mineralization and availability (Felzer et al. 2011, McFarlane et al. 2010).

Finally, changes in plant communities could also alter soil environments, soil biota, nutrient cycling processes, and soil nutrient availability, with potential effects on net primary productivity. Tree invasions into shrub-steppe of the Great Basin have altered the spatial distribution of soil carbon and nutrients (Klemmedson and Tiedemann 2000, Rau et al. 2011b), while tree removal in Texas caused a slow reversal of tree effects on soils (Tiedemann and Klemmedson 1986a, 1986b). Similarly, experimental field studies have shown that grassland species can significantly alter nitrogen cycling rates (Craine et al. 2002, Wedin and Tilman 1990) and the amount and vertical distribution of soil carbon and nitrogen (Rau et al. 2011a).

Carbon Storage

Storing carbon in forests has been proposed as a strategy for mitigating increasing atmospheric CO_2 concentrations and their effects on current and future climate (Malmsheimer et al. 2008, McKinley et al. 2011). Through increased net primary production and ecosystem carbon exchange, anthropogenic carbon emissions could be partially offset by carbon uptake and long-term storage in terrestrial ecosystems, particularly in trees and shrubs (perennial woody tissue) and soils. It is estimated that extensive afforestation efforts and active management following disturbances could allow increased forest carbon storage to offset 10 to 20 percent of anthropogenic carbon emissions in the United States (McKinley et al. 2011).

Disturbance regimes (and their responses to changing climate) will be important for determining whether woody plant biomass can store atmospheric carbon effectively (McKinley et al. 2011), particularly in aboveground biomass. Large-scale insect outbreaks (Kurz et al. 2008), fires (Kashian et al. 2006, Westerling et al. 2006), or drought-mediated mortality (van Mantgem et al. 2009) could convert forests from carbon sinks to carbon sources, at least in the short term. If regeneration and growth eventually returns forests to their former condition (e.g., biomass, coarse woody debris, and soil carbon), the long-term effect on carbon storage is neutral (Hyvönen et al. 2007, Kashian et al. 2006). However, if disturbances convert forests to stable savannas, grasslands, or shrublands, the long-term effect on carbon storage is likely to be negative (Kashian et al. 2006).

Soils store significant amounts of carbon for long periods of time and hold the majority of terrestrial carbon stocks. Carbon enters the soil in the form of woody debris (e.g., branches and roots), plant litter (e.g., leaves and fine roots), dead algal or bacterial cells, and root exudates (Kilham 1994). Residence times are short for many types of soil carbon, as physical processes and soil biota cause rapid decomposition, but other soil organic carbon stocks are much more stable and could provide long-term storage of carbon (Norby and Zak 2011). Soil warming has been shown to increase biological activity; soil respiration; and decomposition rates of litter, fine woody debris, and other (unspecified) forms of soil carbon (Berbeco et al. 2012, Dieleman et al. 2012, Hyvönen et al. 2007, Melillo et al. 2011, Rustad et al. 2001, Zak et al. 2011), thereby offsetting or reversing increased carbon inputs from increased net primary production.

Until recently, there was general belief that effects of elevated CO_2 on litter chemistry would offset or reverse warming effects on decomposition and soil carbon storage in forests by increasing carbon inputs, reducing nitrogen concentrations (increasing carbon:nitrogen ratios) and increasing concentrations of secondary compounds in litter. Recently, however, results from long-term experiments with elevated CO_2 suggest that elevated CO_2 could actually accelerate decomposition of soil organic matter and reduce soil carbon storage (Cheng et al. 2012, Drake et al. 2011, Kowalchuk 2012, Phillips et al. 2012, Schleppi et al. 2012, Zak et al. 2011). Unfortunately, it is unclear how these results, derived primarily from experiments in temperate deciduous forests, translate to western coniferous forests and rangelands with significant seasonal water limitations that can influence soil carbon turnover (Norton et al. 2011).

Invasive Species

Invasive plants are introduced nonnative, exotic, or nonindigenous species that potentially can become successfully established or naturalized, and that spread into new localized natural habitats or ecoregions and potentially cause economic or environmental harm (Lodge et al. 2006). Familiar examples include the shrub scotch broom (*Cytisus scoparius* L. Link) and the exotic annual grass cheatgrass (*Bromus tectorum*). Some native species like juniper (*Juniperus* spp.) have expanded their range in recent decades and are treated as invasive in certain ecosystems (Miller and Wigand 1994, Miller et al. 2005). This document only considers nonnative invasive plants, but we note that climate change could cause additional native plants to exhibit invasive behavior; indeed, many would have to do so to migrate at currently projected rates.

Climate change could cause some native plants to exhibit invasive behavior; indeed, many would have to do so to migrate at currently projected rates.

There is considerable evidence that future climate change will further increase the likelihood of invasion of forests and rangelands and the consequences of those invasions, largely because of the potential for increased ecosystem disturbance (e.g., wildfire, landslides), the impact of warming on species distributions, the enhanced competitiveness of invasive plants as a result of elevated CO_2, and increased stress to native species and ecosystems (Dukes and Mooney 1999, Pauchard et al. 2009, Ziska and Dukes 2011). Pauchard et al. (2009) noted that high levels of natural disturbance in alpine systems (e.g., landslides) are forecast to increase in frequency and extent owing to climate change. Numerous studies have documented the positive relationship between fire and the spread of invasive plants (D'Antonio et al. 2000, Kerns et al. 2006, Keeley and McGinnis 2007). Postdisturbance invasion may be particularly problematic in areas adjacent to seed sources.

With warming temperatures, the upper elevational and latitudinal limit of many invasive plants may expand. For example, the current distribution of cheatgrass is limited by soil temperature at the higher elevations and soil moisture at lower elevations (Chambers 2007). Theoretically, as the soil temperature regime warms at higher elevation and the soil moisture regime dries in the lower elevation, cheatgrass could shift upward in elevation assuming no significant change in the precipitation regime. Recent evidence suggests that invasive plants may be better able to adjust to rapid changes in abiotic conditions by tracking seasonal temperature trends and shifting their phenologies (e.g., earlier spring warming) (Willis et al. 2010). Invasives might also be able to migrate more rapidly than most native species owing to the rapid dispersal ability and genetic flexibility that allowed them to become invasives in the first place.

Increases in productivity in response to elevated CO_2 have also been documented for many invasive plant species including cheatgrass, Canada thistle (*Cirsium vulgare* (Savi) Ten.), spotted knapweed (*Centaurea stoebe* L.), yellow star-thistle (*Centraurea solstitialis* L.), and kudzu (*Pueraria montana* (Lour.) Merr.) (Dukes et al. 2011, Ziska and Dukes 2011). However, plant species response to CO_2 enrichment is less predictable when they are grown in diverse communities and in the field (Dukes and Mooney 1999, Ziska and Dukes 2011) and actual response to CO_2 enrichment may be limited by other nutrient constraints and water availability. The expansion of cheatgrass into salt desert shrub areas, which generally occur in areas of lower precipitation than sagebrush-steppe ecosystems (Jessop and Anderson 2007), may suggest that improved water-use efficiency (e.g., as a result of elevated CO_2 concentrations) is allowing cheatgrass to expand into areas previously considered too dry.

Species performance such as growth, phenology, and productivity may also change in novel conditions (Willis et al. 2010). The ability of the native plant community to resist an invasion may also change in the future. For example, invasive plants may be exposed to above- and belowground biotic interactions different from those in their current range, and "enemy-release" may occur (Engelkes et al. 2008). Climate change will also alter numerous aspects of propagule supply. Most invasive species reach new regions by purposeful or accidental human-aided transport (tourism, commerce). Human population (urban, visitation) is positively correlated to plant invasions (Eschtruth and Battles 2009, Lonsdale 1999). Atmospheric patterns (hurricanes, wind patterns) that transfer seeds will also change in the future. Climate change may also result in increased management actions that cause new disturbances (e.g., biofuel production, thinning).

Chapter 4: Vegetation Sensitivity to Changing Disturbance Regimes

Disturbances are a major driver of vegetation change, as they kill or damage mature vegetation and release resources that can be used by newly established individuals. Disturbances typically alter vegetation structure, which can alter understory environments, particularly in forests. Disturbances produce compositional changes in vegetation if new species replace those killed by disturbance. They can also facilitate genetic shifts within existing populations or alter the relative abundance of existing species. Some of the most common and influential disturbance types in the Pacific Northwest are also influenced by climate and climatic changes in some way. We therefore also discuss the effects of past and future climatic changes on stress-related mortality, fire, and insect and disease outbreaks as indirect conduits for exposing vegetation to environmental changes.

Intact plant communities are often difficult for new species to invade. Resource niches are partially or completely filled, limiting potential invaders to those that can tolerate lower resource availability (for at least one resource) than established species (Tilman 1982, 2004) or to periods of additional resource availability (Davis et al. 2000). Seed deposition from local populations is typically much more abundant than that from distant populations, giving local species an advantage in claiming open growing space and available resources. Mature trees and shrubs are able to buffer themselves (and sometimes their neighbors) against climatic variability and resource limitations, thereby reducing climate-related stress. Long-lived woody species can persist as relict populations for hundreds of years and maintain the potential to regenerate during occasional periods of favorable climate (Hampe and Jump 2011).

Climate-driven vegetation mortality is expected to be an important driver of vegetation changes in response to changing climate. In severe cases, climate-driven vegetation mortality may directly alter vegetation by causing local extinction of one or more species (on the "trailing edge"). Plant mortality can also facilitate new species colonization and changes in relative abundance of previously present species by opening up physical growing space, reducing competition for critical soil resources, reducing local seed abundance, and altering site microclimate. In this chapter, we briefly review three major sources of climate-driven vegetation mortality—physiological stress, fire, and insects and diseases—and their interactions, and how each may be affected by a changing climate.

Physiological Stress—Drought

Climatic variability and change can kill plants by inducing stress beyond the tolerances of individual plants, either in terms of intensity or duration (Allen et al.

Disturbances are a major driver of vegetation change, as they kill or damage mature vegetation and release resources that can be used by newly established individuals.

2010). The most common physiological stress for Pacific Northwest vegetation is probably low soil water availability (drought), though low temperatures and late snowmelt can also produce significant physiological stress in subalpine, alpine, and boreal ecosystems. Future warming is likely to increase the frequency and severity of plant drought stress, while potentially reducing stress from extreme cold or short growing seasons at high elevations.

Drought is a common physiological stress that limits establishment and productivity at lower and middle elevations throughout much of western North America. Physiological stress from drought can be amplified by high temperatures, reducing the time required for drought-induced mortality (Adams et al. 2009). Episodes of widespread drought-induced mortality have been reported for ponderosa pine (*Pinus ponderosa* Lawson and C. Lawson) and pinyon pine (*P. edulis* Engelm.) in the Southwestern United States (Adams et al. 2009; Allen and Breshears 1998; Breshears et al. 2005, 2009; Koepke et al. 2010) and for aspen (*Populus tremuloides* Michx.) in western Canada (Hogg et al. 2008). Increased drought stress due to warmer temperatures has also been implicated in observed increases in mortality throughout forests of western North America (Ganey and Vojta 2011, van Mantgem and Stephenson 2007, van Mantgem et al. 2009).

The proximate mechanisms causing tree mortality during drought can be difficult to determine, largely because there are often multiple contributing factors (Anderegg et al. 2012). Plants typically reduce stomatal conductance in response to drought—which can reduce net carbon uptake—and reduce growth (Anderegg 2012). Droughts can produce extended periods of net carbon loss, particularly if maintenance respiration rates are high, and this can reduce resistance to bark beetles (Breshears et al. 2009, Ganey and Vojta 2011). Severe droughts can cause widespread tree mortality through reductions in nonstructural carbon reserves, cavitation and loss of hydraulic conductance, and increased susceptibility to insect outbreaks (Adams et al. 2009; Anderegg et al. 2012; Breshears et al. 2009; Frey et al. 2004; Hogg et al. 2008; Leuzinger et al. 2009; McDowell et al. 2008, 2011; Plaut et al. 2012).

Species differ in their tolerances of heat and drought stress, so stress-related mortality tends to favor some species over others and can produce significant changes in vegetation structure and composition (Koepke et al. 2010, Mueller et al. 2005). For example, mortality rates were considerably higher for pinyon pine than for its common associate, one-seeded juniper (*Juniperus monosperma*), during the 2002–2003 drought in the Southwestern United States, leading to lower tree densities and increased overstory dominance by junipers (Koepke et al. 2010, Mueller et al. 2005). Furthermore, high rates of mortality and dieback for associated shrubs during the drought produced dramatic reductions in total woody canopy cover, allowing herbaceous understory populations to expand rapidly (Rich et al. 2008). Drought-related mortality could also alter vegetation structure by reducing plant density, perhaps reducing future demands on limited soil water (but see Ganey and Vojta 2011), and produce persistent shifts in biome boundaries (Allen and Breshears 1998).

Warming temperatures under future climate change are likely to increase the frequency and severity of droughts throughout the Pacific Northwest, regardless of small changes in mean annual precipitation. We are not aware of any modern accounts of extensive tree mortality caused by drought stress in the Pacific Northwest (comparable to those recently reported for the Southwestern United States). If drought frequency and intensity increases in the future, however, we would expect to start seeing widespread regeneration failures and dieback or mortality episodes, along with insect outbreaks and fire (see below). Although future droughts may be most obvious in the water-limited ecosystems of the interior Pacific Northwest and Siskiyou Mountains, species in those regions are also the best adapted to drought, so we should not expect drought-related mortality to be limited to those regions.

Fire

Climate is an important factor influencing the spatial distribution of fire regimes from landscape to global scales, including fire frequency, intensity, seasonality, and size (Krawchuk et al. 2009). At a very basic level, climate controls the distribution and productivity of vegetation that provides fuel for wildfires, excluding wildfires from desert regions with little or no vegetation (Flannigan et al. 2009). Within vegetated regions, climatic controls on plant productivity partially influence fire frequency and intensity by influencing rates of fuel accumulation. Climate also determines the timing and duration of the fire season during which fire can occur through its effects on fuel moisture, fire weather, and ignitions. Finally, climate interacts with topography, soils, and land use to influence fire extent.

Within any given vegetation type and fire regime, climatic variability influences the occurrence and characteristics of individual fire events and fire-year characteristics (Taylor et al. 2008). Climatic variability at annual to decadal time scales can alter fire season length, fuel characteristics (e.g., mean moisture levels), fire weather, and ignition frequencies, thereby influencing fire occurrence, fire intensity, and area burned. Drought years are associated with large area burned and regionally synchronous fire occurrences in forests of western North America (Brown 2006, Gedalof et al. 2005, Hessl et al. 2004, Littell et al. 2009, McKenzie et al. 2004, Trouet et al. 2010), as drought increases fuel flammability and enhances fire spread potential across diverse landscapes. Warm spring and summer temperatures are also positively associated with fire frequency, fire duration, and area burned in these forests, as warm spring temperatures extend the fire season length (providing more opportunity for ignitions) and warm summer temperatures favor more extreme fire behavior and hinder fire suppression efforts (Heyerdahl et al. 2008, Taylor et al. 2008, Westerling et al. 2006). Climate influences fire differently in dry western grasslands, however, where large fires are commonly associated with drought years that follow multiple wet years during which plant productivity and fuel production are elevated (Littell et al. 2009). In both forests and grasslands, however, fire frequency and area burned are related to fuel availability (amount and moisture content), fire season length, and fire weather, all of which are influenced by climate.

Wildfire area burned in the Western United States varied considerably through the course of the 20th century, with decadal trends as well as considerable interannual variability. Average area burned by wildfires was generally high early in the century (around 1916–1930) before declining to low levels during the middle of the century (about 1950 to 1975) and then increasing again with a series of large fire years in the last two to three decades (Littell et al. 2009). Although technological advances improved firefighting effectiveness in the mid-20th century, several studies have concluded that climate played an important role in controlling area burned throughout the 20th century (Littell et al. 2009, McKenzie et al. 2004). An analysis of wildfire area burned since 1970 in forests of the Western United States concluded that a trend toward increasing mean annual area burned was caused by higher spring and summer temperatures and earlier snowmelt that increased the duration of the fire season, particularly in mid-elevation forests (Westerling et al. 2006).

Future climatic changes are likely to alter wildfire regimes and wildfire effects by altering fire season length, fire weather, fuel production, and vegetation structure and composition. Warmer spring and summer temperatures would lengthen the fire season and increase fire frequency in forests, particularly in temperate and high-elevation forests that currently support high- and mixed-severity fire regimes (Westerling et al. 2006). Warming temperatures would also alter mean fire weather conditions (and fuel moisture), producing higher potential fire severity and larger fire sizes in many areas where fire weather is currently suboptimal for fire spread. Over longer periods, climatic changes (and disturbances) could also modify vegetation structure and composition, providing a feedback on fire frequency and severity (Westerling et al. 2006).

In the short term, warming temperatures could increase the frequency and extent of large, high-severity wildfires in Pacific Northwest forests (Krawchuk et

A recent trend toward increasing mean annual area burned is attributed to higher spring and summer temperatures and earlier snowmelt that increased the duration of the fire season, particularly in mid-elevation forests.

al. 2009). Mesic and dry-mesic forests that support high productivity and surface fuels could be a particular concern, but these forest types burn infrequently owing to high mean fuel moisture content and short fire seasons. A warmer climate, with longer fire seasons and lower fuel moisture could allow wildfires to "mine" these fuels over one to several fires, some of which are likely to be of high severity.

Fire regime changes in semiarid shrublands and grasslands are less certain and could, in some cases, be quite different from those of forests. These vegetation types typically have long fire seasons; however, fire frequency and extent are limited by ignitions and fuel continuity. It is not clear what influence climate change might have on ignition frequency (e.g., lightning strikes, human activity). Climate change could alter vegetation productivity, fuel production, and fuel continuity by changing the amount and seasonality of precipitation inputs to soil moisture and rates of evapotranspiration. It is not clear if the net result would be increased or reduced fire frequency, and results may be spatially variable. Cheatgrass (*Bromus tectorum* L.) and other annual exotic grasses have progressively invaded dry shrublands throughout the Western United States in recent decades. These grasses have altered the fire regime by increasing vegetation flammability and horizontal fuel continuity, which greatly increases the potential for fire spread and larger wildfires (Link et al. 2006).

Insects and Diseases

Like fire, insects and diseases facilitate changes in vegetation structure and composition by damaging or killing plants (especially dominant trees and shrubs), releasing suppressed individuals and species, and creating opportunities for colonization by new species. Insects and plant diseases in western North American forests may kill individual trees within stands or more than 50 percent of the trees across large regions (Ganey and Vojta 2011, Raffa et al. 2008). Their long-term effects on vegetation structure and composition depend not only on spatial extent and percentage mortality within the disturbed area, but also on whether disturbance agents are affecting canopy dominants, older or younger individuals, suppressed individuals, or some combination of these (e.g., Klenner and Arsenault 2009).

Climate is one of several factors influencing insect and disease disturbance regimes and the incidence of large disturbance events. Climate influences the geographic distribution, population dynamics, and disturbance effects of insects and diseases through (1) direct environmental influences on the development and survival of insects and disease organisms, (2) altered host susceptibility and defenses, and (3) indirect effects caused by environmental influences on biotic interactions with predators (Ayres and Lombardero 2000, Garrett et al. 2006, Kliejunas et al. 2009, Sturrock et al. 2011).

Temperature is the dominant abiotic factor directly affecting herbivorous insects as it directly affects development, survival, range, and abundance (Bale et al. 2002). In particular, winter temperatures influence survival of herbivorous insects in temperate zones, while spring/summer temperatures influence insect life cycle duration, synchrony of insect life cycle stages with host plant phenology, and insect generation time (Bale et al. 2002). Climatic variability can also alter biotic interactions involving insects and diseases by altering the abundance of predators, parasites, mutualists, and competitors (Ayres and Lobardero 2000). Because of these effects, geographic distributions of insect species have changed in the past in response to climate change (Bale et al. 2002, and references therein).

Climate also influences insect and disease impacts indirectly by modifying vigor and defenses in host plants (Bentz et al. 2010, Raffa et al. 2008). Climatic variability can alter physiological stress levels and carbon fixation in host plants, increasing or reducing their susceptibility to insect attacks and plant diseases. Woody plant mortality in response to heat and drought stress is often mediated by insects and diseases; trees weakened by prolonged drought stress have reduced defenses against the insect and disease attacks that eventually kill the tree (Allen et al. 2010, McDowell et al. 2011). For example, Ganey and Vojta (2011) reported that increased mortality in ponderosa pine and mixed-conifer forests during a period of severe drought was attributable to a suite of insects, mediated by drought. Similarly, extensive, rapid, mortality of aspen (*Populus tremuloides* Michx.) in Colorado during the same drought was attributed to insects and diseases that normally would have had limited impacts if drought had not predisposed the trees to mortality (Worrall et al. 2008).

Insect- and disease-caused mortality tends to be species specific, so large outbreaks can significantly alter vegetation structure and composition in mixed-species stands (Astrup et al. 2008). These outbreaks also open up growing space that could be colonized by new species, but seed source limitations and competition from residual vegetation can make colonization difficult (Astrup et al. 2008). Future vegetation is more likely to develop from residual vegetation and release of advance regeneration (trees and shrubs).

Future climatic changes—particularly temperature changes—are expected to significantly alter insect and disease disturbance regimes in terrestrial ecosystems (Kliejunas et al. 2009). Projecting changes to insect and disease activity is difficult owing to the many potential interacting factors, but some effects of increasing temperatures can be inferred with some certainty. For forests, insect and disease disturbances will probably increase, as the ability of the pathogens to adapt to new climatic conditions will be greater than that of their long-lived hosts (Kliejunas et al. 2009, Sturrock 2010). They will also be able to migrate to locations where climate is suitable for their survival and reproduction at a faster rate than tree species (Logan et al. 2003).

Warming temperatures could increase the potential for insect and disease outbreaks, particularly as a transient response in temperate and boreal zones where pathogen activity has been limited by suboptimal temperatures (Bentz et al. 2010). For example, widespread dieback and mortality of thinleaf alder (*Alnus incana* (L.) Moench ssp. *tenuifolia* (Nutt.) Breitung) in the southern Rocky Mountains has been attributed to an epidemic of cytospora canker (*Valsa melanodiscus*), which may be related to increasing summer temperatures (Worrall et al. 2010). Higher warm-season temperatures should also increase growth rates for most temperate insect herbivores, though the rate of increase will vary by species (Bale et al. 2002). For some species, faster growth rates and reduced development time could enhance juvenile survivorship by reducing predation rates during the larval and nymphal feeding stages (Bernays 1997, cited by Bale et al. 2002). Increased growth rates could reduce generation times for some species, which could significantly increase population growth rates (Bale et al. 2002, Mitton and Ferrenberg 2012). Increasing population success increases the potential for insect outbreaks to develop, though outbreaks can be limited by host and predator constraints as well (Bale et al. 2002, Boone et al. 2011). Warmer temperatures could also increase host stress levels and the ability to defend against insect attacks (Boone et al. 2011).

Increasing temperatures could also facilitate migration of insects and diseases toward higher elevations and latitudes (Bale et al. 2002, Bentz et al. 2010). Higher cold-season temperatures could reduce overwinter mortality in bark beetle populations (Bentz et al. 2010). Similarly, species ranges could contract at lower elevations and latitudes if warm-season temperatures exceed tolerance levels during the juvenile (or other) growth stages (Bale et al. 2002).

Although much attention has been paid to insect and disease responses to increasing temperatures, those responses may be altered by the indirect effects of increasing atmospheric carbon dioxide (CO_2) concentrations. Higher CO_2 levels could reduce insect impacts by increasing carbon availability for defenses and reducing substrate quality in host plants (Stiling and Cornelissen 2007); however, the inhibitory effects of increasing CO_2 concentrations may be offset by the stimulatory effects of warmer temperatures on insect activity (Zvereva and Kozlov 2006).

For forests, insect and disease disturbances will probably increase, as the ability of the pathogens to adapt to new climatic conditions will be greater than that of their long-lived hosts.

Disturbance Interactions

In addition to their primary effects on vegetation, disturbance agents can interact, thus increasing or reducing vegetation susceptibility to other disturbance agents. The links from drought, to insects, to fire is a clear example of interacting disturbances. Windthrow and diseases can also increase risks from insects or fire, and vice versa.

Perhaps the most common interaction among disturbance agents in western forests involves drought stress and insects, particularly bark beetles. Episodes of widespread mortality of ponderosa pine and pinyon pine in the Southwestern United States has been attributed to beetles killing trees weakened by extended regional droughts (Allen and Breshears 1998; Breshears et al. 2005, 2009; Ganey and Vojta 2011; Plaut et al. 2012). The proposed mechanism for this interaction is that prolonged drought reduces photosynthesis and shifts carbon utilization from growth and plant defenses to support basic plant functions (respiration), reducing the ability of trees to fend off insect attacks (Breshears et al. 2009). Similarly, extensive mortality of aspen in southwestern Colorado has been attributed to high temperatures and drought that allowed secondary insect and disease agents to kill trees (Worrall et al. 2008).

Fire can interact with a variety of other disturbance agents, including drought, insects, diseases, and windthrow. Mortality from drought, windthrow, avalanches, or insects can increase fire risks (potential fire intensity, severity, and size) by initiating a process of fuel succession that increases surface fuels over time (Bigler et al. 2005, Hicke et al. 2012, Simard et al. 2011). Crown fire risks may decline, however, if tree mortality reduces overstory canopy densities (Simard et al. 2011). Fire can also set the stage for further overstory tree mortality by attracting bark beetles that attack trees weakened by crown scorch or basal heating (Dale et al. 2001).

Climate change effects on disturbances and their interactions are important not only for their immediate effects on vegetation, but also for their potential feedbacks on atmospheric CO_2 concentrations and climate. Widespread disturbances can convert forests from net carbon sinks to carbon sources, further increasing atmospheric CO_2 concentrations and potential for climatic changes (Ayers and Lombardero 2000, Edburg et al. 2012, Kurz et al. 2008).

Chapter 5: Vegetation Adaptation to Changing Climate and CO_2

Vegetation can adapt to changing climate and local environmental conditions in various ways, thereby avoiding mortality (individual level), local extirpation (population level), or extinction (species level).

- **Individual plants can respond to persistent changes in their environment through phenotypic plasticity** (the ability to alter their physiology), **morphology**, and **reproduction** to improve their performance (growth and reproduction) and survival.

- **Plant populations can adapt to changing climate by altering their genetic makeup through reproduction and natural selection**, improving their ability to grow and persist at a particular location.

- **Species can adapt to changing climate through migration**, which can allow new populations to establish in areas with suitable environmental conditions while other populations are extirpated from areas where environmental conditions are no longer suitable for establishment and persistence.

In this chapter, we review three broad types of vegetation adaptation to changing environmental conditions: (1) phenotypic plasticity, (2) local adaptation through natural selection, and (3) migration. All are likely to be important in influencing the rate and magnitude of vegetation responses to changing carbon dioxide (CO_2) and climate. The relative importance of these adaptation strategies is likely to differ among species and sites and with the rate and magnitude of climate change.

Phenotypic Plasticity

Plants experience a great deal of environmental variability during their lifetimes at varying temporal scales. Incoming radiation changes over short periods within a day owing to changing cloud cover or sunfleck movement, daily and seasonally in response to Earth's rotation and orbital position, and from year to year in response to climatic variability and its effects on cloud cover. Temperatures, precipitation, and soil moisture availability all vary daily, seasonally, and from year to year. As sessile organisms, plants must tolerate or acclimate to these changing conditions if they are to persist and reproduce. Longer term changes in climate and atmospheric CO_2 concentrations add yet another source of environmental variability for plants.

Phenotypic plasticity refers to the range of functional traits that can be expressed by a particular genotype (or individual plant) in response to environmental cues. Categories of functional traits that can differ in response to environmental cues include plant physiological processes (e.g., respiration rates, growth phenology), morphology (e.g., height, allocation to roots), and reproduction

Physiological plasticity allows plants to partially compensate for resource limitations by altering physiological processes.

(e.g., method, timing). Sultan (2000) reviewed the literature on phenotypic plasticity and described four types of plasticity: (1) functional traits plasticity, (2) developmental plasticity, (3) life-history plasticity, and (4) cross-generational plasticity. Trait variation can be expressed over monthly, annual, decadal, or generational timespans. Phenotypic plasticity for specific traits may be adaptive (and selected for in a natural selection sense) if it serves to increase plant performance and survival (Matesanz et al. 2010, Nicotra et al. 2010).

Physiological plasticity allows plants to partially compensate for resource limitations by altering physiological processes and helps plants acclimate to changing environmental conditions at varying time scales, from minutes to months (Sultan 2000). Plants can vary stomatal apertures over short time periods to regulate the exchange of water and CO_2 in response to changing evaporative demand (temperature and humidity) and internal plant water balance (Hetherington and Woodward 2003). Plants can adjust their temperature optima for photosynthesis and respiration processes to improve plant performance under seasonally varying temperatures (Atkin and Tjoelker 2003; Atkin et al. 2005, 2006; Grulke 2010; Gunderson et al. 2010, Ryan 1991).

Functional trait or morphological plasticity can also help plants compensate for resource limitations by altering leaf and root structure and by altering carbon allocation to roots, leaf area, and stemwood. Changes in leaf structure and function can allow plants to adapt to persistent changes in CO_2, light, temperature, and soil water (Apple et al. 2000, Atkin et al. 2006, Fraser et al. 2009, Sprugel et al. 1996, Sultan 2000). Temperatures during leaf development can influence specific leaf area (the ratio of leaf area to leaf mass), with subsequent effects on carbon uptake and plant growth (Atkin et al. 2006, Sultan 2000). Fraser et al. (2009) showed that experimental manipulations of temperature and water availability produced changes in leaf area and stomatal density in bluebunch wheatgrass (*Pseudoroegneria spicata* (Pursh) Á. Löve). Similarly, Apple et al. (2000) found that elevated growth temperatures increased needle length but did not affect stomatal density in Douglas-fir (*Pseudotsuga menziesii* (Mirb.) Franco) saplings, while elevated CO_2 did not significantly alter needle morphology at all. In Pacific silver fir (*Abies amabilis* (Douglas ex Loudon) Douglas ex Forbes), shading by overstory trees strongly influenced needle thickness and specific leaf area (Sprugel et al. 1996). In most cases, plasticity in leaf traits is limited to the period of leaf development.

Changes in biomass allocations—particularly among roots, shoots, and leaf area—also allow plants to acclimate to changing environmental conditions and biotic interactions (Atkin et al. 2006, Lapenis et al. 2005, Niinemets 2010, Sprugel et al. 1996). Varying biomass allocation between roots and shoots can allow trees and other plants to compensate for light or soil resource limitations on growth (Markesteijn and Poorter 2009). Pines have been shown to alter their ratio of leaf area to sapwood conducting area in response to site evaporative demand, apparently to improve water relations and reduce risks of hydraulic failure (DeLucia et al. 2000; Maherali and DeLucia 2000, 2001; Maherali et al. 2002). Biomass allocation responses to environmental variation differ among species and environmental drivers, however (DeLucia et al. 2000).

Another form of morphological plasticity allows plants to alter their growth form in response to environmental conditions and biotic interactions. In subalpine ecosystems, some conifers adopt a stunted "krummholz" growth form that allows them to better tolerate cold temperatures and high winds; these trees retain the ability, however, to develop into upright trees if climatic conditions improve or through facilitative interactions (Hadley and Smith 1987, Smith et al. 2003). In maritime coniferous forests, understory seedlings and saplings often alter their crown and needle morphologies to maximize light capture (Niinemets 2010, Sprugel et al. 1996).

Growth and reproductive phenology is another form of phenotypic plasticity (Sultan 2000). Phenological adjustments help plants adjust their growth and reproduction to periods of favorable resource availability (or reduced herbivory), and potentially lengthen or shorten the growing season (Cleland et al. 2007, Körner and Basler 2010, Kramer et al. 2000). The timing of flowering and leaf-out in plants is often controlled by environmental cues such as air and soil temperatures, but can include both chilling and warming requirements (Campbell and Sugano 1979, Harrington et al. 2010, Menzel et al. 2006, Polgar and Primack 2011). Chuine (2010) has argued that growth and reproductive phenology is an important determinant of species ranges, as failure to complete annual growth cycles limits species expansion into cooler environments, while failure to meet winter chilling requirements limits expansion into warmer environments (or persistence in a warming climate). Phenological responses to climatic variability and change are discussed in more detail in chapter 3.

Finally, cross-generational plasticity allows plants to confer plastic responses on their offspring by varying seed size (and stored resources), seed coat thickness, and seed dormancy, or by influencing initial biomass allocation (Sultan 2000). Seed size can influence initial growth rates and biomass of seedlings, while dormancy can influence the timing of seedling emergence. In some cases, parent plants experiencing resource limitations (e.g., light or nutrients) have been found to produce offspring that allocate biomass preferentially to roots or shoots in a way that promotes acquisition of the dominant limiting resource (Sultan 2000).

Adaptive Value of Plasticity

Phenotypic plasticity allows plant individuals and populations to persist on a site in a changing environment.

Phenotypic plasticity is important in considering potential vegetation responses to changing climate because it allows plant individuals and populations to persist on a site in a changing environment (Matesanz et al. 2010). It allows plants to adjust to seasonal changes in climate as well as interannual and interdecadal climatic variability, and helps avoid radical vegetation responses to most climatic variability. Phenotypic plasticity can also help plants become established and persist under low resource availability caused by decadal climatic variability or biotic interactions (e.g., during forest stand development). The ability to persist as a juvenile (advance regeneration) provides the opportunity to respond rapidly to increased resource availability following disturbance (or a favorable period of climate), while the ability to persist as an adult provides a continuing opportunity to reproduce during favorable periods of climate.

Phenotypic plasticity can also contribute to local adaptation of populations to changing climate and to species migration processes. Phenotypic plasticity may reduce selective pressure on plant genotypes, thereby allowing plants to maintain higher genetic diversity and future adaptation potential within populations. It may also facilitate local adaptation of populations by allowing new individuals to establish under altered environmental conditions (Matesanz et al. 2010). By these mechanisms, phenotypic plasticity can delay or prevent range retraction on the "trailing edge" of a species' range. High plasticity may also be beneficial for facilitating migration through colonization of new sites on the "leading edge" of the species' range, as high plasticity allows a single genotype to occupy varying environments (Matesanz et al. 2010). This is probably why high phenotypic plasticity is associated with ecological generalists and many invasive plant species (Matesanz et al. 2010, Sultan 2000).

Phenotypic plasticity is not without its costs, however, and is less common than one might expect, given the apparent benefits to individuals and populations. Valladares et al. (2007) reviewed a wide range of potential internal and external limitations that could prevent plants from fully responding to environmental cues. Ecological limitations include the reliability of environmental cues, abiotic stresses, biotic interactions, and multiple stresses. Internal limitations include genetic costs, carbon (maintenance) costs, developmental constraints, and lag time of responses. When plasticity cannot allow plants to acclimate sufficiently to changing environmental conditions, genetic adaptation or migration responses may be required to maintain species viability.

Adaptation Through Natural Selection

Local genetic adaptation (or in situ evolution) is another way by which plant populations can adapt to changing environmental conditions (Davis et al. 2005). As part of sexual reproduction, plants recombine genetic material and may develop new genotypes (combinations of genes) that are better suited to current conditions than the genotypes of earlier generations. They are also likely to produce genotypes that are less well suited to current environmental conditions. The better genotypes will be more likely to become established and survive, thereby increasing the frequency of favorable genes in the population and increasing the ability of the population to persist.

The effectiveness of local population adaptation depends on several factors, including genetic variability, fecundity, dispersal, and generation time (Aitken et al. 2008, Brubaker 1986, Jump and Peñuelas 2005). Populations with high genetic variability have a higher potential for adaptation if the genetic variability includes traits that affect performance and reproduction responses to climate (Davis and Shaw 2001, Davis et al. 2005). High levels of seed production and dispersal enhance adaptation potential by producing a large number of new genotypes and distributing them into a wide range of habitats, thereby increasing the chances for finding a favorable combination. Short generation times enhance adaptation potential by increasing selection opportunities over time.

Local genetic adaptation might be most important and effective for annual plants, as they replace their entire population each year (short generation time), typically produce large amounts of seed, and often have good seed dispersal (Jump and Peñuelas 2005). Population adaptation can be rapid in small, annual plant species, with significant changes in traits observed after one generation. For example, Franks et al. (2007) found that flowering time by an annual plant population advanced by 2 to 8 days in response to selective pressure from a summer drought.

Local population adaptation is likely to occur much more slowly for tree species but will still play an important role in determining the effects of changing climate and elevated CO_2 on tree species. In general, tree species have more genetic diversity within their populations than herbaceous plant and shrubs (Hamrick 2004, Petit and Hampe 2006). They also produce large numbers of seeds over their lifespans, and typically have developed effective mechanisms for seed dispersal (Petit and Hampe 2006; Nathan et al. 2008, 2011). Although longer generation times (juvenile periods) reduce their potential for rapid population adaptation, long lifespans supported by phenotypic plasticity may provide time for populations to adapt sufficiently to changing climate to avoid local extinction.

Trees often display high local differentiation for adaptive traits (Petit and Hampe 2006), with the traits involved in local adaptation being the product of the small effects of many genes (Aitken et al. 2008). Common garden studies with seedlings have found local differentiation in species traits like phenology, height, and cold hardiness for ponderosa pine (*Pinus ponderosa* Lawson & C. Lawson), (Keller et al. 2004), Douglas-fir (Monserud and Rehfeldt 1990, Rehfeldt 1989), lodgepole pine (*Pinus contorta*) (Rehfeldt 1988), Engelmann spruce (*Picea engelmannii* Parry ex Engelm.), (Rehfeldt 1994a), western redcedar (*Thuja plicata* Donn ex D. Don), (Rehfeldt 1994b), western larch (*Larix occidentalis* Nutt.) (Rehfeldt 1995), and Sitka spruce (*Picea sitchensis* (Bong.) Carrière) (Mimura and Aitken 2007, 2010). Such responses are not universal, however, and some species are only weakly differentiated genetically to local environmental conditions (e.g., western white pine [*Pinus monticola*] Douglas ex D. Don]), perhaps as a result of strong acclimation through phenotypic plasticity (Chuine et al. 2006, Rehfeldt et al. 1984).

Gene flow via seeds or pollen is common in trees and can accelerate or impede population adaptation to altered environmental conditions (Aitken et al. 2008, Kremer et al. 2012, Petit and Hampe 2006). Long-distance dispersal of pollen and seeds can help introduce new genes and genotypes into an existing population, and it is often assumed that the dominant flow of genes is from the center of a species range toward the periphery. Long-distance gene flow could facilitate adaptation in "leading-edge" populations during species migration by introducing genes that are preadapted for warmer temperatures (assuming the migration pattern is toward higher latitudes or elevations), and can generally increase genetic diversity and adaptation potential (Aitken et al. 2008, Kremer et al. 2012). On the other hand, gene flow toward trailing edge populations may slow or prevent population adaptation by introducing less suitable genes (Aitken et al. 2008, Kremer et al. 2012).

Migration

Migration is perhaps the most widely anticipated and discussed adaptation response of plant species to changing climate. Migration, in theory, allows plant species to maintain their current bioclimatic niches by tracking changes in climate across landscapes and regions. Migration responses of trees and other species in response to postglacial warming during the Quaternary are documented in fossil pollen sequences and macrofossils (Cole 1982, Davis and Shaw 2001, Gugger and Sugita 2010, Petit et al. 2008). Biogeographical models suggest that most plant species will have to migrate in response to changing climate in the next century or face dramatic reductions in species ranges and possible extinction. In this section, we briefly describe existing information about the need for plant species migration and some aspects of migration as an adaptive response to changing climate.

Velocity of Change

Biogeographers have used geographical information systems, regional climate and vegetation databases, and bioclimatic envelope models to translate projected changes in mean annual temperature and precipitation onto real landscapes. This has helped them describe spatial shifts in bioclimatic zones and the rates at which plant and animal species would have to migrate in the future to track their current environmental conditions (Loarie et al. 2009). The rate of migration of bioclimatic conditions across landscapes has been aptly referred to as the "velocity of change," and is a useful concept for evaluating the potential for species migrations to keep up with changing climate. These biogeographical approaches have also proved useful as a first approximation for evaluating the long-term potential for conserving biodiversity in current reserve systems (Ackerly et al. 2010, Loarie et al. 2009).

Studies of spatial shifts in bioclimatic zones under climate change have noted that the velocity of change varies considerably with topography. The velocity (meters/year) needed to track projected changes in climate is much greater in flat terrain like the central Great Plains than in complex topography like the mountainous regions of western North America (Loarie et al. 2009). This is largely because temperature changes much more quickly along elevational gradients than along latitudinal gradients.

Persistence in Refugia

There may be some regions within a species' range that retain climatic suitability despite large changes in climate (Ashcroft 2010). Such refugia may exist because the species has a broad ecological niche or high levels of phenotypic plasticity, because elevated CO_2 or local topography buffer the impact of changing climate on critical resources, or because antagonistic biotic interactions are too weak to cause significant mortality despite poor plant performance. Populations occupying these refugia may be able to persist without adaptation or, more likely, can persist through local adaptation, perhaps with the benefit of gene flow from other parts of the species range.

Recent studies have shown the importance of refugia for supporting relict populations of trees during the last glacial advance. Those populations preserved important components of genetic diversity and contributed significantly to species migration following glacial retreat (Gugger and Sugita 2010, Hu et al. 2009, McLachlan et al. 2005, Petit et al. 2008) and current distribution patterns (Norris et al. 2006). There is now great interest in identifying future refugia for maintaining

Populations occupying these refugia may be able to persist without adaptation or, more likely, can persist through local adaptation, perhaps with the benefit of gene flow from other parts of the species range.

plant biodiversity in general as well as currently threatened species or species of particular conservation value (Ashcroft 2010, Ashcroft et al. 2012, Dobrowski 2011). Areas outside the current distribution of a species could serve as refugia if species migration rates and future landscape permeability would allow the species to colonize and persist in those areas (Ashcroft 2010).

Invasion (Leading Edge)

Invasion or colonization of previously unoccupied or newly suitable habitat is the "leading edge" of a species migration. Invasion success and rates of "leading edge" movement depend on the fecundity of leading edge populations, seed dispersal patterns and distances, landscape barriers, community invasibility, biotic interactions, and generation times (Hampe 2011). Because of differences in fecundity, seed size, dispersal mechanisms, and competitive ability, potential migration rates vary among species, and species have migrated at different rates following the last major glacial retreat (Davis et al. 1986, Nathan et al. 2011). Historically, species migrations have lagged significantly behind climatic changes (Davis 1989, Gavin 2009, Gavin and Hu 2006).

Perhaps the most important factor controlling migration potential is the ability of a plant species to produce sufficient quantities of viable seeds, disperse seeds into new habitats, and have the seeds germinate successfully in the new habitat (Burton et al. 2010, Hampe 2011). Wind and animal (including human) dispersal are the most likely mechanisms for producing successful long-distance dispersal (Nathan et al. 2008) but may not be able to match the rate of changing climate in areas with a high "velocity of change." Maximizing the migration benefits of seed dispersal mechanisms requires leading edge populations to serve as the primary seed source for colonization of new habitat, which requires leading edge populations to be old enough to reproduce and for the climate to support investment in reproduction.

Elevated CO_2 and changing climate could alter seed production and dispersal for some species, thereby altering their migration potential. Elevated CO_2 could increase seed production by making more carbon resources available for reproduction; however, nutrient availability could limit increases in seed production, and increased seed size (owing to greater carbon reserves) could limit dispersal for wind-dispersed seed. Warming temperatures could increase wind speeds and thereby increase potential dispersal distances for wind-dispersed seeds (Kuparinen et al. 2009), while changes in prevailing wind directions could alter spatial patterns of seed dispersal (Ackerly et al. 2010). Similarly, climate change effects on animal behavior could alter the distance and direction of dispersal for animal-dispersed species (Hampe 2011, Nathan et al. 2008). Finally, changing climate and disturbance regimes could alter seed dispersal patterns by altering landscape permeability (Nathan et al. 2008).

Invasion success for migrating species also depends on the invasibility of the plant community being colonized (Pauchard et al. 2009). Intact plant communities with one or more dominant competitors may be difficult to invade unless the invading species is preadapted to the low resource availability produced by the dominant competitor. Disturbances can increase community invasibility by reducing or extirpating established populations and increasing resource availability (Pauchard et al. 2009). Fluctuating resources (e.g., soil water availability) may also facilitate invasion (Davis et al. 2000). Some have argued that highly diverse plant communities will be less invasible because of more complete resource utilization, but empirical evidence suggests otherwise (Lonsdale 1999).

Biotic interactions can also limit invasion rates. The presence or absence of facilitators, mutualists, or antagonists can influence invasion success. Release from pathogens or herbivores may increase establishment success and persistence (Hampe 2011). The presence or absence of mutualist species, like beneficial soil biota or pollinators, may also determine invasion success (Hampe 2011). Competition intensity may also be important, as the species traits that promote invasiveness (high seed production and dispersal) can come at the expense of traits that promote competitive ability (Best et al. 2007, Burton et al. 2010).

Extirpation (Trailing Edge)

Systematic extirpation of populations in areas that can no longer support viable populations of a species defines the "trailing edge" of a species migration. Population extirpation is typically associated with disturbances that kill plants, after which recolonization cannot succeed. In the absence of such disturbances, phenotypic plasticity or local population adaptation may allow populations to persist at reduced fitness levels. Regeneration may be limited to years or decades with favorable climate, or may cease altogether, leaving populations to rely on phenotypic plasticity, vegetative reproduction, and long lifespans of individuals to persist (Chevin et al. 2010, Hampe and Jump 2011). This latter condition has been called an "extinction debt," in which local extinction is expected but not yet realized (Dullinger et al. 2012, Jackson and Sax 2010).

Although there are examples of rapid and persistent range retractions driven by extreme climatic events and related disturbances, well-documented examples of systematic population extirpation of trailing edge plant populations are still not common (Allen and Breshears 1998, Allen et al. 2010, Breshears et al. 2009, Jump et al. 2009). In some cases, populations may persist until the arrival (and subsequent population growth) of a superior competitor (Dullinger et al. 2012, Hampe and

Disturbances can increase community invasibility by reducing or extirpating established populations and increasing resource availability.

Population extirpation is typically associated with disturbances that kill plants, after which recolonization cannot succeed.

Jump 2011). While they persist, these populations preserve the potential for the species to respond to future shifts in climate, while also maintaining genotypes adapted to warmer conditions (Hampe and Petit 2005, Jump et al. 2009).

Chapter 6: Simulation Models Used to Project Vegetation Responses

The complexity of climatic influences on vegetation and potential adaptations of plant populations and species to changing climate makes conducting field experiments to assess potential species and community responses to increasing atmospheric carbon dioxide (CO_2) concentrations and climatic changes difficult, expensive, and generally impractical for more than a few species and environments. Instead, models are often used to project vegetation responses to changing CO_2 and climate, including changes in species distributions, biodiversity, community composition, vegetation structure (e.g., biomass, leaf area), and productivity. Model projections may be used to assess vegetation sensitivity or vulnerability to climatic changes, potential rates and magnitudes of change, or the adequacy of conservation reserve systems.

The ideal vegetation model for supporting the development of climate change adaptation strategies would describe the range of climatic and other environmental conditions under which plant species could establish, grow, reproduce, and persist. It would also account for the effects of biotic interactions and disturbances on plant species distributions. If used to project changes in species ranges over time, the model would not only describe the end result, but also indicate the rates of change, intermediate conditions, and the mechanisms producing change. Such ideal vegetation models do not currently exist. Instead, current vegetation models focus on one or more aspects of the overall problem—describing environmental niches, simulating competition, or examining spatial processes—while greatly simplifying other aspects of the problem through assumptions, theory-based approximations, or simply ignoring them altogether.

Several types of vegetation models can and have been used to assess potential impacts of climate change on terrestrial vegetation. Each type has its strengths and weaknesses and addresses vegetation responses at different temporal and spatial resolution. For example, gap models are used to examine species interactions and vegetation change at very fine spatial scales (plots the size of an individual canopy gap or small stand of trees) over daily to annual time steps, while dynamic global vegetation models project changes in vegetation properties (e.g., leaf area and phenology) at very typically broad spatial scales (thousands of square kilometers, although more fine-scale projections are now available, e.g., Rogers et al. 2011) over annual to decadal time steps. In applying vegetation models to inform management adaptations to climate change, it is important to match the spatial and temporal scale of the model with that of the question being asked. It is also important to note that models are developed based on assumptions that are usually reasonable for the

In applying vegetation models to inform management adaptations to climate change, it is important to match the spatial and temporal scale of the model with that of the question being asked.

original scale and purpose of the model, but may be completely unreasonable when models are applied to a different problem or at a different spatial scale.

A frequent quote about models is that they will always be wrong to some degree, but may be useful anyway. In the context of climate change, models may be more useful for illustrating the magnitude of potential vegetation impacts and identifying areas of vulnerability than for making projections about outcomes (Littell et al. 2011, Jackson et al 2009). Many different types of models have been developed, and continue to be developed, to examine how vegetation may change with future climate change, but their strengths, limitations, and best uses are often not made clear to decisionmakers. Vegetation model development often requires considerable investments of time and resources, and there is an understandable tendency for model developers to try to fund continued model development by applying it to new and varied applications, even when another tool (new or existing) might be better suited to the task. Similarly, decisionmakers are often pressed to act quickly and may accept model output as an authoritative basis for decisions without fully understanding the uncertainty in such projections.

This section reviews the major classes of vegetation models; describes their basic function, strengths, and weaknesses; and discusses the contribution each could make toward understanding and projecting vegetation responses to future climatic changes.

Statistical Species Distribution Models
Introduction to Species Distribution Models

Statistical species distribution models (SDM), also known as niche models or bioclimatic envelope models, are used to describe the range of environmental conditions (niche) under which species occur by quantifying relationships between species occurrence data and corresponding environmental descriptors. The SDMs have arisen out of decades of ecological inquiry and analyses related to species-environment relationships (e.g., MacArthur 1972) and share a common philosophy and theoretical foundation with indirect gradient analysis, in that they attempt to relate observed spatial variations in species frequency to associated underlying environmental gradients. Although correlations between species occurrence and environmental conditions can suggest causal mechanisms, the models themselves are purely descriptive and do not directly include processes or mechanisms, although an approach to doing so has been proposed recently (Kearney and Porter 2009).

Species distribution models have been used to address a variety of applied and theoretical questions (Elith and Graham 2009, Guisan and Thuiller 2005, Jeschke and Strayer 2008), including the planning and establishment of conservation reserve networks and identifying potential habitat for species recovery efforts (Araújo et al. 2004). They require little or no knowledge about the ecological requirements of species, which can be an advantage for poorly studied taxa (Kearney and Porter 2009), and are relatively easy to develop and use (Robinson et al. 2008). Their use has grown considerably in recent decades as geographic information system (GIS) technologies have improved and become widely used and as spatial datasets describing interpolated climatic conditions have become available (Elith and Leathwick 2009). Because these models are widely used and there are numerous discussions and projections in the literature using these models, we devote a considerable amount of space to this class of models.

How Species Distribution Models Work

Species distribution models are empirical models describing relationships between observed species occurrences and associated environmental variables based on statistical or other quantitative models (Guisan and Zimmerman 2000). Species data can be presence/absence, presence only, or some measure of species abundance, and are typically obtained from species range maps or extensive networks of vegetation survey plots (e.g., the U.S. Forest Service's Forest Inventory and Analysis monitoring network). Environmental predictor variables typically include summary climatic descriptors (e.g., mean summer temperature, mean annual precipitation, or mean January temperature), but can also include climate-related biophysical descriptors (e.g., potential or actual evapotranspiration), topographic descriptors (e.g., slope aspect or potential solar radiation), disturbance properties, or soil properties (Guisan and Thuiller 2005).

A wide range of quantitative methods have been developed for describing these relationships between species and their environment, including generalized linear models, generalized additive models, and regression trees (Austin 2007). In selecting a quantitative method for an SDM, model developers should ideally consider the relevant ecological theory, whether species responses to modeled environmental gradients are linear or nonlinear, the likely importance of interactions among environmental predictor variables, and properties of the species and environment data (including scales of observation, correlations among environmental predictors, and spatial autocorrelation in species data), though this is often not done (Austin 2007). Similarly, environmental predictor variables should be chosen to represent (directly or indirectly) factors that contribute to establishment, growth, and mortality (e.g., temperature extremes, growing degree-days, water balance).

Depending on the species data and quantitative method used, SDMs will produce estimates of species abundance or the probability of species presence for locations within the study region, given the environmental conditions. In many cases, the most useful way to examine SDM projections, however, is to map those projected abundances or probabilities of species occurrence onto the study region (geographic space) and display those projections using GIS. This can be done by displaying continuous abundance or probability values (using levels of shading) or by establishing threshold abundance or probability values and mapping all areas with values exceeding the threshold as potential species range. Although SDM projections are often interpreted as species range maps, they actually represent a spatial mapping of the environmental conditions within which the model projects the likelihood of species occurrence to be above some minimum threshold level. Not all areas identified as potential suitable climate will be occupied by the target species. Observed species absences within areas modeled as potential suitable climate could to be due to chance alone, barriers to migration, disturbances, or some additional factor that influences the species' distribution but was not included in the model.

For more details about SDM history, development, function, and usage, see reviews by Guisan and Thuiller (2005), Austin (2007), and Elith and Leathwick (2009). For the remainder of this review, we focus on key elements of SDMs that pertain specifically to their use in projecting vegetation vulnerability and responses to climatic changes.

As with most statistical methods, developers of SDMs make assumptions about how the world works and the empirical data from which the models are developed. Some of these assumptions are explicitly acknowledged, while others are less clear, but all have important implications for how the models can be used and their suitability for projecting species responses to climatic changes (Austin 2007, Thuiller et al. 2008). Major assumptions associated with SDMs are summarized in box 6.1.

How Species Distribution Models Are Applied to Climate Change Issues

A carefully developed SDM can characterize the current environmental distribution of a species well and provide evolutionary and ecological insights (Elith and Leathwick 2009, Rehfeldt et al. 2006). For example, examination of the environmental predictors in the model can generate hypotheses about the ecological factors limiting current species ranges that can be subjected to further study. Comparison of SDMs developed for different regions within a species' range can also provide insights about evolutionary changes during prolonged periods of isolation in glacial refugia (Norris et al. 2006).

More recently, SDMs have been increasingly used to project suitable species habitat through interpolation and extrapolation. Projection through interpolation

Box 6.1. Major assumptions associated with widely used species distribution models (SDMs):

- Models assume that the description of the realized niche is suitable for meeting study objectives (Guisan and Thuiller 2005). The SDMs attempt to describe the environmental conditions under which a species **actually** occurs, not the range of conditions under which it **could** occur. The realized niche could be further limited to only those environmental conditions under which a species can reproduce successfully, eliminating relict populations that may be committed to extinction (Guisan and Thuiller 2005); this is not common practice, however, in part because assessments of species reproductive success are often unavailable.

- The target species is in equilibrium with its current environment. If the species is still responding to recent widespread disturbances or past climate changes, or still actively invading, species occurrence data may not adequately represent the species' realized niche.

- Biotic interactions are either of minor importance as determinants of the species' distribution, or are correlated with and adequately represented by environmental variables (Araújo and Luoto 2007).

- The target species does not have unique subpopulations—for which the fundamental/realized niche varies significantly—within the region of interest.

- The environmental predictor variables represent all of the critical elements affecting plant establishment, growth, and survival for a species and have been measured accurately.

- Species and environmental data are being observed and analyzed at appropriate and comparable spatial scales to meet study objectives (the scale at which model predictions are required).

- Relevant environmental gradients have been adequately sampled (Elith and Leathwick 2009, Guisan and Thuiller 2005).

- The statistical methods used are capable of describing changes in species occurrences across the selected environmental gradients and of capturing important interactive effects among the environmental predictor variables.

involves projecting model occurrence probabilities (or projected abundance) onto the current landscape under current environmental conditions; such an approach can be useful for identifying suitable, but unoccupied, habitat for inclusion in reserve planning or species recovery efforts. Projection through extrapolation involves applying model projections to geographic regions or environmental conditions beyond those for which the model was developed. Extrapolating SDM projections in time or space has become increasingly popular, but is much riskier and carries higher levels of uncertainty (Elith and Leathwick 2009). Although SDMs are typically run using data and projections for individual species, they can also be applied to plant functional types (e.g., shrubs) (Kerns and Ohmann 2004).

Species distribution models have been used extensively in climate change research to project potential changes in species geographic ranges in response to changing climate. In a typical application, SDMs are developed for a suite of species occupying a target region using available species and environmental datasets, where the candidate environmental variables include a full range of climatic descriptors thought to represent various limitations on species ranges. After acceptable models have been developed, their projections are projected onto geographic space using both current climatic conditions (interpolation) and one or more scenarios of future climatic conditions (extrapolation) as derived from climate models. The resulting maps (or the underlying projections) can then be compared to address questions about potential changes in species ranges, potential regions for expansion or contraction of species boundaries, and stable habitat areas.

In extrapolating SDMs from current to future climatic conditions, additional assumptions are being made that influence levels of confidence and uncertainty in SDMs, including the following:

- Current fundamental and realized niches are conserved under a new climatic regime (Dormann 2007). This further implies that:

  - Species will not adapt significantly to climatic changes (stability in the fundamental niche).

  - Dominant environmental limiting factors are preserved under future climate.

  - Biotic interactions (e.g., competition or facilitation) and their outcomes are preserved under future climate (stability in the realized niche). This implies that currently interacting species migrate together and that the relative effects of their interactions do not change significantly.

o Changing CO_2 concentrations or altered disturbance regimes
will not alter species-environment relationships or biotic
interactions.

- Model projections can reasonably be extrapolated to project species
responses to novel climates. Novel climates include ranges and combinations of environmental conditions not considered during model
development because they do not occur on the modern landscape
(no current analog) or because data were not available for representative sites.

Strengths and Weaknesses of Species Distribution Models

The major strength of statistical species distribution models is their flexibility and
ease of use. Species distribution models have become very popular because they
are relatively fast and easy to create and apply. Model development requires little
knowledge about species ecophysiology, autecology, or synecology. The necessary
species and environmental data are increasingly available in usable forms, allowing
species models to be generated for many areas and spatial scales. Many of the quantitative methods employed are readily accessible in free software packages (e.g.,
as applications libraries for the free R statistical software) that can facilitate rapid
model development and assessment. The SDMs can often produce a good statistical
fit between available species and environmental data, lending confidence to their
application (though see Chapman 2010 and Beale and Lennon 2012 for cautionary
notes on this topic). Finally, the ability to project model output onto geographic
space and create maps adds to the popularity of the models, as maps are familiar
and appear to be easy to understand and interpret (though this can produce a false
sense of confidence).

A major weakness of SDMs is that they achieve their flexibility and ease of
use through adoption of a suite of simplifying assumptions that allows models to
be created without prior knowledge about species ecophysiology, autecology, or
synecology. Unfortunately, many of these assumptions are likely to be violated,
depending on the species involved and the study question. Many plant species
are unlikely to be in equilibrium with current climate, as climate has changed at
centennial to millennial scales, creating a moving target (Svenning and Skov 2004).
For example, western juniper (*Juniperus occidentalis* Hook.) is still rapidly expand-
ing its range and infilling in less dense areas with almost 90 percent of the western
juniper woodland having developed in the past 150 years (Miller et al. 2000).
Similarly, biotic interactions are poorly studied for most species, but there is sufficient research demonstrating the importance of overstory-understory relationships,
pathogens, herbivory, and mycorrhizal associations on the abundance patterns of

**The major strength
of statistical species
distribution models
is their flexibility and
ease of use.**

selected species to demonstrate the potential importance of biotic interactions for shaping species realized niches. Although the effects of some biotic interactions may be correlated with climate, allowing them to be captured by a statistical model, this is not universally true (Araújo and Luoto 2007).

Climate data availability is another source of weakness for many SDMs, particularly as applied to climate change questions. The SDM methodology assumes that climate variables are accurately measured and can be matched up with associated vegetation data. Weather stations producing high-quality, long-term climate data are distributed sparsely in most regions, particularly in remote areas and mountainous terrain. They are often skewed toward low-elevation sites and clustered near population centers (where they are easiest to monitor and repair). As a result, climatic conditions associated with vegetation sampling plots are usually estimated from spatial interpolations of climate station data (e.g., PRISM) (Daly et al. 2008). The accuracy of such estimates may be adequate for studies at broad spatial scales (coarse spatial resolution), but they are probably not suitable at finer spatial resolutions where topoedaphic influences are strong.

Model development methodologies have also been a source of uncertainty and criticism for SDMs. Many different SDM methodologies are available, each employing different assumptions, algorithms, and parameterizations (Buisson et al. 2010). Unfortunately, models developed from the same data—but with different methods—can produce significantly different results (Buisson et al. 2010, Diniz-Filho et al. 2009). In an ensemble forecasting framework with 8,400 projections of species responses to climate change, Buisson et al. (2010) found that SDM methodology accounted for more variability in model projections than climate model, emission scenario, or initial (training) data used. Clearly, there remains uncertainty about the reliability of SDM projections of species responses to climate change, and it is unlikely that any single statistical approach will be best for all applications and species (Jeschke and Strayer 2008).

For the SDM approach to be effective for projecting species responses to future climate change, the current correlation of species with the environment must be a good predictor of future suitable habitat. Therefore, SDMs implicitly assume niche conservation—that species maintain their current ecological requirements—and constancy in the genetic and phenotypic composition of a species over space and time (Broennimann et al. 2007, Jeschke and Stayer 2008). These assumptions may be ecologically untenable, however, at least for some species. Invasive species provide examples of lack of niche conservation, changing niches from their native to introduced ranges (Broennimann et al. 2007). Recent evidence also suggests that detectable evolution in vegetation occurs at time scales that are comparable to climate change—within years for some annuals, decades for herbaceous species, and centuries for longer lived trees (Franks and Weis 2008, Hairston et al. 2005, Skelly et al. 2007).

Species distribution models also assume that certain processes, such as biotic interactions, are either unimportant or will remain stable with climate change. However, biotic and abiotic factors both constrain species ranges, the relative effects of which may vary in different parts of the species range (Barry and Elith 2006). Changes in climate can alter interactions between plants, as well as plant interactions with herbivores, seed predators, and pathogens (Ayres and Lombardero 2000, Ibanez et al. 2006; see also chapter 4). Higher atmospheric CO_2 levels may also alter biotic interactions through effects on plant growth, carbon allocation, and defenses. A recent review of over 600 studies showed that climate change influenced nearly every aspect of species interactions (Tylianakis et al. 2008). Finally, biotic interactions are likely to change because species have been shown to respond individually to climate change, producing new species assemblages in new environments. Species whose ranges are influenced by biotic interactions are therefore likely to respond in complex ways to novel environments (Elith et al. 2010).

Species distribution model quality also differs by species (Guisan et al. 2007). Species with very specific environmental requirements are modeled more easily than generalists (Elith et al. 2006, Guisan et al. 2007, Hernandez et al. 2006, Luoto et al. 2005, Segurado and Araújo 2004, Thuiller et al. 2004). Early-successional species are often dependent on disturbances to become established and may be excluded from large portions of their potential habitat by competition from late-successional species; it is difficult to determine the environmental requirements for such species (Guisan et al. 2007).

Finally, climate change is expected to result in substantial areas that have no modern analog in terms of climate ("novel climates") (Williams and Jackson 2007, Williams et al. 2007). This may be especially true of the Western United States, where almost half the land area may have novel (or extramural) climatic conditions by the end of the century (Rehfeldt et al. 2006). The more the future state differs from the present (novel climates), the less adequately models will be able to project ecological phenomena such as species distributions (Williams and Jackson 2007) and projections made by correlative models for novel climates may not be defensible (Rehfeldt et al. 2006). In fact, SDMs may produce projections indicating dramatic reductions in suitable habitat for a species simply because future novel climates do not correspond to modern conditions under which the species occurs. Furthermore, as models of modern realized niches increase in complexity (more climatic predictors and interactions), the less likely they are to exist under future climate scenarios.

SDMs may produce projections indicating dramatic reductions in suitable habitat for a species simply because future novel climates do not correspond to modern conditions under which the species occurs.

In some cases, a novel climate could be quite favorable for a species. As a result, novel climates often create a bias in SDM projections toward reduced area for most species under future climate, without identifying which species would replace them.

Using Species Distribution Models

Species distribution models have a number of potentially useful applications in the fields of ecology and conservation, including describing species' environmental niches, suggesting unsurveyed sites with high potential for occurrence of rare species, supporting appropriate management plans for species recovery and mapping reintroduction sites, and supporting conservation planning and reserve selection (Guisan and Thuiller 2005). These applications focus on describing the current environmental niche for a species and using interpolation to identify potential species habitat on the current landscape.

With respect to climate change, SDMs have proven highly valuable for raising awareness about the potential magnitude of climate change impacts on terrestrial biota. At their most basic level, SDM procedures can be used to show how the "bioclimatic envelope" or climatic conditions currently associated with the geographic range of a particular species or functional group would move across a landscape or region in response to projected climatic changes. By comparing current and future geographic distributions, one can estimate the distances and migration rates needed for species to maintain their current environmental niches in the face of climate change (Shafer et al. 2001). These rates will differ among species and can be highly influenced by topographic complexity, with mountainous terrain requiring shorter migration distances and slower migration rates, in general, than flat terrain (Loarie et al. 2009).

Species distribution models may also be useful for identifying core habitat for species that is likely to remain suitable (within that of the current species range) under future climate scenarios. For example, SDMs could be used to quantify sustainability of current reserve systems for maintaining key species or communities. Such an application limits SDM use to current climatic conditions and avoids problems with extrapolating species responses to novel climates (a negative response indicates higher vulnerability, not guaranteed commitment to extinction).

Species distribution models could also be valuable in a research context by generating empirically based hypotheses about what environmental factors limit the distribution of a species in different parts of its range. Depending on the SDM methodology used, it may be possible to examine which predictor in a model is most limiting (or producing a projection of "no occurrence") and use that knowledge to infer a causal factor. For example, if total annual precipitation is a significant statistical predictor for a species, it should be possible to identify locations within the study area where the model indicates that annual precipitation is low enough to significantly reduce the likelihood of occurrence (or prevent occurrence altogether). Such a projection would be useful to researchers, who could design studies to test that projection and either confirm the validity of the model and the associated inference, provide information to change the inference, or identify a flaw in the model (incorrect predictor variable, missing interaction, or incorrect model structure).

Projecting species distributions into the future is the most uncertain usage of SDMs.

Although SDMs can be used in an illustrative or precautionary sense to identify potential species vulnerabilities, Elith and Graham (2009) noted that projecting species distributions into the future is the most uncertain usage of SDMs. Projections of species migrations should be interpreted and used with great caution. Such projections may be useful for identifying target zones for future species colonization or extirpation that could be subject to more intensive monitoring as an early warning of change. The uncertainty levels associated with those projections—including uncertainty in emissions scenarios, climate responses, species environmental requirements and adaptation potential, the effects of biotic interactions, and SDM methodology—are probably too great to allow these models to motivate proactive management activities (e.g., assisted migration). However, they may lend additional support to conducting management activities that would be justified for other purposes ("no-regrets" activities).

Gap-Replacement Models
Introduction to Gap-Replacement Models

Gap models are a class of forest succession models developed to simulate the effects of gap-phase disturbances on forest structure and composition (Bugmann 2001). Originally developed primarily for eastern deciduous forests and later applied to western coniferous forests, these models simulate the establishment, growth, and mortality of individual trees within small forest stands (Bugmann 2001). They have been used to project forest responses to chestnut blight (Shugart and West 1977), air pollution (Kercher and Axelrod 1984a, West et al. 1980), fire (Keane et al. 1990, Kercher and Axelrod 1984b), and climate change (Dale and Franklin 1989, Pastor and Post 1988, Solomon 1986, Zolbrod and Peterson 1999), though their application to climate change has raised questions about model assumptions and the way climate was incorporated into the establishment, growth, and mortality processes (Bugmann 2001). Gap models have largely been replaced by SDMs and other model types in recent efforts to project vegetation responses to climate change, but offer an approach that largely complements those taken by SDMs. Whereas SDMs

Gap models simulate the establishment, growth, and mortality of individual trees in small forest stands as stochastic processes that are driven primarily by resource availability.

project future vegetation condition without specifying the "how" or "when," gap models simulate the process of change in forest stands.

How Gap-Replacement Models Work

Gap models simulate the establishment, growth, and mortality of individual trees in small forest stands as stochastic processes that are driven primarily by resource availability, which is itself a function of climate and competition from neighboring trees (Bugmann 2001). Gap models are process models that simulate processes using mathematical functions that can be parameterized from a basic knowledge of the physiology and allometry of the species of interest (Perry and Enright 2006), though biogeographical knowledge can also assist in developing parameters. Functional relationships and parameters used in major gap models were originally developed from a combination of theory and field data (Botkin et al. 1972, Pacala et al. 1993, Ribbens et al. 1994).

Changes in structure and composition are typically modeled on an annual time step, based on stochastic simulation of establishment, growth, and mortality of individual trees within small stands. The establishment ("birth") process typically includes the effects of seed production/availability, understory light availability, soil moisture, temperature, and herbivory on tree establishment. Growth of trees is regulated by shading (light), crowding (soil nutrients), soil water availability, and temperature. Mortality is a random process, with a low background probability of mortality that increases if the tree is under stress (low growth rate). Mortality can also result from discrete natural disturbances like fire or logging. At each annual time step, tree inventories are updated and summarized to produce new descriptors of stand-level structure and composition.

Gap models typically employ an ensemble approach for generating projections. One simulation produces a single potential outcome, given the starting conditions. Repeating the simulation many times for the same starting conditions provides an assessment of the range and variability of outcomes arising from random chance. Repeating the simulation many times with varying starting conditions (e.g., representing spatial variability in structure and composition within a stand) produces a more general assessment of overall variability in future structure and composition.

Gap models have been modified (adapted) to project forest responses to a variety of disturbance types, including chestnut blight in eastern deciduous forests (Shugart and West 1977), air pollution in coniferous forests of California (Kercher and Axelrod 1984a,1984b), and fire in the inland Pacific Northwest (Keane et al. 1990). In most cases, this has involved modifying the mortality ("kill") procedure to produce periodic pulses of mortality on a fixed interval (e.g., silvicultural treatment) or as a random process (e.g., fire), and examining the resulting effects.

How Gap-Replacement Models Are Applied to Climate Change Issues

Gap models were among the first models used to project the potential impacts of rising atmospheric CO_2 levels and changing climate on forest vegetation. The original gap models (e.g., JABOWA and FORET) were created to simulate climatic influences on establishment, growth, and mortality, largely through temperature and precipitation influences on growing degree-days and soil moisture. These process-based models can therefore simulate both transient and equilibrium forest responses to climate change if given a suitably modified climatic time series as input to the simulations. For transient responses, gap models can be either set to an initial structural state or run for a long period under current climate conditions to establish equilibrium baseline conditions, after which climatic inputs are altered and simulated structural and compositional changes are observed. For equilibrium responses, gap models can simply be run for a long period under projected future climate conditions. By simulating vegetation responses for a network of plots within a region (with suitable initial vegetation states and climatic inputs), gap models can also project changes in species ranges and regional vegetation dynamics.

Strengths and Weaknesses of Gap-Replacement Models

The major advantage of gap models is that they explicitly model the basic processes that drive forest structural and community dynamics, including tree establishment, growth, competition for resources, and mortality. In addition to simulating forest succession, they provide information about the ecological processes driving succession. The projected outcomes and mechanisms can be subjected to validation through well-crafted field studies, providing a way to improve model performance and increase confidence in model projections. Their performance can also be assessed by comparing model projections to forest succession data from long-term monitoring plots (Pabst et al. 2008).

Another advantage of gap models is their flexibility. Gap models can be adapted to new regions and forest types through modification of species pools, defining or modifying species descriptors, and modifying process parameters. The establishment, growth, and mortality functions can be modified to include locally important disturbances (e.g., fire, insects) or to better represent factors influencing establishment, growth, and mortality. Additional processes can be added to accommodate new applications (e.g., new disturbance types or stressors) and forest management scenarios (Pabst et al. 2008). If necessary, functional relationships can be updated as they become better understood.

The emphasis of gap models on simulating processes that drive forest succession has also limited their utility for many applications. Properly simulating tree responses to disturbances, resource limitations, and climate requires a theoretical or empirical understanding of vegetation-environment relationships that has not yet been developed for many species and vegetation types. Although much effort has been invested in modeling tree growth, there has been less in formulating tree establishment and mortality, although these will certainly be important under climate change scenarios (Bugmann et al. 2001). Little or no effort has gone into modeling growth, establishment, and mortality for other life forms, such as shrubs and herbaceous species. Even climate-growth relationships are not well understood for sites where there is no obvious single limiting factor (e.g., upper and lower treeline). Relationships also vary among regions and climatic settings. Species and process parameters developed for eastern deciduous forests are unlikely to work well for simulating forest succession in western coniferous forests. Although parameters and response curves can be developed for new species and regions, such an effort requires time and resources that are often not available.

Most gap models are not spatially explicit and assume no interactions among simulated plots. This has limited their ability to simulate neighborhood effects on seed inputs and other spatial processes within forest stands. This problem has been partially resolved in more recent gap models like SORTIE (Pacala et al. 1993), in which simulated plots are larger, tree locations are explicitly "mapped," crown shapes conform to available gap sizes and locations, and processes such as competition and dispersal are modeled as continuous functions (Perry and Enright 2006). This increased functionality comes with increased parameterization and computation costs, however (Perry and Enright 2006), and still does not resolve problems with spatial interactions at broader spatial scales. For example, topographic influences, sharp climatic gradients, large wildfires, and seed dispersal processes can all produce spatially autocorrelated effects on vegetation dynamics that exceed the spatial extent of gap models. Capturing these processes typically requires a spatially explicit landscape model (see below). However, gap models can be linked with landscape models (e.g., Johnson et al. 2007), and a new class of individual tree models can operate at landscape scales (Seidl et al. 2012).

A major weakness of typical gap models with respect to climate change applications has been the lack of information about climatic influences on forest tree establishment, growth, and mortality, particularly in the juvenile stages (seedlings and saplings). In the absence of such information, assumptions must be made regarding climate response curves and climatic thresholds associated with mortality at different life stages. When gap models were initially applied to studies of forest successional responses to disturbance, climatic influences on tree growth were parameterized based on species geographic distributions, with minimal growth (and mortality thresholds) corresponding to climatic conditions at the margins (typically northern and southern limits) and optimal growth associated with intermediate climatic conditions. This approach was reasonable for projecting successional responses to disturbances in eastern deciduous forests, as it limited the pool of potential species to locally adapted species and allowed gap sizes and relative shade tolerances among species to drive gap replacement processes. However, this approach implicitly assumes either a stable climate (which is a problem for climate change applications) or the same sort of equilibrium conditions assumed by SDMs. The parameterization method was of questionable utility for climate change studies, as warming temperatures automatically produced mortality of existing forest trees and replacement with species from warmer climates, much the same as with statistical species distribution models. Although such a vegetation response is certainly possible, a better understanding and modeling of climate-growth and growth-mortality relationships would likely produce much less formulaic results and be more informative.

Finally, differences in gap model structure and parameterization can produce a broad range of simulated outcomes among models for the same simulation data (initial conditions, climate, and species traits), generating considerable uncertainty about the reliability of model projections. A review of six gap models in several undisturbed European forests found that tree species composition was correctly projected under the current climate about half of the time (Badeck et al. 2001). Tree species with very wide geographical distributions may differ significantly across their range in autecological properties (local adaptation), so local parameterization may be required (Badeck et al. 2001). Gap models and input data need to be improved to provide a more robust assessment of the effects of climate change (Badeck et al. 2001). For example, CO_2 interactions with vegetation are not explicitly represented in most existing models. Lastly, gap models have largely been only applied to forested environments, although the structure of the models, with appropriate parameterization, could be applicable to any ecosystem type.

Using Gap-Replacement Models

Well-designed and locally calibrated gap models could be very useful in stand-to landscape-level management planning (tactical). Their focus on individual trees and stands allows them to provide estimates of rates and trajectories of change in response to disturbances, management treatments, species invasions, or changes in climate and atmospheric CO_2 concentrations. Their ability to simulate future forest responses to a wide variety of disturbances (including management treatments) could be useful in evaluating and choosing among alternative treatment options.

They could also be useful for improving our understanding of forest species invasion processes, as species with known (or hypothetical) characteristics can be introduced to stands with varying initial structure and composition.

With respect to climate change, gap models appear to be best suited to evaluating "what-if" scenarios generated by theory, other models, or proposed management plans. If the climate at a site became suitable for a new, highly competitive species (based on an SDM projection), how long might it take the species to establish itself and become dominant, and how long might the current species persist? How might thinning dry forest stands for restoration and fire management purposes influence the sensitivity of those stands to changing climate? If intense summer droughts caused dieback of a species (or promoted insect outbreaks), how would this alter future stand structure and composition? In some cases, resource managers may be comfortable using model simulations as reasonable projections of the range of potential outcomes. In other cases, the management questions or simulations may raise questions about the adequacy of our knowledge about key processes.

Finally, relationships or outcomes from gap models may be useful for calibrating landscape models (see below).

Landscape Models

Introduction to Landscape Models

Landscape models are a class of models that simulate spatial dynamics of vegetation in response to disturbance and succession (Keane et al. 2004). Some have the ability to characterize transient changes in vegetation in response to climate as well. They simulate the interactions of vegetation, disturbances, and climate across broad spatial scales and through time (Xi et al. 2009). Like gap models, landscape models can model successional processes within stands (grid cells), but typically do so with less detail than in gap models. Unlike gap models, landscape models are designed to allow distance-based spatial interactions in abiotic and biotic processes, such as fires and seed dispersal, among stands or grid cells. Like gap models, landscape models were originally developed to investigate the influences of disturbances and spatial variation in environmental conditions on vegetation (vegetation structure, species composition, and landscape spatial patterns) and have subsequently been adapted for use in climate change research and planning.

How Landscape Models Work

Landscape models attempt to simulate dynamic interactions among vegetation, climate, and disturbances (including management activities). Landscape models typically model vegetation changes within a grid of cells (or a cluster of polygons), where each cell (polygon) represents a "stand" of some size and the entire grid (cluster) represents a landscape. Individual cells can represent stands of varying sizes (Yang et al. 2011), from hundreds of square meters (e.g., 900 m^2 in LANDIS and LANDSUM) (Keane et al. 2008, Yang et al. 2011) to one or more square kilometers (e.g., 1 km^2 in LANDIS-2) (Scheller and Mladenoff 2008). Modern landscape models can simulate up to 1 million grid cells on a single landscape, thereby representing landscape areas of thousands to millions of hectares (Yang et al. 2011).

Vegetation succession is modeled within each grid cell, with the level of complexity and the driving processes varying from model to model. At the high end of the complexity continuum, a landscape model could include a fully functional individual-based gap model or biogeochemical model to simulate vegetation growth and compositional changes as a function of climate, disturbances, and site factors (e.g., FIRE-BGC, Keane et al. 1996; iLand, Seidl et al. 2012). Other landscape models reduce within-cell computing requirements by modeling vegetation structure and composition simply as a function of time since disturbance or by modeling growth of species cohorts rather than individuals (Yang et al. 2011). At the low end of the complexity spectrum are landscape models that represent vegetation as a collection of predefined, static communities that can migrate on the landscape (e.g., MAPSS and TELSA) (Kurz et al. 2000, Neilson 1995).

Most landscape models allow explicit representation of multiple spatial processes and operate in a spatially explicit environment. A key feature of landscape models is the ability to simulate the effects of spatial processes on vegetation dynamics within and among stands, and to allow analysis of the resulting landscape patterns. Important spatial processes can include disturbances such as fires, windstorms, and insect outbreaks, as well as biological processes such as pollination and seed dispersal (Scheller and Mladenoff 2007). Landscape models could also use spatial variability in site characteristics like topographic setting, soil properties, or biophysical environment to simulate spatial variability in vegetation composition, successional patterns, or responses to disturbances or climate.

How Landscape Models Are Applied to Climate Change Issues

As with gap models, some landscape models can address climate change questions by simulating vegetation responses to various scenarios. If the within-cell vegetation succession model allows direct input of climate data, climate data can be altered to match projected future conditions under the proposed scenario, with multiple simulations used to define a range of outcomes for that scenario. Many different types of outcomes could be assessed, including individual species frequencies on the landscape, landscape-level changes in species abundance, patch size distributions, or overall landscape heterogeneity or species diversity. Even

The primary strength of landscape models is the ability to include spatial processes as drivers of vegetation change on landscapes.

if climate is not an explicit driver of vegetation succession in a landscape model, climate change effects could still be evaluated indirectly by simulating the effects of altered processes (e.g., disturbance regimes, seed availability) on vegetation, and landscape patterns.

Strengths and Weaknesses of Landscape Models

The primary strength of landscape models is the ability to include spatial processes as drivers of vegetation change on landscapes, including disturbances like fire and human activities and seed dispersal and species migration processes. Large disturbances like wildfires, insect outbreaks, and human management activities often initiate vegetation change by killing dominant species or individuals, releasing growing space and available resources, and altering microclimate. Seed-dispersal processes influence migration rates and pathways for species and, in turn, regulate rates of potential change in species composition. These spatial processes can significantly influence vegetation change and landscape patterns, but are largely absent from most other types of models. They are also important for modeling transient responses to climate change.

Landscape models also benefit from being, at varying levels of detail, process-based models. Landscape models can be developed to include simulation of stand development or biogeochemical processes, as needed to meet model objectives. They can therefore share many of the strengths of gap models and biogeochemical models for addressing climate change questions.

One limitation with landscape models is that they are computationally demanding, forcing users to make choices about the complexity of processes simulated within each cell (e.g., stand dynamics, biogeochemical cycling), the number and types of spatial processes to be simulated, and the spatial extent of the simulation (cell size and number of cells). Although advances in software design and computer hardware have improved landscape model capabilities, they still cannot do everything over large areas.

An even more basic limitation that landscape models share with gap models is the lack of basic understanding of the effects of climate on vegetation dynamics, disturbances, and their interactions, and on nonforested ecosystems. Simulating processes adequately requires basic knowledge about those processes. Parameterizing process-rich landscape models for use over large spatial and temporal scales requires a great deal of information about species responses to climate, disturbances, drivers of landscape pattern and process, and the spatial and temporal scales at which processes are expressed (Perry and Enright 2006). This information typically does not exist and must be estimated or omitted. Even fully parameterized landscape models may fail to produce realistic results, particularly if key processes are not included in the model. Parameterization problems can be useful for revealing data and knowledge gaps, but they limit the immediate utility of landscape models for addressing climate change questions.

Using Landscape Models

The best use of landscape models may be as tools for designing and testing strategies for managing disturbances and landscape patterns, including potential interactions with specific climate change scenarios. However, as with all models, they should not be used to make specific projections about future conditions or as the basis for making specific conservation predictions (Perry and Enright 2006, Wennergren et al. 1995). For example, a landscape model might be used to examine the effects of projected changes in fire frequency or extent on landscape patterns. Or, it might be used to examine the potential effects of restoration treatments on landscape fire resilience under current and future climate scenarios. It could also estimate potential species migration rates across a landscape once climate becomes suitable (native or exotic species). Such applications make good use of the ability of landscape models to model spatial processes, but do not require the models to predict the nature or timing of direct climate change effects on vegetation.

Biogeochemical Models

Introduction to Biogeochemical Models

Biogeochemical models are process-based models that simulate carbon, water, and mineral (nutrient) cycles in terrestrial ecosystems, including forests and rangelands (Aber and Federer 1992, Running and Nemani 1991, Waring and Running 1998). Biogeochemical models are commonly used to simulate ecosystem net primary productivity and carbon storage, and this is their primary usage in climate change research. Biogeochemical models may also simulate site water balances and nutrient availability at varying levels of detail associated with varying spatial and temporal scales (Schimel et al. 1997a, 1997b).

How Biogeochemical Models Work

Biogeochemical models represent sites by describing one or more soil layers (e.g., depth, water-holding capacity, fertility), climate (input time series at daily to monthly time steps), and any topographic factors that might influence waterflows or solar radiation inputs. Vegetation is generally described in terms of foliage (e.g., leaf area index, leaf nitrogen concentration), structural wood (e.g., stems, branches, and coarse roots), and fine roots. Some biogeochemical models (e.g., Biome-BGC or pNET) treat vegetation on the landscape as a single leaf layer (Aber and Federer 1992, Boisvenue and Running 2010), while others may simulate multiple canopy layers and light attenuation through the canopy. Such models can be parameterized to capture the broad ecophysiological characteristics of plant functional types and are generally not species specific, or to represent the observed characteristics of particular species (e.g., Pietsch et al. 2005). Biogeochemical models "grow" vegetation by determining net carbon uptake through photosynthesis and respiration, which is regulated by temperature and availability of light, water, and soil nutrients. Growth (carbon) is then allocated to different biomass pools, where it may contribute to future resource acquisition (fine roots), photosynthesis (foliage), or structure (wood). Climate data are input as drivers of ecosystem changes through time (Boisvenue and Running 2010), interacting with site environmental conditions and vegetation ecophysiological traits.

How Biogeochemical Models Are Applied to Climate Change Issues

Biogeochemical models can be applied to climate change issues by simulating transient and equilibrium responses of vegetation and, in some cases, ecosystem services to changing climate (Aber et al. 1995). Responses of particular interest may include net carbon uptake and storage, site water balances, and changes in sustainable vegetation characteristic (e.g., leaf area index). As with gap and landscape models, transient and equilibrium responses to climate change can be studied by altering the climate data input stream to reflect projected future changes in climate (with or without a transition period).

Strengths and Weaknesses of Biogeochemical Models

Biogeochemical models directly address ecosystem responses to climate change that are important in natural resources management. Carbon uptake and storage directly address questions about the role of forests and rangelands as sources or sinks for atmospheric CO_2. Estimates of soil water balances and nutrient cycling can help inform assessments of climate change effects on water quality and yields. Describing vegetation changes in terms of changes in foliage leaf area and nitrogen content can also be useful for suggesting ways that vegetation structure and composition might be managed to increase resilience to climate change.

Biogeochemical models are relatively amenable to validation, increasing confidence in model projections. For example, model projections of ecosystem productivity responses to past climatic variability may be tested against data from long-term ecosystem studies, or compared to growth indices derived from tree-ring records. Simulated ecophysiological processes such as photosynthesis and respiration can be measured under field conditions. Soil moisture and runoff can also be measured in the field and compared to model projections. As model projections improve for past and current conditions, confidence in future projections improves.

Biogeochemical models that do not consider individual species or biotic interactions make it difficult to forecast vegetation responses to climatic changes in terms of future species composition or biodiversity. They also do not explicitly model spatial processes, but can be incorporated into spatially explicit landscape models (e.g., Fire-GBC; Keane et al. 1996) or into dynamic global vegetation models (e.g., MC1; Bachelet et al. 2001a). However, unlike other model types, these models can be used across a range of ecosystem types (grasslands, woodlands, forests).

Using Biogeochemical Models

Biogeochemical models are probably best used to simulate climate and management effects on site carbon and water balances, and to identify key climatic factors limiting ecosystem productivity (environmental stressors). Biogeochemical models could also be used effectively in tandem with gap or landscape models to achieve additional objectives.

Dynamic Global Vegetation Models

Introduction to Dynamic Global Vegetation Models

Dynamic global vegetation models (DGVMs) are a class of process models developed to model ecosystem processes and the distribution of major vegetation biomes at continental to global scales. They have been developed primarily for addressing questions related to global ecology, biogeography, and climate change, including interactions among atmospheric CO_2 concentrations, climate, and terrestrial plant productivity. Dynamic Global Vegetation models can be run independently using historical or future projected climate data, or they can be coupled with GCMs for use in generating future climate scenarios.

How Dynamic Global Vegetation Models Work

Dynamic global vegetation models are mechanistic models that integrate many processes—plant biogeography, ecophysiology, biophysics, biogeochemistry, and sometimes disturbances and vegetation dynamics—to simulate land-atmosphere interactions (Cramer et al. 2001). They simulate changes through time for vegetation types, not species, where vegetation types are described by properties like vegetation height, growth phenology, rooting depth, leaf area index, photosynthetic pathway, and stomatal resistance (not species). Climate is one of the main drivers of DGVMs, and climate variables and CO_2 are incorporated directly into process simulations.

Dynamic global vegetation models share characteristics with modern biogeo-chemical models and statistical species distribution models. Like biogeochemical models, DGVMs seek to simulate climate and vegetation effects on carbon and water cycling. In fact, some DGVMs have directly incorporated biogeochemical models into their model structure (e.g., the CENTURY biogeochemical model was incorporated into the MAPSS biogeographical model to produce the MC1 DGVM). Like species distribution models, some DGVMs simulate shifts in the spatial distribution of broad plant functional types (rather than species) by using statistical relationships between vegetation types and either climatic conditions or modeled vegetation characteristics.

How Dynamic Global Vegetation Models Are Applied to Climate Change Issues

Dynamic global vegetation models have been used to project vegetation responses to increasing atmospheric CO_2 concentrations and changing climate at global, national, and regional scales (Bachelet et al. 2004, Cramer et al. 2001, Pan et al. 1998, Rogers et al. 2011). As noted above, climate is one of the main drivers of DGVMs, and climate variables and CO_2 are incorporated directly into process simulations.

Strengths and Weaknesses of Dynamic Global Vegetation Models

Because processes are specified and constraints on new responses are limited, these models may respond well to novel climates. However, many important processes are also faster than the minimum model time steps, and simplified equations that roughly represent the process must be used instead of detailed mechanisms (Neilson et al. 2005). The models are typically evaluated through observation and experimentation.

Dynamic global vegetation models were designed to operate at continental to global extents, with individual grid cells representing thousands of square kilome-ters (Neilson et al. 2005). At such broad scales, climate is often a dominant driver of spatial variability in vegetation structure and ecosystem processes. The models have also been applied at landscape to regional spatial scales (Rogers 2009, 2011). Their use is not limited to one particular ecosystem type or plant functional type, so they are broadly applicable. However, their use at finer spatial scales could greatly increase the uncertainty of model output, as the models often do not simu-late the influence of local drivers on ecosystem processes (e.g., topographic effects).

Differences between models are noteworthy and not easily linked to differences in model process formulations or model complexity (Cramer et al. 2001). Cramer et al. (2001) also noted that regional details of DGMV simulations are not to be taken as predictions. Although these models do include some disturbance processes (notably fire), other important processes, such as insect and disease dynamics, are lacking. Although all models require some sort of future climate data for parameterization, these models are spatially and temporally dynamically coupled to output from GCMs, and highly sensitive to GCM output.

Using Dynamic Global Vegetation Models

These models are best used at the broad global scales for which they were developed. They can be very useful in combination with GCMs for projecting carbon and water fluxes. They can also be used to make broad-scale projections about the capacity of terrestrial ecosystems to take up and sequester (or release) atmospheric carbon. They may also be useful for examining possible changes in terrestrial productivity and environmental limiting factors in response to future climate change scenarios (Neilson et al. 2005).

Dynamic global vegetation models do not appear to be suitable for regional planning efforts, although they are being incorporated into other models used for planning (e.g., Kerns et al. 2012). Their best contribution would likely be estimates of potential sustainable vegetation characteristics (e.g., maximum leaf area), but these could be obtained from biogeochemical models as well. The DGVMs do not try to model vegetation at the species level, so they are not particularly useful for species-level conservation planning. However, some applications have shown that DGVMs can be applied to simulate vegetation dynamics on the species level (Hickler et al. 2004). As noted earlier, DGVMs generally ignore important local drivers of vegetation structure, composition, and productivity (as they should for global-scale applications) making results from their application at fine spatial scales problematic. Adding such drivers would likely convert the model to some form of gap-biogeochemical or SDM-biogeochemical hybrid. Indeed, some hybrid models have recently been developed to address these concerns (e.g., LPJ-GUESS, Smith et al. 2001; HYBRID, Friend et al. 1997).

Growth and Yield Models

Introduction to Growth and Yield Models

Growth and yield models are used in forest management to estimate future growth and yield of forest stands based on site characteristics (e.g., site index) and mathematical or statistical representations of tree growth through time. They typically

Dynamic global vegetation models do not appear to be suitable for regional planning efforts, although they are being incorporated into other models used for planning.

model forest growth and biomass accumulation for entire stands or species cohorts, but some simulate growth at the tree level. A stand growth model simulates the growth, mortality, and other changes in stand composition and structure, and mathematically describes the growth and yield of trees and stands. Growth and yield models have also been coupled with stand visualization systems to provide visual representation of the stand structural conditions being simulated by the models.

How Growth and Yield Models Work

Growth and yield models begin with site information and an initial stand inventory. They then simulate forest stand development by growing existing trees, establishing new cohorts (given growing space availability), and killing trees based on established rules and probabilities. Model parameters can be modified to better suit local conditions or to conduct "what-if" investigations.

The Forest Vegetation Simulator (FVS) is widely used in forest management applications and can serve as a good example of how modern growth and yield models work. The FVS is an individual-tree, semidistance-independent growth and yield model (Crookston et al. 2010, Dixon 2002). Inputs include an inventory of site conditions and a set of measurements on a sample of trees (e.g., tree size, species, crown ratio, recent growth and mortality rates). Outputs include summaries of tree volume, species distributions, and growth and mortality rates that are often customized for specific user needs. Model "variants" have been developed for specific geographic areas of the United States by calibrating model equations to local field data. Because it simulates individual trees, FVS can simulate growth and yield responses to a wide range of silvicultural treatments across a wide range of forest types and initial stand conditions.

How Growth and Yield Models Are Applied to Climate Change Issues

Growth and yield models have traditionally assumed static climatic conditions on a site and have not incorporated temporal climatic variability into establishment, growth, and mortality functions. As such, they have had limited utility for climate change applications.

Recently, climate considerations have been integrated into FVS so that stand-level impacts of climate change can be simulated (Crookston et al. 2010). This was accomplished by (1) adding functions that link mortality and regeneration of species to climate variables expressing climatic suitability, (2) constructing a function linking site index to climate and using it to modify growth rates, and (3) adding functions accounting for changing growth rates resulting from climate-induced genetic responses. This model incorporates climate by using information and data from the species distribution modeling approach that closely parallels Rehfeldt et al. (2006, 2009) (Crookston et al. 2010). It can be argued, however, that in adding these climate considerations to a model that was already simulating individual trees, FVS is becoming more of a gap or hybrid model. The newest model version (2.1) also includes "genetic" variation in the mortality model, largely for species that have very large ranges. For example, the modification in version 2.1 will likely kill off Douglas-fir (*Pseudotsuga menziesii* (Mirb.) Franco) at a given location even if Douglas-fir from elsewhere in the range of the species would grow well. The model may regenerate Douglas-fir in that case under the assumption that the new trees will be genetically adapted to the site.

Strengths and Weaknesses of Growth and Yield Models

Growth and yield models have the benefit of being relatively simple to parameterize and run. To the extent that parameters are derived from local growth and yield data, the models can produce reasonably accurate projections for the local area. These models have proved to be very useful in forest planning efforts and designing silvicultural strategies.

The primary weakness of growth and yield models is the basic assumption of a static climate, such that climatic variability is not a driver of establishment, growth, and survival. Climate functions simply as an invariant site descriptor. Growth and yield models are also most reliable when calibrated against local field data; however, uncertainties about future climate make it difficult to find appropriate model parameters to use to simulate future stand growth. Growth and yield models have also been developed only for forested stands and species.

Using Growth and Yield Models

We do not recommend the use of traditional growth and yield models for projecting forest responses to climate change. Hybrid models like FVS-Climate may have some utility as pseudo-gap models, but this new modeling approach has not yet been widely applied and assessed in the literature.

Chapter 7: Using Model Projections

Chapter 6 highlights the many different types of models that have been developed, and continue to be developed, to examine how vegetation may change with future climate change. We reviewed the major classes of vegetation models; described their basic function, strengths, and weaknesses; and discussed the contribution each could make toward understanding and projecting vegetation responses to future climatic changes. It is clear from this review that the literature is not mature enough at this time to suggest which modeling approach is "best," or which models within a particular approach are "best" although we know some things that are "better" (e.g., using direct gradients not proxies). Our assessment revealed numerous caveats associated with commonly applied empirical species distribution approaches, and suggests that process-based approaches may be more robust to prediction. Yet all process models rely on parameter estimates from experimentation or the literature, which are themselves estimates. Each equation or parameter input into a model has associated uncertainty (Beale and Lennon 2012), which may propagate through the model. The more complex the model is, the better it may deal with novel conditions, but the more uncertainty in results there may be with so many parameters estimated (Sklar and Hunsaker 2001). Overfitting a model with lots of parameters limits extrapolation into novel condition as well. Despite the potential complexity of process models, critical processes may still be omitted (Verboom and Wamelink 2005). In addition, scale issues, lack of data for parameterization of more species, model complexity, lack of management-relevant model output information, and lack of species-specific output from dynamic global vegetation models (DGVMs) like MC1, has often been a barrier to use by the management community.

Despite the specific strengths and weaknesses of the different modeling approaches, there are certain caveats specific to all the models. For example, most of the models do not deal with inertia in vegetation, although some landscape models have the capacity to deal with inertia if they are parameterized to include climate change. None of the models we examined deal with dispersal or genetic adaptation, although some models are starting to do so (Gibson 2011). A new generation of models incorporating climate variability along with dispersal and establishment are clearly needed (Gray et al. 2006). Most of the models also do not incorporate disturbance processes, or may only address fire. The inclusion of disturbance and extreme events in most models is still early in the process (Keane et al. 2004, Lenihan et al. 1998, Thonicke et al. 2001). Many models are also often used without being calibrated and analyzed for sensitivity and uncertainty (Verboom and Wamelink 2005). And for all models, the more future conditions differ from current conditions, the more our understanding of ecological patterns and processes will be incomplete and the less accurate our models will be at predicting ecological phenomena (Williams and Jackson 2007).

The more future conditions differ from current conditions, the more our understanding of ecological patterns and processes will be incomplete and the less accurate our models will be at predicting ecological phenomena.

Ensemble Approaches

Because there is no consensus on which modeling approach is "best," ensemble approaches, such as used in chapter 8, are important. Ensemble approaches are commonly used when looking at climate projections with global climate models (GCMs). Such ensemble forecasting using multiple GCMs and multiple vegetation models can be used to find consistent projections, which may be more likely to be correct (Araújo and New 2007, Bradley 2010). Use of different models in combination also provides information at multiple taxonomic levels (e.g., species vs. vegetation type) about how climate might affect vegetation change, and the difference between projections and their sources are themselves useful tools with which to assess uncertainty (Littell et al. 2011).

In general, agreement among ecological models with different underlying principles and different conceptual approaches when climate inputs are similar (e.g., same scenarios), or across multiple climate models and multiple ecological models, suggests scientific agreement (if not consensus) on sensitivity of the vegetation response to climate (Littell et al. 2011). However, model development, lineages, and model input data are sometimes shared (e.g., sibling models), so it may be important to note that if there is agreement, the models need to be independent in their assumptions for potential reductions in uncertainty to hold. In particular, species distribution models share a similar conceptual approach and many tend to use similar data for training (e.g., Forest Inventory and Analysis data sources for tree presence/absence). Thus it is unclear how independent these types of models are from each other and not surprising that these models often produce quite similar results, despite very different analytical approaches. Agreement among several species distribution models may not be as meaningful in terms of uncertainty as agreement among species distribution and process models. Moreover, process models tend to differ considerably in their conceptual approaches and development (e.g., gap models, DGVMs) and to be truly independent of each other. Therefore, agreements among several process models may be potentially more meaningful than agreement among several species distribution models.

Frequent disagreement among ecological models when climate is similar suggests different assumptions and sensitivities of ecosystem response to climate among models. Frequent disagreement in output from a single ecological model with variable climate inputs suggests high sensitivity of vegetation to climate model input. When models disagree and uncertainty is large, local knowledge, monitoring, observations of historical patterns, and knowledge from other sources may help decrease uncertainty. Even when models agree, there is a need for local knowledge, especially when translating the results into management actions.

When interpreting and using model output, it is key to try to understand why the output may differ so dramatically. Chapter 6 provides some background information that can help inform managers about why there might be differences in model output. For example, the differences in model output shown may be due to the fact that some models contain the disturbance fire and include processes such as nitrogen fertilization (e.g., MC1). However, more than the modeling approaches can differ. For example, modelers often develop or downscale their historical climate data and future climate data differently. Assessing the exact mechanism of why the models differ is a complicated task, which could only realistically be undertaken by running the models using similarly generated input data and extensive sensitivity analyses.

Using Model Projections Wisely

Models have been critical for alerting us to the potential magnitude of the effects of climate change (Sinclair et al. 2010). Furthermore, while the broad scales and long time periods in model simulations make them hard to validate, they also highlight the fact that empirical studies are limited in time and space and that models are needed to fill this gap. Although imperfect, models are necessary for projecting future conditions and likely perform better than expert opinion (Verboom and Wamelink 2005). The role of models in this context is not to predict the future, but rather to help manage uncertainty by narrowing the possible range of futures to a subset of plausible futures that pertain directly to vulnerabilities for specific resources and management objectives (Littell et al. 2011). This is why we often use the term "projection" in reference to simulated model output about the future. There is always the fundamental problem that extremely simplifying assumptions are necessary in modeling exercises (Green and Sadedin 2005). In these cases, simulations are best used to examine general ecological principles rather than predict the behavior of a specific ecosystem (Green and Sadedin 2005).

Models may be insufficient to answer specific management questions at a local scale, but can provide insight into the effects of climate change (Guisan and Thuiller 2005). Therefore, use of model output is better suited for informing strategic decisionmaking or land use planning, rather than tactical stand management decisions (Robinson et al. 2008). A hierarchical approach may be useful where first the climatic suitability is evaluated, then more specific relationships based on soils, land use, and other factors can be used to fine tune the assessment (Bradley 2009, Larson et al. 2001, Pearson and Dawson 2003). For example, potential habitat suitability can be projected for an invasive exotic species under climate change scenarios (Kerns et al. 2009). Combining this information with local information on

The role of models is not to predict the future, but rather to help manage uncertainty by narrowing the possible range of futures to a subset of plausible futures that pertain directly to vulnerabilities for specific resources and management objectives.

the species distribution could alert managers to areas that have a higher probability of being invaded and help focus monitoring and early eradication efforts. Modeling is also a very good way to clarify policy concerns and begin to identify processes that are likely to be important (Perry and Enright 2006).

Littell et al. (2011) suggested asking the following questions when choosing which models to select:

1. Are multiple scenarios and multiple GCMs needed, or is an ensemble mean sufficient? Because it is likely that the mean may not be relevant for impact modeling, and that extremes are important, we suggest using multiple GCMs, emission scenarios, and multiple vegetation models.

2. Do the models and emission scenarios selected match the risk framework (risk tolerant vs. risk averse)?

3. Do the models chosen have good fidelity to 20th century observations for the region of focus?

4. Is the spatial and temporal scale of the climate information appropriate to planning or decisionmaking?

5. If downscaled information is being used, is the extra detail both necessary and realistic?

6. How does the scale of information match the detail of the ecosystem impact model being used?

After model selection is complete, keep in mind the best uses of model output (box 7.1).

Box 7.1. After vegetation model selection is complete, the best uses of simulation model output include (based on Littell et al. 2011):

- Examining general ecological principles and identifying processes that are likely to be important.

- Providing insight into the range of potential effects of climate change.

- Informing strategic, not tactical decisionmaking.

- Helping to narrow the possible range of futures to a subset relevant to vulnerabilities for specific resources and management objectives.

- Clarifying policy concerns.

Chapter 8: Climate Change and Major PNW Biomes

The Pacific Northwest supports a diverse array of environmental settings, from dry deserts of the interior Columbia Basin to the wet Pacific Coast and from warm, low-elevation areas to high-elevation alpine and subalpine areas of the Cascade and Olympic Mountains. These diverse environments support an equally diverse suite of vegetation types, including subalpine forests and meadows, maritime coniferous forests, dry coniferous forests, juniper savannahs and woodlands, and shrub-steppe. Because each of these vegetation types is associated with distinct climatic conditions, environmental stressors, and disturbance regimes, they are likely to respond differently to future climate change. In the following sections, we provide a general description of five major vegetation types in the Pacific Northwest, highlighting their unique features with respect to climate, vegetation, and disturbance, and describe past vegetation changes in response to climate change. We then review the relevant field- and model-based research for each vegetation type (key species and communities) and highlight key findings, projections, and uncertainties about vegetation responses to future climatic changes.

In particular, we seek to answer the following questions:

1. What are the major climate-related factors limiting vegetation growth, reproduction, and survival and how are they likely to change?

2. What are the dominant climate-related disturbance regimes and how are they likely to change?

3. What do we know about vegetation sensitivity and adaptation to elevated carbon dioxide (CO_2) and climatic variability?

4. What are the likely vegetation responses to changing CO_2 and climate?

Synthesis of Model Projections for the Pacific Northwest

We synthesized model projections by biome from relatively recent and peer-reviewed literature (although level of peer review differs). Table 8.1 summarizes the data sources we used with brief information about the global climate models (GCMs) and vegetation models. We combined projections of vegetation change from these different types of models, essentially creating a qualitative ensemble of projections. Table 8.2 provides a summary ensemble of projected responses for some key Pacific Northwest species to climate change by the end of the 21st century based on multiple model output. This summary is based on a qualitative assessment using classes: some loss, moderate loss, major loss, no habitat remaining, some gain, moderate gain, major gain, or little to no change, or shift in habitat. We

Table 8.1—Description of data sources for model output

Model name	Model output source	Species modeled	GCM(s)	Model type	Species occurrence data	Time period
1. Random forests	Plant Species and Climate Profile Predictions. http://forest.moscowfsl.wsu.edu/climate/species/index.php (Crookston et al. 2010, Rehfeldt et al. 2006)	Many trees of North America	GCM3, HADCM3 model	Species distribution	Forest inventory and research plot data	2090
2. ANUCLM	Plant Hardiness of Canada website, Natural Resources Canada, http://planthardiness.gc.ca/ (McKenney et al. 2007, 2011)	Many trees and shrubs of western North America	HADCM3, CGM31, CSIRO mk35, MIROC 32mr	Species distribution model	Forest inventory plot data additional sources	2071–2100
3. MSTC	The ForeCASTS Project http://www.geobabble.org/~hnw/global/treeranges3/climate_change/atlas.html (Hargrove and Hoffman 2005)	Many trees and shrubs of North America	HADCM3, with A1F1 emission scenario	Species distribution model	Forest inventory plot data; additional sources for rare species	2100
4. Bradley	Publication figures and descriptions (Bradley 2009)	*Bromus tectorum* (cheatgrass)	Summary of 10 GCMs, with A1B emission scenario	Species distribution model	Remote sensing (AVHRR) map for the Great Basin	2090–2100
5. MC1	The Conservation Biology Institute website Data Basin http://databasin.org/ (Rogers et al. 2011)	Broad potential vegetation type	HADCM3, SCIROmk3, MIROC32r	Dynamic global vegetation model	None	2070–2099

Table 8.1—Description of data sources for model output (continued)

Model name	Model output source	Species modeled	GCM(s)	Model type	Species occurrence data	Time period
6. FORCLIM	Publication figures and descriptions (Busing et al. 2007)	Maritime forest trees of western North America	Summary of seven GCMs	Gap model	Forest inventory plot data (USDA and USDI)	2050
7. 3-PG	Publication figures and descriptions (Coops et al. 2005)	*Pinus ponderosa* (ponderosa pine)	HadCM2, with IS92a emission scenario	Biogeochemical model	Species range map	2080–2090
8. Hybrid 3-PG Model	Pacific Northwest Species Change website, http://www.pnwspecieschange.info/index.html (Coops and Waring 2011a)	*Pinus contorta* (lodgepole pine)	CGCM2	Hybrid of biogeochemical and species distribution models	Forest inventory plot data	2071–2100
9. Hybrid 3-PG Model	Pacific Northwest Species Change website, http://www.pnwspecieschange.info/index.html (Coops and Waring 2011b)	Trees of Pacific Northwest	CGCM3	Hybrid of biogeochemical and species distribution models	Forest inventory plot data (U.S. and Canada)	2080

Model number are referenced in table 8.2. Most global climate model (GCM) data used for model input were generated from the Intergovernmental Panel on Climate Change 4th assessment report (IPCC 2007b) and only the A2 emission scenario was examined, except as noted.

Table 8.2—Projected response of some key Pacific Northwest species to climate change by the end of the 21st century based on multiple model output

Biome	Key species	Projected response	List of model output (table 8.1)
Subalpine forests			
	Unspecified	Major to total loss	5
	Abies lasiocarpa	Moderate to total loss	1, 2, 3, 9
	Tsuga mertensiana	Increase to total loss, some shifts	1, 2, 3, 9
	Pinus albicaulis	Increase to total loss, some shifts	1, 2, 3, 9
Maritime coniferous forests			
	Unspecified	Moderate to major loss	5
	Pseudotsuga menziesii	No change to total loss	
	Tsuga heterophylla	Increase to total loss, some shifts	1, 2, 3, 6[a], 9
	Abies grandis	Moderate to total loss	1, 2, 3, 6[a], 9
	Thuja plicata	No change to total loss, some shifts	1, 2, 3, 9
	Picea sitchensis	Some to total loss	1, 2, 3, 9
Dry coniferous forests			
	Unspecified	Moderate to major gain	5
	Pinus ponderosa	Moderate to total loss; gains	1, 2, 3, 7, 9
	Pinus contorta	Moderate to total loss	1, 2, 3, 8, 9
	Pseudotsuga menziesii	No change to total loss	1, 2, 3, 9
	Abies grandis	Moderate to total loss	1, 2, 3, 9
	Populus tremuloides	Total loss	3[b]
Savannas and woodlands			
	Unspecified	Moderate to major gain	5
	Juniperus occidentalis	Moderate to total loss	1, 2
	Quercus crysolepsis	Highly variable	1, 2, 3
	Quercus garryana	Highly variable	1, 2, 3
	Quercus kelloggii	All show shifts, mostly gains	1, 2, 3

Note: Model output refers to climate habitat, rather than actual species range. Loss of habitat is based on a qualitative assessment and ranked into classes: some loss, moderate loss, major loss, no habitat remaining, some gain, moderate gain, major gain, little to no change, or shift in habitat. Details on models and sources are provided in table 8.1. Some of the models listed in table 8.1 are not summarized in this table because of the lack of spatial information associated with the maps.

[a] Note that the Busing et al. (2007) projections only go to the middle of the century.

[b] Only one model was available for assessment. Random Forests and ANUCLIM (models 1, 2 in table 8.1) have data available for this species but do not project suitable climate in the Cascades for this species under historical (current) conditions.

examined only a handful of representative species within each biome, and only included models with sufficient spatial information to examine output by biome (see table 8.2). Background information about the vegetation models used to project future response of vegetation to climate is summarized in chapter 6. We tried to assess only output across common GCMs and emission scenarios, but that was not practical given the wide variety of scenarios that researchers have used. We also limited our assessment to recent models and scenarios associated with the Intergovernmental Panel on Climate Change (IPCC) fourth assessment report (IPCC 2007), although there was an exception. It is important to note that differences in projected changes in temperature and especially precipitation in the Pacific Northwest differ more among GCMs than among emissions scenarios. The emissions scenarios and climate models used in the next IPCC assessment will reflect this. We also limited our assessment to the A2 or A1FI emission scenarios as these scenarios have higher emissions and demonstrate potential "worst case scenarios." If the A2 emission scenario was not used for a particular effort (e.g., ForCASTS), then we selected the scenario with the highest future CO_2 emissions. Although the A2 and A1FI emission scenarios may represent the worst case scenario compared to other scenarios, current trajectories of greenhouse gas emissions are either at the upper end or surpass these scenarios (Raupach et al. 2007). Therefore, it is unclear if these scenarios really represent a "worst case." Only the MC1 model output from Rogers et al. (2011) included any disturbance processes, and only fire was modeled.

Subalpine Forests and Alpine Meadows

General Description

Within the Pacific Northwest, subalpine forests and alpine meadow vegetation occupy high-elevation sites in the Cascade, Olympic, and Rocky Mountains and the Okanogan Highlands. We define subalpine forests as high-elevation forests with short growing seasons produced by deep, persistent winter snowpack (5 months or longer, on average) and relatively cool summer temperatures. This includes primarily the mountain hemlock (*Tsuga mertensiana* (Bong.) Carriere) forest zone in the western Washington and Oregon Cascades, Olympic Mountains, and northern Rocky Mountains, and the subalpine fir (*Abies lasiocarpa* (Hook.) Nutt.) forest zone of the eastern Washington and Oregon Cascades, Rocky Mountains, and Okanogan Highlands. Commonly associated tree species include Pacific silver fir (*Abies amabilis* (Douglas ex Loudon) Douglas ex Forbes), Alaska yellow cedar (*Chamaecyparis nootkatensis* (D. Don) Spach), Engelmann spruce (*Picea engelmannii* Parry ex Engelm.), lodgepole pine (*Pinus contorta* Douglas ex Loudon), whitebark pine (*P. albicaulis* Engelm.), and subalpine larch (*Larix lyallii* Parl.) (Franklin and Dyrness 1973). Alpine meadow vegetation includes the heath shrub (*Phyllodoce-Cassiope-Vaccinium*), lush herbaceous (*Valeriana sitchensis* Bong.-*Carex spectabilis* Dewey), dwarf sedge (*Carex nigricans* C.A. Mey), rawmark and low herbaceous, and grass (*Festuca viridula* Vasey) communities (Franklin and Dyrness 1973).

Subalpine forests and alpine meadows are characterized by relatively short growing seasons, low air and soil temperatures, and slow nutrient cycling rates.

The climate in the subalpine and alpine zones is characterized by cold, wet winters, and mild, relatively dry summers. Mean annual precipitation in the subalpine and alpine zones varies considerably across the west-to-east gradient from highest amounts in the Olympic Mountains and western Cascades, to lesser amounts in the eastern Cascades, Okanogan Highlands, and Rocky Mountains. In all cases, however, much of the cool season precipitation falls as snow and is stored in a persistent snowpack that typically forms in November and December and persists until June or later.

Environmental Controls

Subalpine forests and alpine meadows are characterized by relatively short growing seasons, low air and soil temperatures, and slow nutrient cycling rates. Short growing seasons are primarily the result of late-melting snowpack throughout much of the region, while cool air and soil temperatures become more important from west to east. Cool soil temperatures limit nutrient cycling rates, which could lead to nitrogen limitations on growth and reproduction.

Deep, late-melting snowpack and cold soils have a strong influence on plant flowering and growth phenology in subalpine forests and alpine meadows (Canaday and Fonda 1974; Dunne et al. 2003; Inouye 2008; Worrall 1983, 1993). Worrall (1983) found that budburst in subalpine fir and Pacific silver fir plantations varied considerably from year to year, apparently in response to differences in the timing of snowmelt and soil heating. Subalpine fir budburst preceded that of Pacific silver fir, indicating a lower temperature threshold for accumulating heat sums that trigger budburst (Worrall 1983). Budburst phenology in subalpine larch appears to be controlled primarily by air temperatures, as leaves commonly emerge while the snowpack is still present (Worrall 1993). Cessation of growth and cold hardening in true firs (*Abies* spp.) and other subalpine tree species has generally been attributed to a combination of day length (photoperiod) and nighttime air temperatures, so that snowpack duration is also correlated with growing season length for these species (Worrall 1983, but see also Worrall 1993 for a possible exception).

Snowpack melting and subsequent soil heating have been shown to influence flowering, growth phenology, and vegetation community patterns in alpine meadows. Snow removal and soil heating manipulations have shown that both factors influence the timing of flowering in alpine meadows (Dunne et al. 2003, Inouye 2008). Spatial variability in snowpack persistence influences flowering and growth phenology within species and, to the extent that spatial patterns of snowmelt are consistent among years, also influences species composition and community types in alpine meadows (Canaday and Fonda 1974, Evans and Fonda 1990).

Interannual variability in subalpine tree growth has often been linked to effective growing season length. Tree ring studies of subalpine conifers often find that annual diameter increment is negatively correlated with winter precipitation or spring snowpack depth (Ettl and Peterson 1995b; Graumlich and Brubaker 1986; Heikkinen 1985; Peterson and Peterson 1994, 2001; Peterson et al. 2002), particularly in the western subalpine zones that receive more winter precipitation and develop deeper snowpacks. Summer drought may also be a common factor limiting growth in some of the drier, interior subalpine forests (Ettl and Peterson 1995b, Peterson and Peterson 2001, Peterson et al. 2002).

Growing season length and summer drought also influence subalpine tree reproduction, establishment, and mortality particularly at upper treeline. Woodward et al. (1994) found that the production of large cone crops in subalpine fir and mountain hemlock were influenced by multiyear patterns of climatic variability, including factors associated with prior-year growing season length. Seedling demographic studies have shown that regeneration is often episodic in subalpine forests and alpine meadows and associated with decadal climatic variability. Tree invasions of subalpine meadows in the western Cascades and Olympics during the 20th century have been attributed to extended periods (up to a decade or more) of warm temperatures, earlier snowmelt, and extended growing seasons (Fonda and Bliss 1969, Franklin et al. 1971, Heikinnen 1984, Taylor 1995, Zald et al. 2012). Late summer soil moisture can also influence regeneration, as studies have associated successful seedling establishment on drier subalpine sites with a combination of early snowmelt, mild summer temperatures, and above-average summer precipitation that produces a longer growing season while limiting late summer soil water deficits (Little et al. 2004, Taylor 1995, Woodward et al. 1995). Bigler et al. (2007) investigated possible linkages between regional drought and subalpine tree mortality and found that mortality rates for subalpine fir and Engelmann spruce increased for up to a decade following drought, but lodgepole pine appeared to be more drought-resistant.

Air and soil temperatures also influence physiological processes and growth in trees, organic matter decomposition, and soil nutrient cycling. Cold soil and air temperatures limit photosynthesis outside of the growing season (Runyon et al. 1994). Low nighttime temperatures during the growing season can inhibit photosynthesis in subalpine conifer seedlings for up to several days, thereby limiting carbon uptake (Germino and Smith 1999, Johnson et al. 2004). Cold soils can limit leaf water conductance and photosynthesis (Day et al. 1989, Teskey et al. 1984). However, because temperature limitations on growth are stronger than temperature limitations on photosynthesis, growth may be considered temperature rather than carbon limited in subalpine forests (Grace et al. 2002, Harsch and Bader 2011). Cold soils also limit belowground biological processes associated with organic matter decomposition and nutrient cycling, thereby limiting nutrient availability to support plant growth (Hobbie 1996).

Biotic Interactions

Facilitation plays an important role in plant establishment and survival in subalpine and alpine communities, with its importance increasing from sites with lower to higher stress levels (Callaway et al. 2002, Smith et al. 2003). Highly stress-tolerant conifers in subalpine and alpine meadows can facilitate establishment by less tolerant (but potentially more competitive) tree species by ameliorating stress from deep snowpack, cold temperatures, or high light levels, or by reducing competition from herbaceous vegetation (Bansal et al. 2011, Little et al. 1994, Smith et al. 2003, Stueve et al. 2009, Zald et al. 2012). For example, subalpine fir trees are often able to establish under the canopies of large subalpine larch or whitebark pine trees and, being more shade tolerant, may later be able to grow up through the canopy and overtop the pioneer tree (Arno and Habeck 1972, Tomback et al. 2001).

Mutualistic relationships can also be important in subalpine and alpine vegetation communities. Presence of mycorrhizal fungi can help determine plant community composition and primary succession following glacial retreat in alpine ecosystems (Cázares et al. 2005, Jumpponen et al. 2012). The Clark's nutcracker (*Nucifraga columbiana*) depends on seeds from whitebark pine trees as a major part of its diet. In collecting and storing seed for later use, the bird disperses and "plants" the seeds, with an apparent preference for sites with early snowmelt (and hence greater accessibility).

Disturbances

Large-scale disturbances are infrequent in the subalpine and alpine zones but can still play an important role in shaping vegetation. Wildfires are infrequent in subalpine forests, as deep snowpacks produce a very short fire season, fuels are often wet, and spatial discontinuities can inhibit fire spread (Agee 1993). However, forest vegetation can be dramatically altered by rare wildfire events, as recovery from stand-replacing wildfires can be very slow (Little et al. 1994). In fact, it can take decades to centuries for tree reestablishment in burned subalpine forests that do not include lodgepole pine (Agee and Smith 1984, Little et al. 1994). Wildfire has probably played an important historical role in creating or maintaining subalpine and alpine meadows (Griggs 1938, Kuramoto and Bliss 1970). Recovery of subalpine forests following wildfire probably requires nearby seed sources, an extended period of favorable climate, and favorable biotic and abiotic microsite conditions (Bansal et al. 2011, Stueve et al. 2009, Zald et al. 2012).

Responses to Elevated CO_2 and Climate Change

Across all scenarios, species distribution models (models 1 through 3, table 8.1) project that the suitable climate available for most key subalpine species will be moderately reduced to nonexistent by the end of the century (table 8.2). Suitable climate is either nonexistent or only available in the far northern Cascade Mountains at high elevations. Similarly, output from MC1 (model 5, table 8.1) shows that the subalpine forest type will be severely reduced in the future, with only a very minor amount of this type remaining in the northern Cascade Mountains for a relatively cool and wet scenario (CSIRO A2). Interpretation of model output from the species distribution models and MC1 are quite similar. For the 3-PG hybrid model (model 9, table 8.1), projections were in agreement for subalpine fir (*Abies lasiocarpa* (Hook.) Nutt.). However, the model projected that mountain hemlock habitat may actually increase to the west in Oregon, and whitebark pine may have more suitable habitat in interior Washington and southern Oregon. It is apparent that there is some model agreement on the sensitivity of the subalpine forest ecosystem responses to similar future climate scenarios, that this ecosystem might be highly vulnerable to climate change, and that the northern high-elevation Cascade Mountains may serve as refugia for subalpine species. Although there is some disagreement among the models, there is more model agreement for this biome than any other biome examined. Note that information regarding the nontree (meadow) alpine component of alpine systems is lacking.

Projected model results suggest that this forest type may be severely reduced in the future. However, results from experimental and observational studies are not as clear and even suggest potential contrary responses. Warming temperatures, reduced snowpack accumulations, and earlier snowmelt are likely to produce significant changes in alpine and subalpine vegetation over time, including changes in plant growth phenology, establishment and persistence of trees in current meadow communities, and establishment of alpine meadow vegetation in new habitats exposed by melting snow and ice. Earlier snowmelt will facilitate earlier soil warming and likely shift plant flowering and growth phenology earlier in the growing season. This will increase mean growing season length but could also expose plants to early season frost damage (Martin et al. 2010). Longer growing seasons should also promote tree seedling establishment in subalpine meadows on snow-dominated sites, as occurred during warmer periods in the last century (Franklin et al. 1971, Taylor 1995, Woodward et al. 1995).

The effects of warming and earlier snowmelt on treeline and alpine meadow advance are less clear. Migration of tree species or alpine meadow communities to higher elevations or into previously hostile microtopographic positions may be limited by the simultaneous development of the soil fungal communities needed for mycorrhizal associations. Facilitation may also be limited if benefactor trees and shrubs are not yet established. On the other hand, release of previously suppressed tree seedlings and saplings could allow rapid development of new tree clumps within subalpine meadows as well as rapid advance of the forest line. Strong treeline advances have been found in some areas, such as Mount Rainier National Park (Stueve et al. 2009), but treeline responses to recent warming have been inconsistent (Harsch et al. 2009). The influence of broad-scale climate on treeline is modified by the local environment, orographic and edaphic factors, and disturbances (Holtmeier and Broll 2005).

Warming temperatures and elevated CO_2 could also increase carbon uptake and growth by subalpine forest trees. Warmer summer nighttime temperatures should reduce the frequency of cold-temperature photoinhibition, thereby increasing photosynthetic carbon fixation. Warmer summer temperatures, elevated CO_2, and increased nutrient availability could also increase subalpine tree growth. Tree ring studies have linked decadal trends in past tree growth rates to decadal fluctuations in summer temperatures (Graumlich et al. 1989, Peterson and Peterson 2001), but it is unclear how much summer temperatures could increase before growth became limited by other factors (e.g., soil water). Experimental tests of warming and CO_2 enrichment effects suggest that responses differ among species, which could also influence community structure (Dawes et al. 2011, Lambrecht et al. 2007).

Maritime Coniferous Forests

General Description

Evergreen coniferous forests currently occupy much of western Oregon and Washington, occupying low to middle elevations between the Pacific Ocean and the Cascade Mountains. Deciduous broadleaf forests are also common in the region but are mostly limited to recently disturbed forests (e.g., red alder [*Alnus rubra* Bong.] and bigleaf maple [*Acer macrophyllum* Pursh]) or stressful sites (e.g., Oregon white oak [*Quercus garryana* Douglas ex Hook.]) (Franklin and Dyrness 1973). For this discussion, we consider forests of the Sitka spruce (*Picea sitchensis* Bong.) Zone, western hemlock (*Tsuga heterophylla* (Raf.) Sarg.) Zone, and lower portions of the Pacific silver fir Zone (see Franklin and Dyrness (1973) for indepth descriptions of these forest types). We do not explicitly include the moist coniferous forests of the Selkirk Mountains in northeastern Washington, but note that they have similar characteristics to maritime coniferous forests of the western Cascade Mountains in terms of environmental conditions, disturbance regimes, and forest species composition.

Maritime coniferous forests are characterized by strong conifer dominance, great size and longevity for dominant trees, and high forest productivity and biomass accumulation. The dominant species in this region (e.g., Douglas-fir [*Pseudotsuga menziesii* (Mirb.) Franco], western hemlock, and Sitka spruce) can achieve great heights (up to 50 to 75 m) and large diameters (1 to 2 m) and are generally long lived with lifespans of 400 to 800 years (Franklin and Dyrness 1973). These forests can be highly productive and retain high productivity for centuries, resulting in high biomass accumulations (both above- and belowground). These forests also accumulate large amounts of coarse woody debris, making them especially well-suited for sequestering large amounts of carbon per unit area.

Maritime coniferous forests are supported by a maritime climate that features high annual precipitation, most of which falls as rain during the winter and spring (November through April), mild winter temperatures, and relatively mild, dry summers. Although maritime coniferous forests all receive considerable precipitation, there is considerable variability within the region; for example, precipitation at selected sites in the western hemlock zone ranges from about 145 to 321 cm per year (Franklin and Dyrness 1973). Mean annual temperatures also vary considerably within this region. This shows that although maritime coniferous forests are favored by certain climatic features, they are able to tolerate a fairly wide range of environmental settings. Snowpack water storage does not play a significant role in most of these forests.

Environmental Controls

Photosynthesis, net primary productivity, and tree growth are limited primarily by vapor-pressure deficits, low soil water availability, and freezing temperatures in the winter (Runyon et al. 1994). Mild, wet winters favor evergreen conifers by allowing them to assimilate much of their annual carbon requirements during the cool months (fall, winter, and spring) when deciduous trees have no leaves (Waring and Franklin 1979). Cold winter temperatures reduce photosynthesis, which can also impact growth and productivity by reducing carbon reserves (Gholz 1982, Runyon et al. 1994).

Dry summers with high vapor pressure deficits and low precipitation limit summer photosynthesis and productivity in maritime coniferous forests but also favor conifers over temperate deciduous tree species owing to differences in hydraulic architecture, stomatal conductance, water storage capacity, and rooting depths (Waring and Franklin 1979). Warm temperatures coupled with low humidity during the summer growing season can create high vapor pressure deficits, which can reduce photosynthesis by inducing partial or complete stomatal closure. Severe soil water deficits are uncommon, but evaporative demand can often exceed rates of water uptake, requiring trees to reduce leaf water conductance through stomatal closure or make use of internal water stores to buffer diurnal fluctuations in demand. Tree ring studies have shown that interannual variability in tree growth is positively correlated with summer soil moisture (Case and Peterson 2005; Chen et al. 2010; Little et al. 1995, 2008). Site water balance also appears to control the distribution of some important species, like western hemlock (Gavin and Hu 2006).

Photosynthesis and productivity could also be considered to be light-limited in much of the maritime coniferous forest zone, at least during certain seasons. Studies of maritime coniferous forests in western Oregon suggest that undisturbed forests develop high leaf area index values that allow them to intercept more than 90 percent of incident photosynthetically active radiation (IPAR) and that leaf area is positively correlated with mean site water balance (Grier and Running 1977, Runyon et al. 1994). Standing biomass and productivity increase with increasing leaf area, except at very high levels (Gholz 1982). It appears that maritime coniferous forests develop toward canopy structures and leaf area indices that maximize light capture subject to the constraints imposed by site water availability (Grier and Running 1977). Interannual variability in IPAR could therefore influence net primary productivity (indicating a light limitation), unless changes in IPAR are strongly correlated with changes in vapor pressure deficits, soil water availability, or winter temperatures.

Finally, there is evidence for nutrient limitations on growth in Douglas-fir forests of western Washington and Oregon. Studies have shown that fertilization treatments increase forest productivity in Douglas-fir stands and that fertilization can increase productivity more than supplemental water (Gessel et al. 1990). Although nitrogen enhancement could increase leaf area somewhat, the primary benefit of fertilization might be to increase photosynthetic rates and light-use efficiency. Such an effect could be important if warming temperatures or elevated CO_2 increase nutrient cycling rates and nutrient uptake rates.

Biotic Interactions

Competition for light is the dominant biotic interaction in maritime coniferous forests, though facilitation may be important as forests recover from severe disturbances. Early successional species like Sitka spruce and Douglas-fir maintain access to light by growing tall and persisting for up to hundreds of years. Forest succession favors species that can establish and persist under low light levels, eventually reaching the overstory canopy through slow growth (given a less dense canopy) or through a canopy gap replacement process.

Disturbances

The major disturbances in maritime coniferous forests include timber harvesting, windstorms, land use changes, and high-severity wildfires. High forest productivity and high timber values have led to extensive harvesting of old- and second-growth forests and replacement of mixed-species forests with single-species plantations. Human population growth and economic development have led to replacement of large areas of forest by agriculture, housing, and urban infrastructure (e.g., roads, stores, factories, and office buildings).

Wind and wildfire are the primary natural disturbances. Wind can cause significant tree mortality, particularly in late fall and winter, when windstorms occur in conjunction with heavy rains or wet snow, saturated soils, and ice storms. Although most wind disturbances involve individual trees or small groups of trees (gap processes), large blow-down events also occur periodically. Wildfires are relatively rare in these forests owing to mild temperatures, high fuel moisture levels, and very low levels of natural ignitions (e.g., lightning ignitions are uncommon). However, high levels of coarse woody debris, litter, and live biomass can produce occasional large, high-severity wildfires when ignitions coincide with favorable fire weather and dry fuel conditions (Agee 1993).

Responses to Elevated CO$_2$ and Climate Change

Species distribution models (models 1–3, table 8.1) projected that most species would have less suitable climate habitat by the end of the century with changes occurring by the midcentury, even for models that project less warming such as CSIRO. Climate habitat losses are primarily in the south and west, while climate habitat remains in the north and for the Cascade Mountains. Model output from MC1 (model 5, table 8.1) projected moderate to more extreme loss of this vegetation type, particularly for the HADCM3 model, which is considered a comparatively warm (especially summer) and dry GCM (Rogers et al. 2011). Losses are largely in the southern and eastern part of the existing climate habitat for MC1. The 3-PG hybrid model (model 9, table 8.1) projects little change for Douglas-fir, western redcedar (*Thuja plicata* Donn ex D. Don), and Sitka spruce and only a slight decrease for western hemlock. Model output from FORCLIM (Busing et al. 2007, model 6, table 8.1) indicated no change in forest dominance as of 2050 for either future scenario for Douglas-fir or western hemlock. It is apparent that there is some model agreement that this ecosystem is somewhat vulnerable to climate change, particularly the southwestern part of the region.

Projected model results suggest that this forest type may be reduced in the future, particularly in the southern part of the region. However, there was limited model agreement, and some models predicted little to no change for this forest type. Important aspects of future climate change for maritime coniferous forests probably include the effects on winter temperatures, seasonal precipitation patterns and amounts, vapor pressure deficits, and perhaps elevated CO_2. Winter temperatures are already mild in this zone. Warmer fall, winter, and spring temperatures would further enhance the mildness of Pacific Northwest winters, potentially enhancing cool-season photosynthesis and nutrient cycling. The Pacific Ocean would likely continue to ameliorate temperature extremes, generate coastal fog, and promote high levels of annual precipitation in coastal areas, maintaining suitable habitat for Sitka spruce forests, but this is not certain. Reduced snowfall and winter snowpack accumulation could also allow slow expansion of western hemlock into the Pacific silver fir zone.

Warmer winter temperatures could also alter the phenology of Douglas-fir shoot growth, with implications for tree growth and forest productivity. Although warmer temperatures are typically associated with earlier budburst and longer growing seasons, field studies and subsequent phenological models suggest that substantially warmer winter temperatures could delay spring budburst in Douglas-firs because chilling requirements that serve to prevent premature budburst would not be met (Bailey and Harrington 2006, Campbell and Sugano 1979, Harrington et al. 2010). Predicted temperatures are still within a suitable range to allow Douglas-fir to maintain dominance in these wet coniferous forests (Dale and Franklin 1989, Franklin and Dryness 1973), but populations may need to adapt their phenological cues to match changing climatic conditions.

Warmer summer temperatures could affect maritime coniferous forests by increasing vapor pressure deficits, stomatal conductance, and transpiration (Apple et al. 2000); reducing soil water availability; and increasing the length or intensity of the summer dry period. Douglas-fir productivity could decline with warming temperatures at severely moisture-limited sites, while increasing at high-elevation sites (Case and Peterson 2005; Littell et al. 2008, 2010). Elevated CO_2 levels and changes in nutrient availability could alter these simple responses to temperature and moisture, however, by altering water- and light-use efficiency. For example, Lewis et al. (2004) reported that elevated temperatures increased needle nitrogen concentrations and net photosynthesis in Douglas-fir seedlings, while elevated CO_2 increased photosynthetic rates.

The effects of changing climate on precipitation patterns are likely to significantly influence vegetation responses in these forests. Increases in precipitation (and humidity) outside of the winter months could help to offset the effects of increasing temperatures on vapor pressure deficits and soil water availability, with subsequent effects on productivity. Unfortunately, this remains an area of great uncertainty.

Extending the summer dry period could also increase wildfire frequencies in the maritime coniferous forests (Littell et al. 2010). However, even with warmer temperatures and shorter fire-return intervals, most maritime coniferous forests would continue to support low-frequency, high-severity fire regimes. In addition, the primary effect of severe fire is to reduce total standing biomass rather than change forest composition, as forests usually recover well after individual wildfires (Franklin and Dryness 1973).

Dry Coniferous Forests

General Description

The dry coniferous forest biome occupies the lower to middle elevations of the eastern slopes of the Cascade Mountains; the Okanogan Highlands and Rocky Mountains in eastern Washington; and the Blue, Ochoco, and Wallowa Mountains in eastern Oregon (Franklin and Dyrness 1973). Dry coniferous forests in this region typically feature ponderosa pine (*Pinus ponderosa* Lawson & C. Lawson) and Douglas-fir as early seral dominant species, but may also include significant components of true firs (*Abies grandis* [Douglas ex D. Don] Lindl., *A. concolor* [Gord. & Glend.] Lindl. Ex Hildebr., *A. magnifica* A. Murray bis, and *A. lasiocarpa*), western larch (*Larix occidentalis*), western white pine (*Pinus monticola*), lodgepole pine, and western redcedar (*Thuja plicata*) (Franklin and Dyrness 1973). In eastern Oregon, western juniper (*Juniperus occidentalis* Hook.) often occupies the ecotone between the dry coniferous forest and interior steppe biomes (Franklin and Dyrness 1973). Dry coniferous forests also occupy much of the forested area in the Klamath Mountains of southwestern Oregon, though they often also contain a significant component of deciduous trees and shrubs.

The climate of the dry coniferous forest biome varies with elevation, but common features include warm, dry summers, with warm to hot daytime temperatures and cool nighttime temperatures, and cold, moist winters. Much of the annual precipitation falls as snow in winter or during spring rainstorms. Mean annual precipitation can range from about 35 cm per year in ponderosa pine forests to over 100 cm per year in mixed-conifer forests. Most dry coniferous forests in the region support a persistent winter snowpack, but the mean duration of the snowpack varies from about 1 to 5 months, depending on elevation and winter temperatures. The snowpack serves to store winter precipitation onsite and transfer it to soil water storage during spring snowmelt.

Environmental Controls

Dry coniferous forests experience a significant period of summer drought every year during which high vapor pressure deficits and low soil water availability limit tree establishment and growth (Barrett 1979, Boisvenue and Running 2010, Runyon et al. 1994). In some ponderosa pine forests, regeneration pulses are associated with one or more consecutive wet years (Barrett 1979, Brown 2006). Drought stress is prevalent, but most species are adapted to dry summers. Interannual variation in tree growth is positively correlated with precipitation or negatively correlated with summer temperatures for ponderosa pine (Carnwath et al. 2012, Knutson and Pyke 2008, Kusnierczyk and Ettl 2002), Douglas-fir (Carnwath et al. 2012, Case and Peterson 2005, Chen et al. 2010, Griesbauer and Green 2010, Littell et al. 2008), and lodgepole pine (Case and Peterson 2007). There is little evidence that summer drought is the direct cause of significant tree mortality; rather, drought may indirectly cause mortality through its effects on wildfires and forest health.

Cold winter temperatures also limit forest productivity by limiting winter photosynthesis and increasing the importance of cold hardening and frost tolerance (Runyon et al. 1994). Growth is largely confined to spring and early summer, when mild temperatures and high soil moisture availability produce favorable conditions.

Biotic Interactions

Facilitation and competition both influence vegetation dynamics in dry coniferous forests. Competition for soil water is undoubtedly the primary form of competition, as annual soil water deficits force plants to either compete directly or partition soil water use in time and space. For example, many forbs and grasses complete their annual growth and reproduction in the spring and early summer, when soil water is relatively abundant. Trees (and some shrubs) can extend the growing season by tapping into deep soil water resources.

Facilitation is probably most important during seedling establishment. Shading from overstory trees, tall shrubs, or neighboring saplings could facilitate establishment and persistence by reducing evaporative demands and improving plant water balance, more than offsetting negative effects of reduced light on plant performance (Fajardo et al. 2006, Holmgren et al. 1997).

Disturbances

Summer drought creates a long fire season during which surface and live fuels are dry enough to carry wildfires. Most dry coniferous forests in this region historically supported low- or mixed-severity fire regimes (Agee 1993, Everett et al. 2000, Hessburg and Agee 2003, Perry et al. 2011, Wright and Agee 2004). Low-severity fire regimes were concentrated in dry, low-elevation ponderosa pine forests, while mixed-severity fire regimes were concentrated in mesic Douglas-fir and mixed-conifer forests. Logging, livestock grazing, and fire suppression have reduced fire frequencies in most dry coniferous forests over the past century, producing changes in forest structure, fuel profiles, and fire behavior (Hessburg and Agee 2003). Higher tree densities, higher fuel loadings, and greater fuel continuity (horizontal and vertical) now predispose these forests to larger and more severe wildfires than the historical norms, despite efforts to restore historical structure and fire behavior in these dry forests.

Insects and diseases are also common disturbance agents in dry coniferous forests (Fettig et al. 2007). Mortality from bark beetles and defoliators is generally low, but can rise dramatically during periodic outbreaks (Fettig et al. 2007). For example, a mountain pine beetle (*Dendroctonus ponderosae*) outbreak in southern British Columbia killed more than 75 percent of ponderosa pines with diameter greater than 7.5 cm and almost 95 percent of large ponderosa pines (diameter > 30 cm) (Klenner and Arsenault 2009).

Responses to Elevated CO_2 and Climate Change

The species distribution models (models 1 through 3, table 8.1) indicate that suitable climate available for interior forest tree species by the end of the century will be severely reduced, particularly for Oregon and the Blue Mountains. However, MC1 (model 5, table 8.1) projects a dramatic increase in the temperate needleleaf forest type in eastern Oregon and Washington, which is representative of this biome (Rogers et al. 2011). The 3-PG model for ponderosa pine also suggested an increase in species habitat (model 7, table 8.1), which is consistent with the MC1 projections (Coops et al. 2005). However, the more recent 3-PG hybrid model (model 9, tables 8.1 and 8.2) projected loss of suitable climate for ponderosa pine in the Pacific Northwest (Coops and Waring 2011b). Variability in model projections for ponderosa pine, and the analogous MC1 vegetation type temperate needleleaf forest for the HADCM2 models (except as noted) are shown in figure 8.1. There seems to be little model agreement on the sensitivity of the dry coniferous forest species to similar future climate scenarios based on the model output. If we assume that the process models are more robust to prediction, then the vulnerability of this forest type may not be high. However, the dramatic disagreement in model output suggests that caution should be used in any interpretation.

Projected model results showed no model agreement regarding potential changes for this forest type and major species such as ponderosa pine (fig. 8.1).

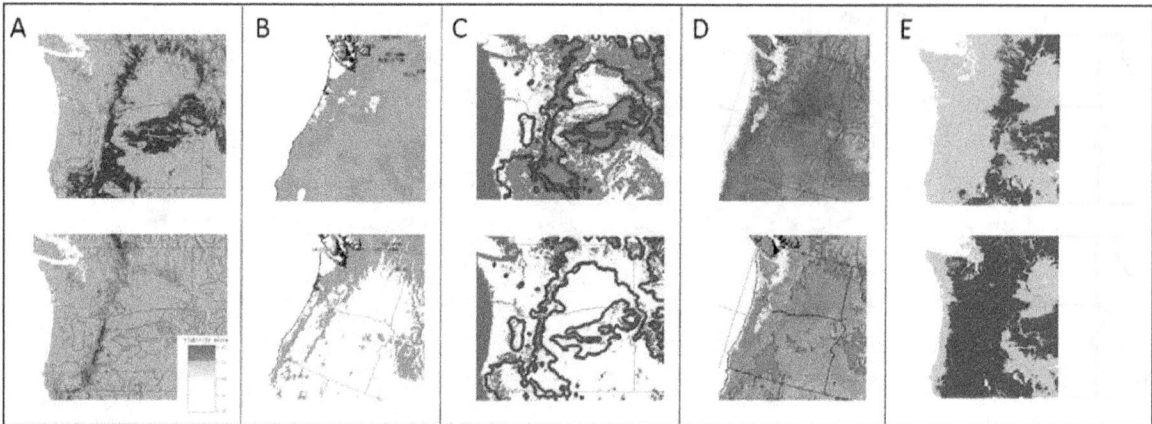

Figure 8.1—Projections of *Pinus ponderosa* (ponderosa pine) climate habitat based on modeled current (top) and end-of-century (bottom) climates. (A) Rehfeldt et al. (2006) HADCM3 A2, (B) McKenney et al. (2007) HADCM3 A2, (C) Hargrove and Hoffman (2005) HADCM3 A1F1, (D) Coops and Waring (2011b) CGCM3 A2, and (E) temperate needleleaf forest type, Rogers et al. (2011) HADCM3 A2. End of century is defined as 2090 for Rehfeldt, 2071–2100 for McKenney, 2100 for Hargrove, 2080 for Coops, and 2070–2099 for Rogers.

The dry coniferous forest biome is potentially vulnerable to future warming temperatures and their effects on winter snowpack (water storage), summer drought, and disturbance regimes.

Yet, the dry coniferous forest biome is potentially vulnerable to future warming temperatures and their effects on winter snowpack (water storage), summer drought, and disturbance regimes. Warming winter temperatures would reduce the fraction of winter precipitation that falls as snow as well as snowpack accumulation and snowpack duration. Earlier snowmelt and warmer spring and summer temperatures would promote earlier onset of summer drought and increase the mean drought duration and intensity. Future increases in spring and summer precipitation and higher CO_2 concentrations could partially offset the effects of reduced snowpack and higher temperatures on evapotranspiration and summer drought, but the net result is still likely to be longer and more intense summer drought.

Longer and more intense summer droughts may reduce productivity in dry coniferous forests at lower elevations, and especially near the lower treeline. Kusnierczyk and Ettl (2002) found that ponderosa pine growth was positively correlated with precipitation in the fall and winter prior to the growing season but was not significantly correlated with temperatures, suggesting that ponderosa pine growth is more sensitive to changes in site water balance than to temperature itself. Similarly, Littell et al. (2008) found that water availability limited Douglas-fir growth across much of its range in the Pacific Northwest. Increasing atmospheric CO_2 levels could limit drought-related losses in productivity by reducing stomatal conductance and delaying soil water depletion but are unlikely to fully offset the effects of warmer temperatures on evapotranspiration.

Some evidence indicates that ponderosa pine could adapt to increased summer drought stress by altering biomass allocation (Callaway et al. 1994). Desert ponderosa pine allocated more biomass to sapwood conducting area, reducing the ratio of leaf area to sapwood area and presumably reducing risks of hydraulic failure (Callaway et al. 1994). Maherali et al. (2002) concluded that this was likely an example of phenotypic plasticity and not genetic adaptation, suggesting that this could be a future response to changing climate.

Longer mean summer drought would likely alter disturbance regimes in dry coniferous forests. Increased summer drought stress could further increase susceptibility to insects and diseases. Dale and Franklin (1989) noted that climate change may change the intensities of disturbances such as bark beetle outbreaks that may result in greater changes than gap models predict.

Longer summer droughts would also lengthen the fire season for most dry coniferous forest types and may increase the risk of large wildfires, particularly in areas that historically supported mixed-severity fire regimes (Westerling et al. 2006). Increased frequency and duration of summer drought would allow wildfires to burn wetter and cooler sites, where high fuel loads become more available owing to reduced fuel moisture (effectively mining fuels that accumulated in a wetter climate). Stand-replacing wildfires could present problems for forest managers as warmer temperatures and reduced water availability could lead to reduced postfire tree establishment or regeneration failures (on planted sites).

Longer summer droughts would also lengthen the fire season for most dry coniferous forest types and may increase the risk of large wildfires, particularly in areas that historically supported mixed-severity fire regimes.

Savannas and Woodlands

General Description

Western juniper savannas and woodlands occupy the biome transition zone between the Interior Steppe and Dry Coniferous Forest biomes in eastern Oregon but are scarce in eastern Washington (Gedney et al. 1999, Miller et al. 2005). It is a Pacific Northwest version of the more widespread pinyon-juniper woodlands of the Great Basin and other dry regions of western interior North America (Franklin and Dyrness 1973). Western juniper is the dominant tree species, with occasional ponderosa pines found on mesic microsites (Miller et al. 2005). Common shrubs include big sagebrush (*Artemisia tridentatea* Nutt.) and bitterbrush (*Purshia tridentatea* Pursh DC.) (Miller et al. 2005). Western juniper savannas occupy much of the transition zone, but denser juniper woodlands can also develop.

Western juniper savannas and woodlands occupy the driest of the tree-dominated vegetation zones in eastern Oregon. Summers are hot and very dry, while winters are cold and relatively wet. Annual precipitation in western juniper savannas and woodlands ranges from 13 to 75 cm per year, but most sites fall within the range of 25 to 50 cm per year (Gedney et al. 1999). Much of this precipitation falls during the winter as rain or snow (Franklin and Dyrness 1973).

Environmental Controls

Drought, high vapor pressure deficits, and cold winter temperatures all serve as environmental controls on vegetation in western juniper savannas and woodlands (Runyon et al. 1994). High summer temperatures coupled with low relative humidity produce high evaporative demand and require vegetation to exercise strong controls on water loss or tolerate high levels of moisture stress. Much of the annual precipitation falls during the winter and is stored in a shallow snowpack or soil layers. With relatively little recharge during the active growing season, soil water becomes severely limiting during the growing season, forcing plants to concentrate their growth and reproduction during the spring and early summer.

Tree ring analyses suggest that western juniper growth is driven primarily by soil moisture availability and drought (Knapp et al. 2004, Knutson and Pyke 2008). Growth was positively correlated with winter and spring precipitation (October through June) and negatively correlated with spring and summer temperatures (Knutson and Pyke 2008). Growth sensitivity to drought was greatest at lower elevations and on steep, rocky sites.

Cold winter temperatures also exert influence on vegetation communities and performance. Runyon et al. (1994) reported cold winter temperatures to be almost as important as drought for limiting photosynthesis in juniper woodlands. Extreme cold temperatures can also function as a disturbance agent (Knapp and Soulé 2005).

Biotic Interactions

Facilitation and competition are both important in juniper savannas and woodlands. Western juniper often established initially in shrub understories, apparently benefiting from altered microclimate and soil fertility during the establishment phase. As junipers grow, however, they compete strongly with their neighbors for soil water, relying on their evergreen nature and cold tolerance to take up and use (preempt) soil water early in the growing season. Large junipers can fully utilize soil water under and near their canopies, limiting tree densities and creating patches with few or no understory plants.

Disturbances

Historical fire regimes are not well described for juniper savannas and woodlands in Oregon (Agee 1993, Young and Evans 1981). Young junipers have thin bark and are readily killed by fires. Junipers that avoid fires early in their lifespan can subsequently escape injury and death from fire by having thicker bark and suppressing understory herbaceous fine fuels through competition for water (Agee 1993). Consequently, fire-scarred junipers are limited to microsites with limited fine fuel production. Fire scars in scattered or adjacent ponderosa pine forests suggest a mixed-severity fire regime, with mean fire-return intervals of 15 years to more than a century and occasional large fires (Agee 1993, Miller and Rose 1999, Miller et al. 2005). In this predominantly fuel-limited biome, climate change effects on fire frequency and severity will likely depend on changes in soil water availability and its effect on understory plant productivity (fuel generation).

Juniper has expanded its range in the interior Pacific Northwest during the past 130 years, invading and creating savannas and woodlands in semiarid ecosystems that were formerly shrub-steppe and grassland communities (Miller et al. 2000). More than 90 percent of the 3.2 million hectares of current juniper savannas and woodlands developed in the past 100 years (Miller et al. 2000). The area of juniper forest and woodland is estimated to have increased fivefold between 1936 and 1988 (Gedney et al. 1999). Much of this expansion is attributable to heavy livestock grazing and reduced fire frequencies from fuel reductions and active fire-suppression efforts (Miller et al. 2000), but there is some indication that woodland expansion was initiated between 1850 and 1870 in some areas owing to wet and mild climatic conditions (Miller et al. 2005). The combination of reduced fire occurrences as a result of European settlement and optimal climatic conditions for establishment at the turn of the century were probably the two dominant factors that initiated postsettlement western juniper expansion (Miller et al. 2005). Junipers can live for up to a thousand years (Miller et al. 2000); therefore, once established, they may persist for a very long time in the absence of disturbance.

Climate influences the dynamics of juniper woodlands much like the shrub-steppe biome, with winter temperatures and soil water availability being the most important influences. Wet, mild conditions promote vigorous growth in western juniper and are associated with prior periods of expansion in the Pacific Northwest (Miller et al. 2005). Junipers are generally cold tolerant, but an extreme October freeze produced significant damage and mortality in Oregon juniper woodlands, as the freeze occurred before trees were fully cold hardened (Soulé and Knapp 2007). Mortality was highest in high-density patches, on recently colonized sites, and on warmer microsites, suggesting some degree of self-regulation in the system (Soulé and Knapp 2007).

Tree growth and productivity in juniper woodlands are sensitive to soil water availability and drought. A tree ring analysis of interannual growth variability found that growth was positively correlated with fall, winter, and spring precipitation (October to June), suggesting the importance of deep soil water storage for supplying water during the growing season (Knutson and Pyke 2008). Drought has produced dramatic changes in pinyon-juniper woodlands of southwestern North America (pinyon pine [*Pinus edulis* Engelm.] and oneseed juniper [*Juniperus monosperma* (Engelm.) Sarg.]) in the past century. A severe drought in the 1950s caused extensive ponderosa pine mortality and favored advance of pinyon-juniper woodlands into former ponderosa pine forest (Allen and Breshears 1998). A more recent drought (2002 to 2003) produced high mortality of pinyon pine, leading to increased dominance by oneseed juniper (Breshears et al. 2005, 2009). We are not aware of any similar episodes of widespread tree mortality in Pacific Northwest juniper woodlands, however.

As temperatures warmed during the early Holocene, western juniper began migrating north into its present range in the Pacific Northwest. Since the arrival of western juniper in central and eastern Oregon (circa 6600–4800 BP), northeastern California, and southeastern Idaho, its abundance and distribution have fluctuated (see Miller et al. 2005 for an excellent presentation of juniper paleohistory). Dry climatic periods tend to result in regional declines of juniper, with wet (particularly summer precipitation) and mild (mild winters) periods resulting in expansion.

Responses to Elevated CO_2 and Climate Change

Model projections for the savannas and woodlands and shrub-steppe vegetation types were too limited to synthesize in table 8.2, but we do discuss the limited available model output. For western juniper, the species distribution models (models 1 through 3, table 8.1) projected that this species would have substantially less or no suitable climate habitat by the end of the century. MC1 (model 5, table 8.1) projects minor changes in the temperate evergreen needleleaf woodland vegetation type; although a minor reduction for the MIROC model is noted, as well as some redistribution. It is apparent that there is little model agreement on the sensitivity of juniper savannas and woodlands to similar future climate scenarios.

For oak species (*Quercus* spp.), some species distribution models (models 1 through 3, table 8.1) project increases and shifts in distribution, although there is no consensus among the models. Many of the models also performed poorly in predicting the historical climate habitat for oak species. Unlike most of the other species' distribution model output, agreement for the sign of change differed between the models. Projections vary widely by species and generalizations are difficult. MC1 (model 5, table 8.1) projects an increase for temperate warm and cool mixed forests across all GCM scenarios, with significantly more of this vegetation type emerging for the MIROC scenario (Rogers et al. 2011). There appears to be little model agreement on the sensitivity of oak and mixed-woodlands species to similar future climate scenarios. Potential response of oak species to future climate change is highly uncertain based on this analysis.

Little or no experimental work has been done on the response of junipers to elevated CO_2 or warming temperatures. As noted above, modeling studies are also somewhat limited for this biome, and provide little agreement about potential future change. Junipers might be expected to benefit from increasing atmospheric CO_2 if it reduces stomatal conductance and delays depletion of deep soil water; however, it is unclear if improved water-use efficiency would significantly increase growth, or simply reduce drought stress. Increased growth of western juniper in recent decades suggests that elevated CO_2 may be increasing growth through increased water-use efficiency (Knapp et al. 2001), but such evidence is not conclusive.

Shrub-Steppe

General Description

Steppe (grassland) and shrub-steppe vegetation covers much of eastern Washington and Oregon, occupying the basins between the Cascade Mountains and the Rocky Mountain foothills (or Blue Mountains). The steppe biome encompasses numerous grass- and shrub-dominated vegetation community types that differ according to the dominant grasses and shrubs, and whose distribution largely reflects underlying gradients in annual mean precipitation and soil properties (Franklin and Dyrness 1973). Characteristic species include cool season (C_3) bunchgrasses (e.g., bluebunch wheatgrass [*Pseudoroegneria spicata* (Pursh A. Love)], Idaho fescue [*Festuca idahoensis* Elmer], and Sandberg bluegrass [*Poa sandbergii* J. Presl.]) and sagebrushes (e.g., big sagebrush, little sagebrush [*A. arbuscula* (Nutt.) A. Gray], and scabland sagebrush [*A. rigida*]). The climate is classified as arid to semiarid with low precipitation, hot dry summers, and relatively cold winters, and the region has often been described as cold desert or high desert (Franklin and Dyrness 1973).

Vegetation in the steppe biome often forms complex mosaics at ecotones. In eastern Washington, it forms an ecotone with the dry coniferous forest biome (Franklin and Dyrness 1973). In eastern Oregon, the steppe biome more often forms an ecotone with juniper (*Juniperus* spp.) woodlands, which occupy a narrow ecological niche between the steppe and dry coniferous forest biomes (Franklin and Dyrness 1973).

Steppe communities have long occupied parts of the interior Pacific Northwest, but their abundance and distribution has changed considerably through time. At Waits Lake in northeastern Washington state, steppe and sage-steppe vegetation alternated with dry coniferous (pine) forest for thousands of years following the last glacial period before being replaced by the current Douglas-fir (*Pseudotsuga menziesii* Mirb. Franco)-dominated forest vegetation around 2,300 years ago (Mack et al. 1978). At Carp Lake in southern Washington state, a 125,000-year pollen record shows that the site has alternated between periods of montane coniferous forest, pine forest, and steppe vegetation; it currently supports dry coniferous forest

(Whitlock et al. 2000). In southeastern Washington, a 100,000-year record of silica phytoliths (fossil records from grasses) indicated large shifts in vegetation over time, with a low-elevation site alternating between different grassland communities, and two higher elevation sites transitioning from cold sage-steppe and subalpine parkland vegetation to dry forest and grassland vegetation, before transitioning to modern dry mixed-conifer and subalpine forests (Blinnikov et al. 2002).

Environmental Controls

Soil moisture and winter temperatures are the major environmental limiting factors influencing vegetation composition and productivity in Pacific Northwest steppe communities, with precipitation, temperature, soil texture, and soil depth being the primary abiotic determinants of soil moisture (Bates et al. 2006, Comstock and Ehleringer 1992, Schlaepfer et al. 2011). Winter precipitation (snow and rain) is important for recharging water storage in deep soil layers (Schlaepfer et al. 2011, Schwinning et al. 2003), and most of the Great Basin and Columbia Basin in Oregon and Washington receive the greatest amount of precipitation in the winter and spring (Bates et al. 2006). However, high temperatures and low summer precipitation combine to produce extended periods of soil moisture deficits each summer. Although summers are warm and dry, winters can be quite cold throughout much of the steppe region in the Pacific Northwest (Comstock and Ehleringer 1992).

Steppe vegetation is generally well adapted to both cold winter temperatures and summer drought. Grasses and forbs can avoid summer drought stress by concentrating growth in the spring and early summer, when soil water is still available and cooler temperatures promote high water-use efficiency (Comstock and Ehleringer 1992). Some shrubs are able to tolerate drought and remain photosynthetically active during periods of water and heat stress (DePuit and Caldwell 1975) or avoid severe drought stress by developing deep root systems that allow them to access deep soil water reserves throughout the summer (Franklin and Dyrness 1973).

Biotic Interactions

As with other stressful environments, facilitation plays an important role in the shrub-steppe biome. Established shrubs can facilitate establishment and growth of other species by enhancing soil water and nutrient availability while reducing light levels and evaporative demand. Some deep-rooted shrubs employ "hydraulic lift" mechanisms to transfer soil water between deep and shallow soil layers (Caldwell and Richards 1989, Caldwell et al. 1998). Hydraulic lift can provide soil water to neighboring plants but may also promote nutrient cycling and fine root growth during the dry summer season and deep soil water recharge in the winter and spring months (Caldwell and Richards 1989, Caldwell et al. 1998). Griffith (2010) found that modification of microclimate and soil fertility by two shrubs, big sagebrush and bitterbrush (*Purshia tridentatea*), increased understory establishment and reproduction of cheatgrass (*Bromus tectorum* L.) compared to areas between shrubs.

Disturbances

Steppe ecosystems have been strongly affected by human activities, including livestock grazing, introduction of exotic species, and cultivation for agricultural crops (Franklin and Dyrness 1973). Grazing first became a major factor in Pacific Northwest steppe communities with the introduction of cattle grazing in 1834 and sheep grazing in 1860. Settlers also introduced numerous alien grasses, including cheatgrass, which was well adapted to climate within parts of the steppe region (Mack 1981). Heavy grazing allowed alien grasses to invade native communities, where they became highly persistent (Mack 1981). In addition to grazing, much of the steppe region in the Columbia River Basin has been cultivated for dryland agricultural crops like winter wheat or irrigated to produce summer fruits, vegetables, and grains.

Few studies have documented fire regimes across shrub-steppe communities and woodlands throughout this region (Miller et al 2005), in part because it is difficult to find the equivalent of fire-scarred trees that provide a biological record of past fire activity. In productive mountain big sagebrush (*Artemisia tridentatea* ssp. *vaseyana* (Rydb.) Beetle) plant associations, such as those characterized by Idaho fescue, mean fire-return intervals ranged between 10 to 25 years, with large fires every 38 years (Miller et al. 2005). However, fire was much less frequent in the more arid plant associations such as Wyoming big sagebrush/Thurber needlegrass (*A. tridentatea* ssp. *wyomingensis/Achnatherum thurberianum* J. Presl.) (50 to 70 years) and low sagebrush/Sandberg bluegrass (*A. arbuscula/Poa sandbergii*) (Miller and Rose 1999, Young and Evans 1981), where fire-free periods of 90 (Young and Evans 1981) and 138 years (Miller and Rose 1999) were reported in northern California and south-central Oregon, and fire-free periods probably exceeded 150 years for some sites. Baker (2006) argues that historical fire rotations were 70 to 200 years in mountain big sagebrush and longer in other types. An examination of long-term charcoal records suggests that fire regimes in these types are climate and fuel driven; sagebrush densities and fire frequencies increased during wet periods (decades to centuries) and declined during dry periods (Mensing et al. 2006).

Most of the dominant bunch grasses and some of the shrubs recover well from fires by resprouting from belowground organs. However, two of the major shrub species in the region, big sagebrush and bitterbrush are fire sensitive and can be temporarily eliminated from a site by burning. Recovery of shrub canopy cover to predisturbance levels can require 10 to 50 years or more, with recruitment of new shrubs from soil seed banks being an important factor controlling recovery time (Ziegenhagen and Miller 2009). Short fire-return intervals can cause significant vegetation change if shrub communities have not fully recovered between disturbances (Davies et al. 2012). In some areas, introductions of invasive plant species such as cheatgrass and medusahead (*Taeniatherum caput-medusae* (L.) Nevski) have significantly altered fire regimes by producing sufficient fine fuels to carry wildfires (D'Antonio and Vitousek 1992).

Responses to Elevated CO_2 and Climate Change

Only one species distribution model had projections available for shrub-steppe species. The ANUCLIM species distribution model (model 2, table 8.1) projected severe reductions in suitable climate for bitterbrush, big sagebrush, mountain mahogany (*Cercocarpus ledifolius* S. Watson), and gray rabbitbrush (*Ericameria nauseosa* (Pall. Ex Pursh) G.L. Nesom & Baird) (McKenney et al. 2007, 2011). The MC1 model (model 5, table 8.1) projects some decrease in this vegetation type, with the largest decreases for the CSIRO model (Rogers et al. 2011). There appears to be some model agreement on the general sign of a potential response for this biome, indicating some vulnerability to climate change. However, the difference in the magnitude of response among the models is striking, and only two models are available for comparison.

Bradley (2009) reported that for a "worst case future climate scenario," cheatgrass (model 4, table 8.1) climatic habitat will either be maintained or decrease. The worst case future climate scenario was characterized by the maximum decrease in summer precipitation out of all the climate models assessed. However, it is important to note that the current distribution of cheatgrass in eastern Oregon and Washington only covered a fraction of the modeled current climate habitat, indicating that the species has not yet fully invaded all suitable climate habitats. Therefore, although changes in future climate habitat may not be great according to this analysis, there still could be considerable risk for the expansion of cheatgrass.

The only model available with relevant output for grassland or steppe vegetation was MC1 (model 5, table 8.1) (Rogers et al. 2011). MC1 projected that for the warmer scenarios, grasslands will experience some reductions in spatial extent. The less warm and wetter MIROC model projected little to no change. However, only one impact model is available for assessment, and there are no species-specific model outputs for grass species.

There is little model information regarding relevant grassland and steppe species; however, predicted climatic changes could alter environmental conditions in the steppe region in important ways that ultimately affect soil water availability. Grasslands are largely structured by climate and soils (Fay et al. 2012). Higher winter temperatures could reduce the percentage of winter precipitation that falls as snow, thereby reducing winter snowpack water storage and possibly increasing winter runoff (Schlaepfer et al. 2011, 2012). Warming spring temperatures would likely melt winter snowpack, warm soils, and begin evaporating soil water earlier in the spring, causing earlier onset of seasonal drought (Schlaepfer et al. 2012). Warmer summer temperatures would further increase potential evapotranspiration and increase drought stress.

Vegetation responses to climatic change in the steppe region of the Pacific Northwest are likely to be strongly influenced by changes in precipitation patterns, particularly total annual precipitation and the timing, frequency, and intensity of precipitation events. Cool season precipitation (late fall to early spring) is important for recharge of shallow and deep soil water reserves, so changes in net cool season water infiltration—a function of both precipitation and runoff—could influence the intensity and duration of warm season drought, particularly for deep-rooted shrubs. Winter precipitation and deep soil water recharge are also important for grass productivity (Bowling et al. 2010). Changes in the frequency and intensity of dry season precipitation events could also alter plant water and nutrient availability, but are unlikely to have significant effects on vegetation productivity and composition until summer precipitation becomes abundant and regular enough to reduce summer drought stress significantly. Unfortunately, predictions of future precipitation patterns from global climate models carry a high degree of uncertainty, and this uncertainty may be magnified by regional topographic effects on the spatial and seasonal distribution of precipitation.

Increasing atmospheric CO_2 concentrations may also influence vegetation patterns by increasing water-use efficiency for some species. Higher CO_2 concentrations are expected to be particularly beneficial for cool-season plant species that employ the C_3 photosynthetic pathway. Morgan et al. (2011) reported that a CO_2 enrichment treatment (600 parts per million by volume) increased water-use efficiency sufficiently to offset increased desiccation from a warming treatment (1.5/3.0 °C day night warming) and maintain soil water content equivalent to that of a control treatment in a semiarid grassland. Dukes et al. (2005) found no effect of modest warming or CO_2 enrichment on root and shoot production, however, in California grassland. McMurtrie et al. (2008) suggested that CO_2 enrichment will have the greatest benefits for plants on sites where water is highly limiting, but nitrogen is not. Fay et al. (2012) demonstrated that an increase in aboveground net primary productivity associated with CO_2 enrichment in grasslands depends strongly on soil type.

It is not clear whether predicted climatic changes would alter disturbance regimes in the steppe region. Wildfire occurrences are generally limited by lack of ignitions during the fire season or by lack of continuous fuels. Elevated CO_2 concentrations have been shown to increase biomass production of cheatgrass and other exotic annual grasses, which could lead to increased buildup of matrix fuels that could promote the spread of fires (Lucash et al. 2005, Smith et al. 2000. Increased drought stress could reduce fire frequencies as in the past (Ziegenhagen and Miller 2009), unless increased evaporative demand is offset by increased precipitation or CO_2-induced reductions in stomatal conductance (Lucash et al. 2005, Naumburg et al. 2003). It is also possible that climatic changes could alter the frequency of lightning ignitions during summer thunderstorms, but we are not aware of any research in this area.

Several studies also show that grasslands may be resistant to climate change effects (Dukes et al. 2005, Grime et al. 2008). Short-term changes in the interannual precipitation regime may not result in large changes in semiarid vegetation communities (Jankju 2008). Shrub-steppe communities in Idaho have considerable interannual variability in climate and productivity (West and Yorks 2006). Semiarid ecosystems may be able to buffer against the effects of climate change by shifting the type or intensity of plant-plant interactions (Bates et al. 2006, Brooker 2006, Jankju 2008). Sagebrush is tolerant of summer drought and is unresponsive to shifts in the seasonality of precipitation in regard to cover and density (Bates et al. 2006). High spatial and temporal variability in precipitation in semiarid ecosystems (Augustine 2010) may further isolate these systems against climate change effects. However, sagebrush ecosystems may be vulnerable to encroachment from woodlands owing to increasing precipitation (Bachelet et al. 2001b).

Altered climate could have mixed influences on cheatgrass and efforts to manage it. The exotic annual is likely to benefit (and perhaps has already benefited) from the positive effects of elevated atmospheric CO_2 on productivity (Ziska et al. 2005). On the other hand, model projections suggest that the response of cheatgrass to future climate may depend greatly on changes in precipitation, with cheatgrass expected to benefit from reduced precipitation (Bradley 2009, see also chapter 7).

Chapter 9: Conclusions

The goal of this document was to provide insight into the range of potential effects of climate change on vegetation in the Pacific Northwest using information from the literature and modeling studies. Although it is clear that climate change could have profound effects on global and regional vegetation, it is less clear what those effects will be and what activities land managers could or should undertake to preserve values at risk and to continue to achieve a variety of management objectives. Recently, there has been much information published regarding managing for climate change and developing adaptation approaches in the Pacific Northwest (e.g., Aubry et. al. 2011, Halofsky et al. 2011, Littell et al. 2012, Peterson et al. 2011), other forested ecosystems in the United States (Rice et al. 2012, Swanston and Janowiak 2012), and the United States in general (Vose et al. 2012). Much literature focuses on generalizable "toolbox approaches" (Joyce et al. 2009, Millar et al. 2007, Peterson et al. 2011, Spies et al. 2010, Stephens et al. 2010).

Although a complete review of the climate and natural resource adaptation literature is beyond the scope of this document, we note that several of the "toolbox approaches" to managing ecosystem responses to climate change feature three basic adaptive strategies: (1) promoting resistance to change, (2) promoting resilience to change, and (3) facilitating response to change (Joyce et al. 2009, Millar et al. 2007, Spies et al. 2010, Stephens et al. 2010). Resistance strategies seek to delay responses to climate change by reducing climate-related stresses and preventing disturbances; they are used primarily to protect high-value resources from rapid change (Millar et al. 2007). Resistance strategies have long been used in the restoration and management of such fire-prone ecosystems as dry coniferous forests in the Pacific Northwest. Resilience strategies seek to manage ecosystems so that the ecosystem can return to desired conditions following disturbance (Millar et al. 2007). Landscape-scale resilience strategies are currently being developed to manage spotted owl (*Strix occidentalis caurina*) habitat in the dry mixed-conifer forests of the eastern Cascades in Washington and Oregon. Resilience strategies would logically be used in combination with resistance strategies but recognize uncertainty in the success of resistance strategies. Response strategies seek to manage the process of change, allowing for a more orderly transition from current to future conditions; they recognize the inevitability (and potential benefits) of change but seek to manage the rate of change and avoid potentially undesirable outcomes. Managing for high species and genetic diversity is one example of a response strategy across all biomes of the Pacific Northwest.

The contemporary management focus on climate change and uncertainty contrasts sharply with heavily relied on paradigms of ecosystem management such as historical range of variability (HRV). This concept has been widely embraced by

Although it is clear that climate change could have profound effects on global and regional vegetation, it is less clear what those effects will be and what activities land managers could or should undertake to preserve values at risk.

natural resource managers, planners, and policymakers over the past two decades. The concept suggests that past conditions and processes provide context and guidance for managing ecological systems today (Franklin et al. 2002, Landres et al. 1999, Moore et al 1999). However, many forest managers, planners, and policymakers now question whether or not the HRV concept is even applicable. Application of the concept has strayed from the original intent, and some question whether or not the concept is "quaint" (Jackson and Hobbs 2009). Often temporally and spatially static or narrow definitions of past conditions are used as benchmarks for desired future conditions and the focus is largely on structural rather than process-based management. Although this structural focus may be necessary for agencies and landowners in terms of recordkeeping and accountability, process-based approaches do not have to be abandoned. This issue is problematic even now, and becomes increasingly so as both natural and human-induced climatic variability and the potential for a "no analog" future are considered (Williams and Jackson 2007, Williams et al. 2007). If "natural" states are difficult to quantify, the environment is always changing and ecosystems are always coming and going, and if multiple realizations are normal, then the principles underlying ecological restoration, potential natural vegetation, and HRV come under question (Jackson and Hobbs 2009, Jackson 2012).

Millar et al. (2007) noted that attempts to maintain past conditions could result in forests and ecosystems that are not well adapted to current and future conditions and may be more vulnerable to future change. However, understanding the past still is important for thinking about the future and HRV can provide important information about possible future trajectories and ways that species and communities respond to changes in climate and disturbance regimes. Thus a more nuanced view is needed, one that is better aligned with the original focus of the original HRV concept, which emphasized an evolutionary (long-term) context, a focus on process structure, and on ranges rather than means (box 9.1). Moreover, rare and uncommon events need to be incorporated into any HRV framework. A more nuanced HRV framework will provide better guidance for land management, but uncertain future climatic shifts and no analog situations will still arise. Given the certainty of unpredictable changing conditions, forest managers may need to rely more on understanding, accepting, and working with current and future conditions and processes and less on using the past as a benchmark. We provide several suggestions for incorporating HRV into management (box 9.1), and several frameworks are provided in the literature regarding restoration decisionmaking in the context of novel conditions (Belnap et al. 2012, Hobbs et al. 2009). Hobbs et al.

(2009) suggested that developing and evaluating hybrid and novel ecosystems may be inevitable (Hobbs et al. 2009).

Natural resource agencies may want to critically gauge the potential challenges that climate change will have on the success of traditional restoration activities based on HRV and better incorporate climate change in management and planning, including the development of resistance, resilience, and response options that facilitate adaptation of natural resources to potentially adverse effects of climate change. Peterson et al. (2011) outlined the following steps, based on science-management partnerships, that can be used to facilitate adaptation on national forests or any natural resource land base: (1) become aware of basic climate change science and integrate that understanding with knowledge of local resource conditions and issues (review), (2) evaluate sensitivity of natural resources to climate change (rank), (3) develop and implement options for adapting resources to climate change (resolve), and (4) monitor the effectiveness of on-the-ground management (observe) and adjust as needed. Before developing adaptation strategies or a management response to climate change, mangers and others require information to "review" and "rank." This document could serve as a potentially important source of information about climate change science in relation to vegetation in the Pacific Northwest, and a useful source for evaluating the potential sensitivity of vegetation to climate change. We highlight that there are uncertainties about exactly what the effects of climate change will be; however, information does exists and can be used

---

Box 9.1. Suggestions for incorporating historical range of variability (HRV) concepts into contemporary management.

1) Focus on variability, considering past and potential future variability, and do not discount rare events, and/or anomalies. The mean of a particular attribute from the past should not be used alone because rare and extreme events will not be included and boundaries using extreme events need to be considered. Use of spike descriptors, trend descriptors, and probabilistic descriptions can be used to examine rare, uncommon, and extreme or severe events and consistency with past system behavior (Landres et al. 1999). Assess the potential "future range of variability," the estimated range of some ecological condition that may occur in the future (Duncan et al. 2010). Taking a longer view (e.g., paleoecological studies) can also help inform understanding of existing and historical ecosystems, determine the circumstances under which they arose, gauge the range of environmental variability they have experienced, and potentially identify environmental thresholds at which they will require different levels of management. Paleoecological insights, together with modeling, experimentation, and observation, will advance our capacity to successfully manage ecosystems (Jackson and Hobbs 2009).

2) Avoid specific and static benchmarks based on structure and concentrate on process and ecosystem services. Several authors note that use of historical information for identifying desired future conditions does not imply management for static conditions (Moore et al. 1999, Swetnam et al. 1999). However, application of the HRV concept has often resulted in using static benchmarks, often based on forest structure (e.g., tree density). Jackson (2012) noted that vegetation is a dynamic entity, and we need to focus attention on the processes that govern it in order to understand it, manage it and forecast its future states. Management could focus on targeting the maintenance of desirable ecological goods and services, including aesthetic values, rather than focusing on static benchmarks (Jackson and Hobbs 2009). In many cases, this approach will lead to ecosystems unlike those of the past, but more resilient to the future.

3) Apply our understanding of processes, interactions, and conditions to the current biophysical, social, and economic environment: try to manage for change. Without consideration of current conditions and multiple disturbances and stresses, or the realized stress complex, unintended consequences or management surprises are likely (McKenzie et al. 2009, Paine et al. 1998). Livestock grazing, fire suppression, drought, reduced biological legacies, and exotic species introductions are just a few factors currently influencing forest systems and the outcome of management actions. Today, disturbance regimes and ecosystem processes are now interacting with present and future environment conditions that are very different than historical conditions. State-and-transition models can be used to examine a range of future conditions and multiple realizations, and these models are now taking climate change transitions into account (Kerns et al. 2012).

4) Use information from HRV to develop and evaluate hybrid or novel ecosystem models that may provide key ecosystem services but be quite different than past ecosystems. Hybrid ecosystems retain some original ecosystem characteristics as well as novel elements, whereas novel ecosystems comprise different species, interactions, and functions than past ecosystems (Hobbs et al. 2009). In certain ecosystems, novel mixes of species, structure, or processes (e.g., less desirable native species, nonnative species) might be used to maintain valuable hybrid or novel ecosystems and their services (high carbon storage, resistance to fire or invasive species, wildlife habitat).

to begin the adaptation and risk management process and respond to the range of potential effects of climate change on vegetation in the Pacific Northwest.

Acknowledgments

Funding for this work was provided the Bureau of Land Management (BLM), Oregon State Office, and the U.S. Forest Service (USFS), Pacific Northwest Research Station. We thank staff members from the Region 6 Climate Change Working Group (BLM and USFS) for their input and guidance on the project. We especially thank Jim Alegria, Louisa Evers, David Chmura, Crystal Raymond, and Tom Spies for their input and manuscript reviews. Finally, we thank Michelle Day for providing geographic information system assistance for examining model output and editorial reviews.

English Equivalents

When you know:	Multiply by:	To find:
Centimeters (cm)	0.394	Inches
Meters (m)	3.28	Feet
Meters (m)	1.094	Yards
Kilometers (km)	0.621	Miles
Hectares (ha)	2.47	Acres
Square meters (m^2)	10.76	Square feet
Square kilometers (km^2)	0.386	Square miles
Degrees Celsius (°C)	1.8 °C + 32	Degrees Fahrenheit

References

Aber, J.D.; Federer, C.A. 1992. A generalized lumped-parameter model of photosynthesis, evapotranspiration and net primary production in temperate and boreal forest ecosystems. Oecologia. 92: 463–474.

Aber, J.D.; Ollinger, S.V.; Federer, C.A.; Reich, P.B.; Goulden, M.L.; Kicklighter, D.W.; Melillo, J.M.; Lathrop, R.G., Jr. 1995. Predicting the effects of climate change on water yield and forest production in the Northeastern U.S. Climate Research. 5: 207–222.

Ackerly, D.D.; Loarie, S.R.; Cornwell, W.K.; Weiss, S.B.; Hamilton, H.; Branciforte, R.; Kraft, N.J.B. 2010. The geography of climate change: implications for conservation biogeography. Diversity and Distributions. 16: 476–487.

Adams, H.D.; Guardiola-Claramonte, M.; Barron-Gafford, G.A.; Villegas, J.C.; Breshears, D.D.; Zou, C.B.; Troch, P.A.; Huxman, T.E. 2009. Temperature sensitivity of drought-induced tree mortality portends increased regional die-off under global-change-type drought. Proceedings of the National Academy of Sciences of the United States of America. 106: 7063–7066.

Agee, J.K. 1993. Fire ecology of Pacific Northwest forests. Washington, DC: Island Press. 493 p.

Agee, J.K.; Smith, L. 1984. Subalpine tree reestablishment after fire in the Olympic Mountains, Washington. Ecology. 65: 810–819.

Ainsworth, E.A.; Long, S.P. 2005. What have we learned from 15 years of free-air CO_2 enrichment (FACE)? A meta-analytic review of the responses of photosynthesis, canopy properties and plant production to rising CO_2. New Phytologist. 165: 351–372.

Aitken, S.N.; Yeaman, S.; Holliday, J.A.; Wang, T.L.; Curtis-McLane, S. 2008. Adaptation, migration or extirpation: climate change outcomes for tree populations. Evolutionary Applications. 1: 95–111.

Allen, C.D.; Breshears, D.D. 1998. Drought-induced shift of a forest-woodland ecotone: Rapid landscape response to climate variation. Proceedings of the National Academy of Sciences of the United States of America. 95: 14839–14842.

Allen, C.D.; Macalady, A.K.; Chenchouni, H.; Bachelet, D.; McDowell, N.; Vennetier, M.; Kitzberger, T.; Rigling, A.; Breshears, D.D.; Hogg, E.H.; Gonzalez, P.; Fensham, R.; Zhang, Z.; Castro, J.; Demidova, N.; Lim, J.H.; Allard, G.; Running, S.W.; Semerci, A.; Cobb, N. 2010. A global overview of drought and heat-induced tree mortality reveals emerging climate change risks for forests. Forest Ecology and Management. 259: 660–684.

Amaranthus, M.P.; Perry, D.A. 1989. Interaction effects of vegetation type and Pacific madrone soil inocula on survival, growth, and mycorrhiza formation in Douglas-fir. Canadian Journal of Forest Research. 19: 550–556.

Anderegg, W.R.L. 2012. Complex aspen forest carbon and root dynamics. Climatic Change. 111: 983–991.

Anderegg, W.R.L.; Berry, J.A.; Field, C.B. 2012. Linking definitions, mechanisms, and modeling of drought-induced tree death. Trends in Plant Science. 17: 693–700.

Angert, A.; Biraud, S.; Bonfils, C.; Henning, C.C.; Buermann, W.; Pinzon, J.; Tucker, C.J.; Fung, I. 2005. Drier summers cancel out the CO_2 uptake enhancement induced by warmer springs. Proceedings of the National Academy of Sciences of the United States of America. 102: 10823–10827.

Apple, M.E.; Olszyk, D.M.; Ormrod, D.P.; Lewis, A.; Southworth, D.; Tingey, D.T. 2000. Morphology and stomatal function of Douglas fir needles exposed to climate change: elevated CO_2 and temperature. International Journal of Plant Sciences. 161: 127–132.

Araújo, M.B.; Cabeza, M.; Thuiller, W.; Hannah, L.; Williams, P.H. 2004. Would climate change drive species out of reserves? An assessment of existing reserve-selection methods. Global Change Biology. 10: 1618–1626.

Araújo, M.B.; Luoto, M. 2007. The importance of biotic interactions for modelling species distributions under climate change. Global Ecology and Biogeography. 16: 743–753.

Araújo, M.B.; New, M. 2007. Ensemble forecasting of species distributions. Trends in Ecology and Evolution. 22: 42–47.

Arno, S.F.; Habeck, J.R. 1972. Ecology of alpine larch (*Larix lyallii* Parl.) in the Pacific Northwest. Ecological Monographs. 42: 417–450.

Ashcroft, M.B. 2010. Identifying refugia from climate change. Journal of Biogeography. 37: 1407–1413.

Ashcroft, M.B.; Gollan, J.R.; Warton, D.I.; Ramp, D. 2012. A novel approach to quantify and locate potential microrefugia using topoclimate, climate stability, and isolation from the matrix. Global Change Biology. 18: 1866–1879.

Astrup, R.; Coates, K.D.; Hall, E. 2008. Recruitment limitation in forests: lessons from an unprecedented mountain pine beetle epidemic. Forest Ecology and Management. 256: 1743–1750.

Atkin, O.K.; Bruhn, D.; Hurry, V.M.; Tjoelker, M.G. 2005. The hot and the cold: unraveling the variable response of plant respiration to temperature. Functional Plant Ecology. 32: 87–105.

Atkin, O.K.; Loveys, B.R.; Atkinson, L.J.; Pons, T.L. 2006. Phenotypic plasticity and growth temperature: understanding interspecific variability. Journal of Experimental Botany. 57: 267–281.

Atkin, O.K.; Tjoelker, M.G. 2003. Thermal acclimation and the dynamic response of plant respiration to temperature. Trends in Plant Science. 8: 343–351.

Aubry, C.; Devine, W.; Shoal, R.; Bower, A.; Miller, J.; Maggiulli, N. 2011. Climate change and forest biodiversity: a vulnerability assessment and action plan for National Forests in western Washington. Portland, OR: U.S. Department of Agriculture, Forest Service, Pacific Northwest Region. 299 p.

Augustine, D.J. 2010. Spatial versus temporal variation in precipitation in a semiarid ecosystem. Landscape Ecology. 25: 913–925.

Austin, M. 2007. Species distribution models and ecological theory: a critical assessment and some possible new approaches. Ecological Modelling. 200: 1–19.

Ayres, M.P.; Lombardero, M.J. 2000. Assessing the consequences of global change for forest disturbance from herbivores and pathogens. Science of the Total Environment. 262: 263–286.

Bachelet, D.; Johnson, B.R.; Bridgeman, S.D.; Dunn, P.V.; Anderson, H.E.; Rogers, B.M. 2011. Climate change impacts on western Pacific Northwest prairies and savannas. Northwest Science. 85: 411–429.

Bachelet, D.; Lenihan, J.M.; Daly, C.; Neilson, R.P.; Ojima, D.S.; Parton, W.J. 2001a. MC1: a dynamic vegetation model for estimating the distribution of vegetation and associated ecosystem fluxes of carbon, nutrients, and water— technical documentation. Version 1. Gen. Tech. Rep. PNW-GTR-508. Portland, OR: U.S. Department of Agriculture, Forest Service, Pacific Northwest Research Station. 95 p.

Bachelet, D.; Neilson, R.P.; Lenihan, J.M.; Drapek, R.J. 2001b. Climate change effects on vegetation distribution and carbon budget in the United States. Ecosystems. 4: 164–185.

Bachelet, D.; Neilson, R.P.; Lenihan, J.M.; Drapek, R.J. 2004. Regional differences in the carbon source-sink potential of natural vegetation in the U.S.A. Environmental Management. 33(S1): S23–S43. doi:10.1007/s00267-003-9115-4.

Badeck, F.W.; Bondeau, A.; Böttcher, K.; Doktor, D.; Lucht, W.; Schaber, J.; Sitch, S. 2004. Responses of spring phenology to climate change. New Phytologist. 162: 295–309.

Badeck, F.W.; Lischke, H.; Bugmann, H.; Hickler, T.; Honninger, K.; Lasch, P.; Lexer, M.J.; Mouillot, F.; Schaber, J.; Smith, B. 2001. Tree species composition in European pristine forests: comparison of stand data to model predictions. Climatic Change. 51: 307–347.

Bailey, J.D.; Harrington, C.A. 2006. Temperature regulation of bud-burst phenology within and among years in a young Douglas-fir (*Pseudotsuga menziesii*) plantation in western Washington, USA. Tree Physiology. 26: 421–430.

Baker, W.L. 2006. Fire and restoration of sagebrush ecosystems. Wildlife Society Bulletin. 34: 177–185.

Bakker, E.S.; Ritchie, M.E.; Olff, H.; Milchunas, D.G.; Knops, J.M.H. 2006. Herbivore impact on grassland plant diversity depends on habitat productivity and herbivore size. Ecology Letters. 9: 780–788.

Bale, J.S.; Masters, G.J.; Hodkinson, I.D.; Awmack, C.; Bezemer, T.M.; Brown, V.K.; Butterfield, J.; Buse, A.; Coulson, J.C.; Farrar, J.; Good, J.E.G.; Harrington, R.; Hartley, S.; Jones, T.H.; Lindroth, R.L.; Press, M.C.; Symrnioudis, I.; Watt, A.D.; Whittaker, J.B. 2002. Herbivory in global climate change research: direct effects of rising temperature on insect herbivores. Global Change Biology. 8: 1–16.

Bansal, S.; Reinhardt, K.; Germino, M.J. 2011. Linking carbon balance to establishment patterns: comparison of whitebark pine and Engelmann spruce seedlings along an herb cover exposure gradient at treeline. Plant Ecology. 212: 219–228.

Barnett, T.P.; Adam, J.C.; Lettenmaier, D.P. 2005. Potential impacts of a warming climate on water availability in snow-dominated regions. Nature. 438: 303–309.

Barrett, J.W. 1979. Silviculture of ponderosa pine in the Pacific Northwest: the state of our knowledge. Gen Tech. Rep. PNW-GTR-79. Portland, OR: U.S. Department of Agriculture, Forest Service, Pacific Northwest Research Station. 106 p.

Barry, S.; Elith, J. 2006. Error and uncertainty in habitat models. Journal of Applied Ecology. 43: 413–423.

Bates, J.D.; Svejcar, T.; Miller, R.F.; Angell, R.A. 2006. The effects of precipitation timing on sagebrush steppe vegetation. Journal of Arid Environments. 64: 670–697.

Beale, C.M.; Lennon, J.J. 2012. Incorporating uncertainty in predictive species distribution modelling. Philosophical Transactions of the Royal Society Biology. 367: 247–258.

Beaubien, E.; Hamann, A. 2011. Spring flowering response to climate change between 1936 and 2006 in Alberta, Canada. BioScience. 61: 514–524.

Beaumont, L.J.; Hughes, L.; Pitman, A.J. 2008. Why is the choice of future climate scenarios for species distribution modelling important? Ecology Letters. 11: 1135–1146.

Belnap, J.; Ludwig, J.A.; Wilcox, B.P.; Betancourt, J.L.; Dean, W.R.J.; Hoffmann, B.D.; Milton, S.J. 2012. Introduced and invasive species in novel rangeland ecosystems: friends or foes? Rangeland Ecology and Management. 65: 569–578.

Bentz, B.J.; Regniere, J.; Fettig, C.J.; Hansen, E.M.; Hayes, J.L.; Hicke, J.A.; Kelsey, R.G.; Negron, J.F.; Seybold, S.J. 2010. Climate change and bark beetles of the western United States and Canada: direct and indirect effects. Bioscience. 60: 602–613.

Berbeco, M.R.; Melillo, J.M.; Orians, C.M. 2012. Soil warming accelerates decomposition of fine woody debris. Plant Soil. 356: 405–417.

Berry, J.; Björkman, O. 1980. Photosynthetic response and adaptation to temperature in higher plants. Annual Review of Plant Physiology. 31: 491–543.

Best, A.S.; Johst, K.; Munkemuller, T.; Travis, J.M.J. 2007. Which species will successfully track climate change? The influence of intraspecific competition and density dependent dispersal on range shifting dynamics. Oikos. 116: 1531–1539.

Bigler, C.; Gavin, D.G.; Gunning, C.; Veblen, T.T. 2007. Drought induces lagged tree mortality in a subalpine forest in the Rocky Mountains. Oikos. 116: 1983–1994.

Bigler, C.; Kulakowski, D.; Veblen, T.T. 2005. Multiple disturbance interactions and drought influence fire severity in rocky mountain subalpine forests. Ecology. 86: 3018–3029.

Bingham, M.A.; Simard, S. 2012. Ectomycorrhizal networks of *Pseudotsuga menziesii* var. *glauca* trees facilitate establishment of conspecific seedlings under drought. Ecosystems. 15: 188–199.

Blinnikov, M.; Busacca, A.; Whitlock, C. 2002. Reconstruction of the late Pleistocene grassland of the Columbia basin, Washington, USA, based on phytolith records in loess. Palaeogeography Palaeoclimatology Palaeoecology. 177: 77–101.

Boisvenue, C.; Running, S.W. 2006. Impacts of climate change on natural forest productivity-evidence since the middle of the 20th century. Global Change Biology. 12: 862–882.

Boisvenue, C.; Running, S.W. 2010. Simulations show decreasing carbon stocks and potential for carbon emissions in Rocky Mountain forests over the next century. Ecological Applications. 20: 1302–1319.

Bonfils, C.; Santer, B.D.; Pierce, D.W.; Hidalgo, H.G.; Bala, G.; Das, T.; Barnett, T.P.; Cayan, D.R.; Doutriaux, C.; Wood, A.W.; Mirin, A.; Nozawa, T. 2008. Detection and attribution of temperature changes in the mountainous western United States. Journal of Climate. 21: 6404–6424.

Boone, C.K.; Aukema, B.H.; Bohlmann, J.; Carroll, A.L.; Raffa, K.F. 2011. Efficacy of tree defense physiology varies with bark beetle population density: a basis for positive feedback in eruptive species. Canadian Journal of Forest Research. 41: 1174–1188.

Botkin, D.B.; Janak, J.F.; Wallis, J.R. 1972. Some ecological consequences of a computer model of forest growth. Journal of Ecology. 60: 849–852.

Bowling, D.R.; Bethers-Marchetti, S.; Lunch, C.K.; Grote, E.E.; Belnap, J. 2010. Carbon, water, and energy fluxes in a semiarid cold desert grassland during and following multiyear drought. Journal of Geophysical Research. 115, G04026. doi:10.1029/2010JG001322.

Bradley, B.A. 2009. Regional analysis of the impacts of climate change on cheatgrass invasion shows potential risk and opportunity. Global Change Biology. 15: 196–208.

Bradley, B.A. 2010. Assessing ecosystem threats from global and regional change: hierarchical modeling of risk to sagebrush ecosystems from climate change, land use and invasive species in Nevada, USA. Ecography. 33: 198–208.

Breshears, D.D.; Cobb, N.S.; Rich, P.M.; Price, K.P.; Allen, C.D.; Balice, R.G.; Romme, W.H.; Kastens, J.H.; Floyd, M.L.; Belnap, J.; Anderson, J.J.; Myers, O.B.; Meyer, C.W. 2005. Regional vegetation die-off in response to global-change-type drought. Proceedings of the National Academy of Sciences of the United States of America. 102: 15144–15148.

Breshears, D.D.; Huxman, T.E.; Adams, H.D.; Zou, C.B.; Davison, J.E. 2008. Vegetation synchronously leans upslope as climate warms. Proceedings of the National Academy of Sciences of the United States of America. 105: 11591–11592.

Breshears, D.D.; Myers, O.B.; Meyer, C.W.; Barnes, F.J.; Zou, C.B.; Allen, C.D.; McDowell, N.G.; Pockman, W.T. 2009. Tree die-off in response to global change-type drought: mortality insights from a decade of plant water potential measurements. Frontiers in Ecology and the Environment. 7: 185–189.

Briggs, J.M.; Knapp, A.K.; Blair, J.M.; Heisler, J.L.; Hoch, G.A.; Lett, M.S.; McCarron, J.K. 2005. An ecosystem in transition: causes and consequences of the conversion of mesic grassland to shrubland. BioScience. 55: 243–254.

Broennimann, O.; Treier, U.A.; Muller-Scharer, H.; Thuiller, W.; Peterson, A.T.; Guisan, A. 2007. Evidence of climatic niche shift during biological invasion. Ecology Letters. 10: 701–709.

Brohan, P.; Kennedy, J.J.; Harris, I.; Tett, S.F.B.; Jones, P.D. 2006. Uncertainty estimates in regional and global observed temperature changes: a new dataset from 1850. Journal of Geophysical Research. Vol. 111, D12106. doi:10.1029/2005JD006548.

Brooke, R.C.; Peterson, E.B.; Krajina, V.J. 1970. The subalpine mountain hemlock zone. Ecology of Western North America. 2: 148–239.

Brooker, R.W. 2006. Plant-plant interactions and environmental change. New Phytologist. 171: 271–284.

Brooker, R.W.; Maestre, F.T.; Callaway, R.M.; Lortie, C.L.; Cavieres, L.A.; Kunstler, G.; Liancourt, P.; Tielborger, K.; Travis, J.M.J.; Anthelme, F.; Armas, C.; Coll, L.; Corcket, E.; Delzon, S.; Forey, E.; Kikvidze, Z.; Olofsson, J.; Pugnaire, F.; Quiroz, C.L.; Saccone, P.; Schiffers, K.; Seifan, M.; Touzard, B.; Michalet, R. 2008. Facilitation in plant communities: the past, the present, and the future. Journal of Ecology. 96: 18–34.

Brown, P.M. 2006. Climate effects on fire regimes and tree recruitment in Black Hills ponderosa pine forests. Ecology. 87: 2500–2510.

Brown, R.D.; Mote, P.W. 2009. The response of Northern Hemisphere snow cover to a changing climate. Journal of Climate. 22: 2124–2145.

Brubaker, L.B. 1986. Responses of tree populations to climatic change. Vegetatio. 67: 119–130.

Bugmann, H. 2001. A review of forest gap models. Climatic Change. 51: 259–305.

Bugmann, H.K.M.; Wullschleger, S.D.; Price, D.T.; Ogle, K.; Clark, D.F.; Solomon, A.M. 2001. Comparing the performance of forest gap models in North America. Climatic Change. 51: 349–388.

Buisson, L.; Thuiller, W.; Casajus, N.; Lek, S.; Grenouillet, G. 2010. Uncertainty in ensemble forecasting of species distribution. Global Change Biology. 16: 1145–1157.

Burton, O.J.; Phillips, B.L.; Travis, J.M.J. 2010. Trade-offs and the evolution of life-histories during range expansion. Ecology Letters. 13: 1210–1220.

Busing, R.T.; Solomon, A.M.; McKane, R.B.; Burdick, C.A. 2007. Forest dynamics in Oregon landscapes: evaluation and application of an individual-based model. Ecological Applications. 17: 1967–1981.

Butler, S.M.; Melillo, J.M.; Johnson, J.E.; Mohan, J.; Steudler, P.A.; Lux, H.; Burrows, E.; Smith, R.M.; Vario, C.L.; Scott, L.; Hill, T.D.; Aponte, N.; Bowles, F. 2012. Soil warming alters nitrogen cycling in a New England forest: implications for ecosystem function and structure. Oecologia. 168: 819–828.

Caldwell, M.M.; Dawson, T.E.; Richards, J.H. 1998. Hydraulic lift: consequences of water efflux from the roots of plants. Oecologia. 113: 151–161.

Caldwell, M.M.; Richards, J.H. 1989. Hydraulic lift: water efflux from upper roots improves effectiveness of water uptake by deep roots. Oecologia. 79: 1–5.

Callaway, R.M. 1995. Positive interactions among plants. Botanical Review. 61: 306–349.

Callaway, R.M.; Brooker, R.W.; Choler, P.; Kikvidze, Z.; Lortie, C.J.; Michalet, R.; Paolini, L.; Pugnaire, F.I.; Newingham, B.; Aschehoug, E.T.; Armas, C.; Kikodze, D.; Cook, B.J. 2002. Positive interactions among alpine plants increase with stress. Nature. 417: 844–848.

Callaway, R.M.; Delucia, E.H.; Schlesinger, W.H. 1994. Biomass allocation of montane and desert ponderosa pine: an analog for response to climate change. Ecology. 75: 1474–1481.

Callaway, R.M.; Walker, L.R. 1997. Competition and facilitation: a synthetic approach to interactions in plant communities. Ecology. 78: 1958–1965.

Campbell, R.K.; Sugano, A.I. 1979. Genecology of bud-burst phenology in Douglas-fir: response to flushing temperature and chilling. Botanical Gazette. 140: 223–231.

Canaday, B.B.; Fonda, R.W. 1974. Influence of subalpine snowbanks on vegetation pattern, production, and phenology. Bulletin of the Torrey Botanical Club. 101: 340–350.

Cannell, M.G.R.; Smith, R.I. 1983. Thermal time, chill days and prediction of budburst in *Picea sitchensis*. Journal of Applied Ecology. 20: 951–963.

Cannell, M.G.R.; Smith, R.I. 1986. Climatic warming, spring budburst and forest damage on trees. Journal of Applied Ecology. 23: 177–191.

Carnwath, G.C.; Peterson, D.W.; Nelson, C.R. 2012. Effect of crown class and habitat type on climate-growth relationships of ponderosa pine and Douglas-fir. Forest Ecology and Management. 285: 44–52.

Case, M.J.; Peterson, D.L. 2005. Fine-scale variability in growth-climate relationships of Douglas-fir, North Cascade Range, Washington. Canadian Journal of Forest Research. 35: 2743–2755.

Case, M.J.; Peterson, D.L. 2007. Growth-climate relations of lodgepole pine in the North Cascades National Park, Washington. Northwest Science. 81: 62–75.

Casola, J.H.; Cuo, L.; Livneh, B.; Lettenmaier, D.P.; Stoelinga, M.T.; Mote, P.W.; Wallace, J.M. 2009. Assessing the impacts of global warming on snowpack in the Washington Cascades. Journal of Climate. 22: 2758–2772.

Cayan, D.R. 1996. Interannual climate variability and snowpack in the western United States. Journal of Climate. 9: 928–948.

Cázares, E.; Trappe, J.M.; Jumpponen, A. 2005. Mycorrhiza-plant colonization patterns on a subalpine glacier forefront as a model system of primary succession. Mycorrhiza. 15: 405–416.

Chambers, J.C.; Roundy, B.A.; Blank, R.R.; Meyer, S.E.; Whittaker, A. 2007. What makes Great Basin sagebrush ecosystems invasible by *Bromus tectorum*? Ecological Monographs. 77: 117–145.

Chapman, D.S. 2010. Weak climatic associations among British plant distributions. Global Ecology and Biogeography. 19: 831–841.

Chen, P.Y.; Welsh, C.; Hamann, A. 2010. Geographic variation in growth response of Douglas-fir to interannual climate variability and projected climate change. Global Change Biology. 16: 3374–3385.

Cheng, L.; Booker, F.L.; Tu, C.; Burkey, K.O.; Zhou, L.; Shew, H.D.; Rufty, T.W.; Hu, S. 2012. Arbuscular mycorrhizal fungi increase organic carbon decomposition under elevated CO_2. Science. 337: 1084–1087.

Chevin, L.M.; Lande, R.; Mace, G.M. 2010. Adaptation, plasticity, and extinction in a changing environment: toward a predictive theory. PLoS Biology. 8(4): e1000357. doi:10.1371/hournal.pbio.1000357.

Chmura, D.J.; Anderson, P.D.; Howe, G.T.; Harrington, C.A.; Halofsky, J.E.; Peterson, D.L.; Shaw, D.C.; St. Clair, J.B. 2011. Forest responses to climate change in the northwestern United States: ecophysiological foundations for adaptive management. Forest Ecology and Management. 261: 1121–1142.

Chuine, I. 2010. Why does phenology drive species distribution? Philosophical Transactions of the Royal Society, Biological Sciences. 365: 3149–3160.

Chuine, I.; Rehfeldt, G.E.; Aitken, S.N. 2006. Height growth determinants and adaptation to temperature in pines: a case study of *Pinus contorta* and *Pinus monticola*. Canadian Journal of Forest Research. 36: 1059–1066.

Churkina, G.; Running, S.W. 1998. Contrasting climatic controls on the estimated productivity of global terrestrial biomes. Ecosystems. 1: 206–215.

Clarke, L.; Edmonds, J.; Jacoby, H.; Pitcher, H.; Reilly, J.; Richels, R. 2007. Scenarios of greenhouse gas emissions and atmospheric concentrations. Sub-report 2.1. A of synthesis and assessment product 2.1 by the U.S. Climate Change Science Program and the Subcommittee on Global Change Research. Washington, DC: Department of Energy, Office of Biological and Environmental Research. 154 p.

Cleland, E.E.; Chuine, I.; Menzel, A.; Mooney, H.A.; Schwartz, M.D. 2007. Shifting plant phenology in response to global change. Trends in Ecology and Evolution. 22: 357–365.

Cole, K. 1982. Late Quaternary zonation of vegetation in the eastern Grand Canyon. Science. 217: 1142–1145.

Comstock, J.P.; Ehleringer, J.R. 1992. Plant adaptation in the Great Basin and Colorado Plateau. Great Basin Naturalist. 52: 195–215.

Connell, J.H.; Slatyer, R.O. 1977. Mechanisms of succession in natural communities and their role in community stability and organization. American Naturalist. 111: 1119–1144.

Coops, N.C.; Waring, R.H. 2011a. A process-based approach to estimate lodgepole pine (*Pinus contorta* Dougl.) distribution in the Pacific Northwest under climate change. Climatic Change. 105: 313–328.

Coops, N.C.; Waring, R.H. 2011b. Estimating the vulnerability of fifteen tree species under changing climate in Northwest North America. Ecological Modelling. 222: 2119–2129.

Coops, N.C.; Waring, R.H.; Law, B.E. 2005. Assessing the past and future distribution and productivity of ponderosa pine in the Pacific Northwest using a process model, 3-PG. Ecological Modelling. 183: 107–124.

Craine, J.M.; Reich, P.B.; Tilman, G.D.; Ellsworth, D.; Fargione, J.; Knops, J.; Naeem, S. 2003. The role of plant species in biomass production and response to elevated CO_2 and N. Ecology Letters. 6: 623–630.

Craine, J.M.; Tilman, D.; Wedin, D.; Reich, P.; Knops, J. 2002. Functional traits, productivity and effects on nutrient cycling of 33 grassland species. Functional Ecology. 16: 563–574.

Cramer, W.; Bondeau, A.; Woodward, F.I.; Prentice, I.C.; Betts, R.A.; Brovkin, V.; Cox, P.M.; Fisher, V.; Foley, J.A.; Friend, A.D.; Kucharik, C.; Lomas, M.R.; Ramankutty, N.; Sitch, S.; Smith, B.; White, A.; Young-Molling, C. 2001. Global response of terrestrial ecosystem structure and function to CO_2 and climate change: results from six dynamic global vegetation models. Global Change Biology. 7: 357–373.

Crookston, N.L.; Rehfeldt, G.E.; Dixon, G.E.; Weiskittel, A.R. 2010. Addressing climate change in the forest vegetation simulator to assess impacts on landscape forest dynamics. Forest Ecology and Management. 260: 1198–1211.

Dale, V.H.; Franklin, J.F. 1989. Potential effects of climate change on stand development in the Pacific Northwest. Canadian Journal of Forest Research. 19: 1581–1590.

Dale, V.H.; Joyce, L.A.; McNulty, S.; Neilson, R.P.; Ayres, M.P.; Flannigan, M.D.; Hanson, P.J.; Irland, L.C.; Lugo, A.E.; Peterson, C.J.; Simberloff, D.; Swanson, F.J.; Stocks, B.J.; Wotton, B.M. 2001. Climate change and forest disturbances. Bioscience. 51: 723–734.

Daly, C.; Conklin, D.R.; Unsworth, M.H. 2010. Local atmospheric decoupling in complex topography alters climate change impacts. International Journal of Climatology. 30: 1857–1864.

Daly, C.; Halbleib, M.; Smith, J.I.; Gibson, W.P.; Doggett, M.K.; Taylor, G.H.; Curtis, J.; Pasteris, P.P. 2008. Physiographically sensitive mapping of climatological temperature and precipitation across the conterminous United States. International Journal of Climatology. 28: 2031–2064.

D'Antonio, C.M.; Tunison, J.T.; Loh, R.K. 2000. Variation in the impact of exotic grasses on native plant composition in relation to fire across an elevation gradient in Hawaii. Austral Ecology. 25: 507–522.

D'Antonio, C.M.; Vitousek, P.M. 1992. Biological invasions by exotic grasses, the grass/fire cycle, and global change. Annual Review of Ecology and Systematics. 23: 63–87.

Davies, G.M.; Bakker, J.D.; Dettweiler-Robinson, E.; Dunwiddie, P.W.; Hall, S.A.; Downs, J.; Evans, J. 2012. Trajectories of change in sagebrush steppe vegetation communities in relation to multiple wildfires. Ecological Applications. 22: 1562–1577.

Davis, M.A.; Grime, J.P.; Thompson, K. 2000. Fluctuating resources in plant communities: a general theory of invasibility. Journal of Ecology. 88: 528–534.

Davis, M.B. 1981. Quaternary history and the stability of forest communities. In: West, D.C.; Shugart, H.H., eds. Forest succession: concepts and application. New York: Springer-Verlag: 132–153.

Davis, M.B. 1989. Lags in vegetation response to greenhouse warming. Climatic Change. 15: 75–82.

Davis, M.B.; Shaw, R.G. 2001. Range shifts and adaptive responses to Quaternary climate change. Science. 292: 673–679.

Davis, M.B.; Shaw, R.G.; Etterson, J.R. 2005. Evolutionary responses to changing climate. Ecology. 86: 1704–1714.

Davis, M.B.; Woods, K.D.; Webb, S.L.; Futyma, R.P. 1986. Dispersal versus climate: expansion of *Fagus* and *Tsuga* into the Upper Great Lakes Region. Vegetatio. 67: 93–103.

Dawes, M.A.; Hättenschwiler, S.; Bebi, P.; Hagedorn, F.; Handa, I.T.; Körner, C.; Rixen, C. 2011. Species-specific tree growth responses to 9 years of CO_2 enrichment at the alpine treeline. Journal of Ecology. 99: 383–394.

Day, T.A.; DeLucia, E.H.; Smith, W.K. 1989. Influence of cold soil and snowcover on photosynthesis and leaf conductance in two Rocky Mountain conifers. Oecologia. 80: 546–552.

de Graaff, M.-A.; van Groenigen, K.-J.; Six, J.; Hungate, B.; van Kessel, C. 2006. Interactions between plant growth and soil nutrient cycling under elevated CO_2: a meta-analysis. Global Change Biology. 12: 2077–2091.

DeLucia, E.H.; Maherali, H.; Carey, E.V. 2000. Climate-driven changes in biomass allocation in pines. Global Change Biology. 6: 587–593.

DePuit, E.J.; Caldwell, M.M. 1975. Gas exchange of three cool semi-desert species in relation to temperature and water stress. Journal of Ecology. 63: 835–858.

Dickie, I.A.; Schnitzer, S.A.; Reich, P.B.; Hobbie, S.E. 2005. Spatially disjunct effects of co-occurring competition and facilitation. Ecology Letters. 8: 1191–1200.

Dieleman, W.I.J.; Vicca, S.; Dijkstra, F.A.; Hagedorn, F.; Hovenden, M.J.; Larsen, K.S.; Morgan, J.A.; Volder, A.; Beier, C.; Dukes, J.S.; King, J.; Leuzinger, S.; Linder, S.; Luo, Y.; Oren, R.; de Angelis, P.; Tingey, D.; Hoosbeek, M.R.; Janssens, I.A. 2012. Simple additive effects are rare: a quantitative review of plant biomass and soil process responses to combined manipulations of CO_2 and temperature. Global Change Biology. 18: 2681–2693.

Diniz-Filho, J.A.F.; Bini, L.M.; Rangel, T.F.; Loyola, R.D.; Hof, C.; Nogués-Bravo, D.; Araújo, M.B. 2009. Partitioning and mapping uncertainties in ensembles of forecasts of species turnover under climate change. Ecography. 32: 897–906.

Dixon, G.E., comp. 2002. Essential FVS: a user's guide to the Forest Vegetation Simulator. Internal Rep. Fort Collins, CO: U.S. Department of Agriculture, Forest Service, Forest Management Service Center. 226 p. (Revised: January 17, 2013).

Dobrowski, S.Z. 2011. A climatic basis for microrefugia: the influence of terrain on climate. Global Change Biology. 17: 1022–1035.

Donato, D.C.; Fontaine, J.B.; Campbell, J.L.; Robinson, W.D.; Kauffman, J.B.; Law, B.E. 2009. Conifer regeneration in stand-replacement portions of a large mixed-severity wildfire in the Klamath-Siskiyou Mountains. Canadian Journal of Forest Research. 39: 823–838.

Dormann, C.F. 2007. Promising the future? Global change projections of species distributions. Basic and Applied Ecology. 8: 387–397.

Drake, B.G.; Gonzàlez-Meler, M.A.; Long, S.P. 1997. More efficient plants: a consequence of rising atmospheric CO_2? Annual Review of Plant Physiology and Plant Molecular Biology. 48: 609–639.

Drake, J.E.; Gallet-Budynek, A.; Hofmockel, K.S.; Bernhardt, E.S.;
Billings, S.A.; Jackson, R.B.; Johnsen, K.S.; Lichter, J.; McCarthy, H.R.;
McCormack, M.L.; Moore, D.J.P.; Oren, R.; Palmroth, S.; Phillips, R.P.;
Pippen, J.S.; Pritchard, S.G.; Treseder, K.K.; Schlesinger, W.H.; DeLucia,
E.H.; Finzi, A.C. 2011. Increases in the flux of carbon belowground stimulate
nitrogen uptake and sustain the long-term enhancement of forest productivity
under elevated CO_2. Ecology Letters. 14: 349–357.

Dukes, J.S.; Chiariello, N.R.; Cleland, E.E.; Moore, L.A.; Shaw, M.R.; Thayer,
S.; Tobeck, T.; Mooney, H.A.; Field, C.B. 2005. Responses of grassland
production to single and multiple global environmental changes. PLoS Biology.
3: 1829–1837.

Dukes, J.S.; Chiariello, N.R.; Loarie, S.R.; Field, C.B. 2011. Strong response
of an invasive plant species (*Centaurea solstitialis* L.) to global environmental
changes. Ecological Applications. 21: 1887–1894.

Dukes, J.S.; Mooney, H.A. 1999. Does global change increase the success of
biological invaders? Trends in Ecology and Evolution. 14: 135–139.

Dullinger, S.; Gattringer, A.; Thuiller, W.; Moser, D.; Zimmerman, N.;
Guisan, A.; Willner, W.; Plutzar, C.; Leitner, M.; Mang, T.; Caccianiga,
M.; Dirnböck, T.; Ertl, S.; Fischer, A.; Lenoir, J.; Svenning, J.C.; Psomas,
A.; Schmatz, D.R.; Silc, U.; Vittoz, P.; Hülber, K. 2012. Extinction debt of
high-mountain plants under twenty-first-century climate change. Nature Climate
Change. 2: 619–622.

Duncan, S.L.; McComb, B.C.; Johnson, K.N. 2010. Integrating ecological and
social ranges of variability in conservation of biodiversity: past, present, and
future. Ecology and Society. 15(1): article 5. http://hdl.handle.net/10535/6002.

Dunne, J.A.; Harte, J.; Taylor, K.J. 2003. Subalpine meadow flowering
phenology responses to climate change: integrating experimental and gradient
methods. Ecological Monographs. 73: 69–86.

Edburg, S.L.; Hicke, J.A.; Brooks, P.D.; Pendall, E.G.; Ewers, B.E.; Norton,
U.; Gochis, D.; Gutmann, E.D.; Meddens, A.J.H. 2012. Cascading impacts of
bark beetle-caused tree mortality on coupled biogeophysical and biogeochemical
processes. Frontiers in Ecology and the Environment. 8: 416–424.

Elith, J.; Graham, C.H. 2009. Do they? How do they? WHY do they differ?
On finding reasons for differing performances of species distribution models.
Ecography. 32: 66–77.

Elith, J.; Graham, C.H.; Anderson, R.P.; Dudik, M.; Ferrier, S.; Guisan, A.; Hijmans, R.J.; Huettmann, F.; Leathwick, J.R.; Lehmann, A.; Li, J.; Lohmann, L.G.; Loiselle, B.A.; Manion, G.; Moritz, C.; Nakamura, M.; Nakazawa, Y.; Overton, J.M.; Peterson, A.T.; Phillips, S.J.; Richardson, K.; Scachetti-Pereira, R.; Schapire, R.E.; Soberon, J.; Williams, S.; Wisz, M.S.; Zimmermann, N.E. 2006. Novel methods improve prediction of species' distributions from occurrence data. Ecography. 29: 129–151.

Elith, J.; Kearney, M.; Phillips, S. 2010. The art of modelling range-shifting species. Methods in Ecology and Evolution. 1: 330–342.

Elith, J.; Leathwick, J.R. 2009. Species distribution models: ecological explanation and prediction across space and time. Annual Review of Ecology Evolution and Systematics. 40: 677–697.

Elmendorf, S.C.; Henry, G.H.R.; Hollister, R.D.; Björk, R.G.; Boulanger-Lapointe, N.; Cooper, E.J.; Cornelissen, J.H.C.; Day, T.A.; Dorrepaal, E.; Elumeeva, T.G.; Gill, M.; Gould, W.A.; Harte, J.; Hik, D.S.; Hofgaard, A.; Johnson, D.R.; Johnstone, J.F.; Jónsdóttir, I.S.; Jorgenson, J.C.; Klanderud, K.; Klein, J.A.; Koh, S.; Kudo, G.; Lara, M.; Lévesque, E. 2012. Plot-scale evidence of tundra vegetation change and links to recent summer warming. Nature Climate Change. 2: 453–457.

Elsner, M.M.; Co, L.; Voisin, N.; Deems, J.S.; Hamlet, A.F.; Vano, J.A.; Mickelson, K.E.B.; Lee, S.-Y.; Lettenmaier, D.P. 2010. Implications of 21st century climate change for the hydrology of Washington State. Climatic Change. 102: 225–260.

Engelkes, T.; Morriën, E.; Verhoeven, K.J.F.; Bezemer, T.M.; Biere, A.; Harvey, J.A.; McIntyre, L.M.; Tamis, W.L.M.; van der Putten, W.H. 2008. Successful range-expanding plants experience less above-ground and below-ground enemy impact. Nature. 456: 946–948.

Eschtruth, A.K.; Battles, J.J. 2009. Assessing the relative importance of disturbance, herbivory, diversity, and propagule pressure in exotic plant invasion. Ecological Monographs. 79: 265–280.

Ettl, G.J.; Peterson, D.L. 1995a. Extreme climate and variation in tree growth-individualistic response in subalpine fir (*Abies lasiocarpa*). Global Change Biology. 1: 231–241.

Ettl, G.J.; Peterson, D.L. 1995b. Growth response of subalpine fir (*Abies lasiocarpa*) to climate in the Olympic Mountains, Washington, USA. Global Change Biology. 1: 213–230.

Evans, R.D.; Fonda, R.W. 1990. The influence of snow on subalpine meadow community pattern, North Cascades, Washington. Canadian Journal of Botany. 68: 212–220.

Everett, R.L.; Schellhaas, R.; Keenum, D.; Spurbeck, D.; Ohlson, P. 2000. Fire history in the ponderosa pine/Douglas-fir forests on the east slope of the Washington Cascades. Forest Ecology and Management. 129: 207–225.

Fajardo, A.; Goodburn, J.M.; Graham, J. 2006. Spatial patterns of regeneration in managed uneven-aged ponderosa pine/Douglas-fir forests of Western Montana, USA. Forest Ecology and Management. 223: 255–266.

Fay, P.A.; Jin, V.L.; Way, D.A.; Potter, K.N.; Gill, R.A.; Jackson, R.B.; Polley, H.W. 2012. Soil-mediated effects of subambient to increased carbon dioxide on grassland productivity. Nature Climate Change. 2: 742–746.

Felzer, B.S.; Cronin, T.W.; Melillo, J.M.; Kicklighter, D.W.; Schlosser, C.A.; Dangal, S.R.S. 2011. Nitrogen effects on carbon-water coupling in forests, grasslands, and shrublands in the arid western United States. Journal of Geophysical Research. 116: G03023. doi:10.1029/2010JG001621, 2011.

Fettig, C.J.; Klepzig, K.D.; Billings, R.F.; Munson, A.S.; Nebeker, T.E.; Negrón, J.F.; Nowak, J.T. 2007. The effectiveness of vegetation management practices for prevention and control of bark beetle infestations in coniferous forests of the western and southern United States. Forest Ecology and Management. 238: 24–53.

Fisher, B.S.; Nakićenović, N.; Alfsen, K.; Corfee Morlot, J.; de la Chesnaye, F.; Hourcade, J. Ch.; Jiang, K.; Kainuma, M.; La Rovere, E.; Matysek, A.; Rana, A.; Riahi, K.; Richels, R.; Rose, S.; van Vuuren, D.; Warren, R. 2007. Issues related to mitigation in the long term context. In: Metz, B.; Davidson, O.R.; Bosch, P.R.; Dave, R.; Meyer, L.A., eds. Climate Change 2007: Mitigation. Contribution of working group III to the fourth assessment report of the Intergovernmental Panel on Climate Change. Cambridge, United Kingdom and New York: Cambridge University Press: 170–250. Chapter 3.

Flannigan, M.D.; Krawchuk, M.A.; de Groot, W.J.; Wotton, B.M.; Growman, L.M. 2009. Implications of changing climate for global wildland fire. International Journal of Wildland Fire. 18: 483–507.

Fonda, R.W.; Bliss, L.C. 1969. Forest vegetation of the montane and subalpine zones, Olympic Mountains, Washington. Ecological Monographs. 39: 271–301.

Forrest, J.; Inouye, D.W.; Thomson, J.D. 2010. Flowering phenology in subalpine meadows: Does climate variation influence community co-flowering patterns? Ecology. 91: 431–440.

Forrest, J.R.K.; Thomson, J.D. 2011. An examination of synchrony between insect emergence and flowering in Rocky Mountain meadows. Ecological Monographs. 81: 469–491.

Forster, P.; Ramaswamy, V.; Artaxo, P.; Berntsen, T.; Betts, R.; Fahey, D.W.; Haywood, J.; Lean, J.; Lowe, D.C.; Myhre, G.; Nganga, J.; Prinn, R.; Raga, G.; Schulz, M.; Van Dorland, R. 2007. Changes in atmospheric constituents and in radiative forcing. In: Solomon, S.; Qin, D.; Manning, M.; Chen, Z.; Marquis, M.; Averyt, K.B.; Tignor, M.; Miller, H.L., eds. Climate change 2007: the physical science basis. Contribution of working group I to the fourth assessment report of the Intergovernmental Panel on Climate Change. Cambridge, United Kingdom and New York: Cambridge University Press: 129–234. Chapter 2.

Franklin, J.F.; Dyrness, C.T. 1973. Natural vegetation of Oregon and Washington. Gen. Tech. Rep. PNW-GTR-008. Portland, OR: U.S. Department of Agriculture, Forest Service, Pacific Northwest Forest and Range Experiment Station. 427 p.

Franklin, J.F.; Moir, W.H.; Douglas, G.W.; Wiberg, C. 1971. Invasion of subalpine meadows by trees in the Cascade Range, Washington and Oregon. Arctic and Alpine Research. 3: 215–224.

Franklin, J.F.; Spies, T.A.; Van Pelt, R.; Carey, A.B.; Thornburgh, D.A.; Berg, D.R.; Lindenmayer, D.B.; Harmon, M.E.; Keeton, W.S.; Shaw, D.C.; Bible, K.; Chen, J. 2002. Disturbances and structural development of natural forest ecosystems with silvicultural implications, using Douglas-fir forests as an example. Forest Ecology and Management. 155: 399–423.

Franks, S.J.; Sim, S.; Weis, A.E. 2007. Rapid evolution of flowering time by an annual plant in response to a climate fluctuation. Proceedings of the National Academy of Sciences of the United States of America. 104: 1278–1282.

Franks, S.J.; Weis, A.E. 2008. A change in climate causes rapid evolution of multiple life-history traits and their interactions in an annual plant. Journal of Evolutionary Biology. 21: 1321–1334.

Fraser, L.H.; Greenall, A.; Carlyle, C.; Turkington, R.; Friedman, C.R. 2009. Adaptive phenotypic plasticity of *Pseudoroegneria spicata*: response of stomatal density, leaf area and biomass to changes in water supply and increased temperature. Annals of Botany. 103: 769–775.

Frey, B.R.; Lieffers, V.J.; Hogg, E.H.; Landhäusser, S.M. 2004. Predicting landscape patterns of aspen dieback: mechanisms and knowledge gaps. Canadian Journal of Forest Research. 34: 1379–1390.

Friend, A.D.; Stevens, A.K.; Knox, R.G.; Cannell, M.G.R. 1997. A process-based terrestrial biosphere model of ecosystem dynamics (Hybrid v3.0). Ecological Modelling. 95: 249–287.

Ganey, J.L.; Vojta, S.C. 2011. Tree mortality in drought-stressed mixed-conifer and ponderosa pine forests, Arizona, USA. Forest Ecology and Management. 261: 162–168.

Garrett, K.A.; Dendy, S.P.; Frank, E.E.; Rouse, M.N.; Travers, S.E. 2006. Climate change effects on plant disease: genomes to ecosystems. Annual Review of Phytopathology. 44: 489–509.

Gavin, D.G. 2009. The coastal-disjunct mesic flora in the inland Pacific Northwest of USA and Canada: refugia, dispersal and disequilibrium. Diversity and Distributions. 15: 972–982.

Gavin, D.G.; Hu, F.S. 2006. Spatial variation of climatic and non-climatic controls on species distribution: the range limit of *Tsuga heterophylla*. Journal of Biogeography. 33: 1384–1396.

Gedalof, Z.; Peterson, D.L.; Mantua, N.J. 2005. Atmospheric, climatic, and ecological controls on extreme wildfire years in the northwestern United States. Ecological Applications. 15: 154–174.

Gedney, D.R.; Azuma, D.L.; Bolsinger, C.L.; McKay, N. 1999. Western juniper in eastern Oregon. Gen. Tech. Rep. PNW-GTR-464. Portland, OR: U.S. Department of Agriculture, Forest Service, Pacific Northwest Research Station. 53 p.

Germino, M.J.; Smith, W.K. 1999. Sky exposure, crown architecture, and low-temperature photoinhibition in conifer seedlings at alpine treeline. Plant Cell and Environment. 22: 407–415.

Gessel, S.P.; Miller, R.E.; Cole, D.W. 1990. Relative importance of water and nutrients on the growth of coast Douglas fir in the Pacific Northwest. Forest Ecology and Management. 30: 327–340.

Gholz, H.L. 1982. Environmental limits on above-ground net primary production, leaf-area, and biomass in vegetation zones of the Pacific Northwest. Ecology. 63: 469–481.

Gibson, J. 2011. Individualistic response of piñon and juniper tree species distributions to climate change in North America's arid interior west. Logan, UT: Utah State University. 95 p. Ph.D. dissertation.

Glick, P.; Stein, B.A.; Edelson, N.A., eds. 2011. Scanning the conservation horizon: a guide to climate change vulnerability assessment. Washington, DC: National Wildlife Federation. 168 p.

Grace, J.; Berninger, F.; Nagy, L. 2002. Impacts of climate change on the tree line. Annals of Botany. 90: 537–544.

Graumlich, L.J.; Brubaker, L.B. 1986. Reconstruction of annual temperature (1590-1979) for Longmire, Washington, derived from tree rings. Quaternary Research. 25: 223–234.

Graumlich, L.J.; Brubaker, L.B.; Grier, C.C. 1989. Long-term trends in forest net primary productivity: Cascade Mountains, Washington. Ecology. 70: 405–410.

Gray, A.N.; Spies, T.A. 1997. Microsite controls on tree seedling establishment in conifer forest canopy gaps. Ecology. 78: 2458–2473.

Gray, L.J.; Beer, J.; Geller, M.; Haigh, J.D.; Lockwood, M.; Matthes, K.; Cubasch, U.; Fleitmann, D.; Harrison, G.; Hood, L.; Luterbacher, J.; Meehl, G.A.; Shindell, D.; van Geel, B.; White, W. 2010. Solar influences on climate. Reviews of Geophysics. 48, RG4001. doi:10.1029/2009RG000282.

Gray, S.T.; Betancourt, J.L.; Jackson, S.T.; Eddy, R.G. 2006. Role of multidecadal climate variability in a range extension of pinyon pine. Ecology. 87: 1124–1130.

Green, D.G.; Sadedin, S. 2005. Interactions matter—complexity in landscapes and ecosystems. Ecological Complexity. 2: 117–130.

Grier, C.C.; Running, S.W. 1977. Leaf area of mature northwestern coniferous forests—relation to site water-balance. Ecology. 58: 893–899.

Griesbauer, H.P.; Green, D.S. 2010. Regional and ecological patterns in interior Douglas-fir climate-growth relationships in British Columbia, Canada. Canadian Journal of Forest Research. 40: 308–321.

Griffith, A.B. 2010. Positive effects of native shrubs on *Bromus tectorum* demography. Ecology. 91: 141–154.

Griggs, R.F. 1938. Timberlines in the northern Rocky Mountains. Ecology. 19: 548–564.

Grime, J.P. 1979. Plant strategies and vegetation processes. Chichester, United Kingdom: Wiley. ISBN 0-471-99692-0.

Grime, J.P.; Fridley, J.D.; Askew, A.P.; Thompson, K.; Hodgson, J.G.; Bennett, C.R. 2008. Long-term resistance to simulated climate change in an infertile grassland. Proceedings of the National Academy of Sciences of the United States of America. 105: 10028–10032.

Grubb, P.J. 1977. The maintenance of species-richness in plant communities: the importance of the regeneration niche. Biological Reviews. 52: 107–145.

Grulke, N.E. 2010. Plasticity in physiological traits in conifers: implications for response to climate change in the western U.S. Environmental Pollution. 158: 2032–2042.

Guak, S.; Olsyzk, D.M.; Fuchigami, L.H.; Tingey, D.T. 1998. Effects of elevated CO_2 and temperature on cold hardiness and spring bud burst and growth in Douglas-fir (*Pseudotsuga menziesii*). Tree Physiology. 18: 671–679.

Gugger, P.F.; Sugita, S. 2010. Glacial populations and postglacial migration of Douglas-fir based on fossil pollen and macrofossil evidence. Quaternary Science Reviews. 29: 2052–2070.

Guisan, A.; Thuiller, W. 2005. Predicting species distribution: offering more than simple habitat models. Ecology Letters. 8: 993–1009.

Guisan, A.; Zimmermann, N.E. 2000. Predictive habitat distribution models in ecology. Ecological Modelling. 135: 147–186.

Guisan, A.; Zimmermann, N.E.; Elith, J.; Graham, C.H.; Phillips, S.; Peterson, A.T. 2007. What matters for predicting the occurrences of trees: techniques, data, or species' characteristics? Ecological Monographs. 77: 615–630.

Gunderson, C.A.; O'Hara, K.H.; Campion, C.M.; Walker, A.V.; Edwards, N.T. 2010. Thermal plasticity of photosynthesis: the role of acclimation in forest responses to a warming climate. Global Change Biology. 16: 2272–2286.

Hadley, J.L.; Smith, W.K. 1987. Influence of krummholz mat microclimate on needle physiology and survival. Oecologia. 73: 82–90.

Hairston, N.G.; Ellner, S.P.; Geber, M.A.; Yoshida, T.; Fox, J.A. 2005. Rapid evolution and the convergence of ecological and evolutionary time. Ecology Letters. 8: 1114–1127.

Halofsky, J.E.; Peterson, D.L.; O'Halloran, K.A.; Hawkins Hoffman, C., eds. 2011. Adapting to climate change at Olympic National Forest and Olympic National Park. Gen. Tech. Rep. PNW-GTR-844. Portland, OR: U.S. Department of Agriculture, Forest Service, Pacific Northwest Research Station. 130 p.

Hamilton, J.; Zangerl, A.R.; Berenbaum, M.R.; Sparks, J.P.; Elich, L.; Eisenstein, A.; DeLucia, E.H. 2012. Elevated atmospheric CO_2 alters the arthropod community in a forest understory. Acta Oecologica. 43: 80–85.

Hamlet, A.F.; Mote, P.W.; Clark, M.P.; Lettenmaier, D.P. 2005. Effects of temperature and precipitation variability on snowpack trends in the western United States. Journal of Climate. 18: 4545–4561.

Hamlet, A.F.; Mote, P.W.; Clark, M.P.; Lettenmaier, D.P. 2007. Twentieth-century trends in runoff, evapotranspiration, and soil moisture in the western United States. Journal of Climate. 20: 1468–1486.

Hampe, A. 2011. Plants on the move: the role of seed dispersal and initial population establishment for climate-driven range expansions. Acta Oecologia. 37: 666–673.

Hampe, A.; Jump, A.S. 2011. Climate relicts: past, present, future. Annual Review of Ecology, Evolution, and Systematics. 42: 313–333.

Hampe, A.; Petit, R.J. 2005. Conserving biodiversity under climate change: the rear edge matters. Ecology Letters. 8: 461–467.

Hamrick, J.L. 2004. Response of forest trees to global environmental changes. Forest Ecology and Management. 197: 323–335.

Hargrove, W.W.; Hoffman, F.M. 2005. The potential of multivariate quantitative methods for delineation and visualization of ecoregions. Environmental Management. 34: S39–S60.

Harmon, M.E.; Franklin, J.F. 1989. Tree seedlings on logs in *Picea-Tsuga* forests of Oregon and Washington. Ecology. 70: 48–59.

Harmon, M.E.; Franklin, J.F.; Swanson, F.J.; Sollins, P.; Gregory, S.V.; Lattin, J.D.; Anderson, N.H.; Cline, S.P.; Aumen, N.G.; Sedell, J.R.; Lienkaemper, G.W.; Cromack, K., Jr.; Cummins, K.W. 1986. Ecology of coarse woody debris in temperate ecosystems. Advances in Ecological Research. 15: 133–302.

Harrington, C.A.; Gould, P.J.; St. Clair, J.B. 2010. Modeling the effects of winter environment on dormancy release of Douglas-fir. Forest Ecology and Management. 259: 798–808.

Harrington, R.; Woiwod, I.; Sparks, T. 1999. Climate change and trophic interactions. Trends in Ecology and Evolution. 14: 146–150.

Harsch, M.A.; Bader, M.Y. 2011. Treeline form—a potential key to understanding treeline dynamics. Global Ecology and Biogeography. 20: 582–596.

Harsch, M.A.; Hulme, P.E.; McGlone, M.S.; Duncan, R.P. 2009. Are treelines advancing? A global meta-analysis of treeline response to climate warming. Ecology Letters. 12: 1040–1049.

Hays, J.D.; Imbrie, J.; Shackleton, N.J. 1976. Variations in Earth's orbit: pacemaker of the Ice Ages. Science. 194: 1121–1132.

Hegland, S.J.; Nielsen, A.; Lazaro, A.; Bjerknes, A.L.; Totland, O. 2009. How does climate warming affect plant-pollinator interactions? Ecology Letters. 12: 184–195.

Heikkinen, O. 1984. Forest expansion in the subalpine zone during the past hundred years, Mount Baker, Washington, USA. Erdkunde. 38: 194–202.

Heikinnen, O. 1985. Relationships between tree growth and climate in the subalpine Cascade Range of Washington, U.S.A. Annales Botanici Fennici. 22: 1–14.

Hernandez, P.A.; Graham, C.H.; Master, L.L.; Albert, D.L. 2006. The effect of sample size and species characteristics on performance of different species distribution modeling methods. Ecography. 29: 773–785.

Hessburg, P.F.; Agee, J.K. 2003. An environmental narrative of Inland Northwest United States forests, 1800-2000. Forest Ecology and Management. 178: 23–59.

Hessl, A.E.; McKenzie, D.; Schellhaas, R. 2004. Drought and Pacific Decadal Oscillation linked to fire occurrence in the inland Pacific Northwest. Ecological Applications. 14: 425–442.

Hetherington, A.M.; Woodward, F.I. 2003. The role of stomata in sensing and driving environmental change. Nature. 424: 901–908.

Heyerdahl, E.K.; McKenzie, D.; Daniels, L.D.; Hessl, A.E.; Littell, J.S.; Mantua, N.J. 2008. Climate drivers of regionally synchronous fires in the inland Northwest (1651–1900). International Journal of Wildland Fire. 17: 40–49.

Hicke, J.A.; Johnson, M.C.; Hayes, J.L.; Preisler, H.K. 2012. Effects of bark beetle-caused tree mortality on wildfire. Forest Ecology and Management. 271: 81–90.

Hickler, T.; Smith, B.; Sykes, M.T.; Davis, M.B.; Sugita, S.; Walker, K. 2004. Using a generalized vegetation model to simulate vegetation dynamics in northeastern USA. Ecology. 85: 519–530.

Hikosaka, K.; Kinugasa, T.; Oikawa, S.; Onoda, Y.; Hirose, T. 2011. Effects of elevated CO_2 concentration on seed production in C_3 annual plants. Journal of Experimental Biology. 62: 1523–1530.

HilleRisLambers, J.; Harpole, W.S.; Schnitzer, S.; Tilman, D.; Reich, P.B. 2009. CO_2, nitrogen, and diversity differentially affect seed production of prairie plants. Ecology. 90: 1810–1820.

Hobbie, S.E. 1996. Temperature and plant species control over litter decomposition in Alaskan tundra. Ecological Monographs. 66: 503–522.

Hobbs, R.J.; Higgs, E.; Harris, J.A. 2009. Novel ecosystems: Implications for conservation and restoration. Trends in Ecology and Evolution. 24: 599–605.

Hofmann, D.J.; Butler, J.H.; Tans, P.P. 2009. A new look at atmospheric carbon dioxide. Atmospheric Environment. 43: 2084–2086.

Hogg, E.H.; Brandt, J.P.; Michaelian, M. 2008. Impacts of a regional drought on the productivity, dieback, and biomass of western Canadian aspen forests. Canadian Journal of Forest Research. 38: 1373–1384.

Holmgren, M.; Scheffer, M.; Huston, M.A. 1997. The interplay of facilitation and competition in plant communities. Ecology. 1966–1975.

Holtmeier, F.K.; Broll, G. 2005. Sensitivity and response of Northern Hemisphere altitudinal and polar treelines to environmental change at landscape and local scales. Global Ecology and Biogeography. 14: 395–410.

Holtum, J.A.M.; Winter, K. 2010. Elevated [CO_2] and forest vegetation: More a water issue than a carbon issue? Functional Plant Biology. 37: 694–702.

Housman, D.C.; Naumburg, E.; Huxman, T.E.; Charlet, T.N.; Nowak, R.S.; Smith, S.D. 2006. Increases in desert shrub productivity under elevated carbon dioxide vary with water availability. Ecosystems. 9: 374–385.

Hu, F.S.; Hampe, A.; Petit, R.J. 2009. Paleoecology meets genetics: deciphering past vegetational dynamics. Frontiers in Ecology and the Environment. 7: 371–379.

Huang, J.G.; Bergeron, Y.; Denneler, B.; Berninger, F.; Tardif, J. 2007. Response of forest trees to increased atmospheric CO_2. Critical Reviews in Plant Sciences. 26: 265–283.

Hyvönen, R.; Ágren, G.I.; Linder, S.; Persson, T.; Cotrufo, M.F.; Ekblad, A.; Freeman, M.; Grelle, A.; Janssens, I.A.; Jarvis, P.G.; Kellomaki, S.; Lindroth, A.; Loustau, D.; Lundmark, T.; Norby, R.J.; Oren, R.; Pilegaard, K.; Ryan, M.G.; Sigurdsson, B.D.; Strömgren, M.; van Oijen, M.; Wallin, G. 2007. The likely impact of elevated [CO_2], nitrogen deposition, increased temperature and management on carbon sequestration in temperate and boreal forest ecosystems: a literature review. New Phytologist. 173: 463–480.

Ibanez, I.; Clark, J.S.; Dietze, M.C.; Feeley, K.; Hersh, M.; LaDeau, S.; McBride, A.; Welch, N.E.; Wolosin, M.S. 2006. Predicting biodiversity change: outside the climate envelope, beyond the species-area curve. Ecology. 87: 1896–1906.

Inouye, D.W. 2008. Effects of climate change on phenology, frost damage, and floral abundance of montane wildflowers. Ecology. 89: 353–362.

Inouye, D.W.; Barr, B.; Armitage, K.B.; Inouye, B.D. 2000. Climate change is affecting altitudinal migrants and hibernating species. Proceedings of the National Academy of Sciences of the United States of America. 97: 1630–1633.

Intergovernmental Panel on Climate Change [IPCC]. 2007a. Climate change 2007: impacts, adaptation and vulnerability. Contribution of working group II the fourth assessment report of the Intergovernmental Panel on Climate Change. In: Parry, M.L.; Canziana, O.F.; Palutikof, J.P.; van der Linden, P.J.; Hanson, C.E., eds. Cambridge, United Kingdom: Cambridge University Press.

Intergovernmental Panel on Climate Change [IPCC]. 2007b. Climate change 2007: synthesis report. Contribution of working groups I, II and III to the fourth assessment report of the Intergovernmental Panel on Climate Change. In: Pachauri, R.K.; Reisinger, A., eds. Geneva, Switzerland. 104 p. http://www.ipcc.ch/publications_and_data/publications_and_data_reports.shtml. (April 2012).

Intergovernmental Panel on Climate Change [IPCC]. 2007c. Climate change 2007: the physical science basis. Contribution of working group I the fourth assessment report of the Intergovernmental Panel on Climate Change. In: Solomon, S.; Qin, D.; Manning, M.; Chen, Z.; Marquis, M.; Averyt, K.B.; Tignor, M.; Miller, H.L., eds. Cambridge, United Kingdom: Cambridge University Press.

Jablonski, L.M.; Wang, X.; Curtis, P.S. 2002. Plant reproduction under elevated CO_2 conditions: a meta-analysis of reports on 79 crop and wild species. New Phytologist. 156: 9–26.

Jackson, S.T. 2012. Natural, potential and actual vegetation in North America. Journal of Vegetation Science. doi: 10.1111/jvs.12004.

Jackson, S.T.; Betancourt, J.L.; Booth, R.K.; Gray, S.T. 2009. Ecology and the ratchet of events: climate variability, niche dimensions, and species distributions. Proceedings of the National Academy of Sciences of the United States of America. 106: 19685–19692.

Jackson, S.T.; Hobbs, R.J. 2009. Ecological restoration in the light of ecological history. Science. 325: 567–569.

Jackson, S.T.; Overpeck, J.T. 2000. Responses of plant populations and communities to environmental changes of the late Quaternary. Paleobiology. 26: 194–220.

Jackson, S.T.; Sax, D.F. 2010. Balancing biodiversity in a changing environment: extinction debt, immigration credit and species turnover. Trends in Ecology and Evolution. 25: 153–160.

Jankju, M. 2008. Individual performances and the interaction between arid land plants affected by the growth season water pulses. Arid Land Research and Management. 22: 123–133.

Jansen, E.; Overpeck, J.; Briffa, K.R.; Duplessy, J.-C.; Joos, F.; Masson-Delmotte, V.; Olago, D.; Otto-Bliesner, B.; Peltier, W.R.; Rahmstorf, S.; Ramesh, R.; Raynaud, D.; Rind, D.; Solomina, O.; Villalba, R.; Zhang, D. 2007. Paleoclimate. In: Solomon, S.; Qin, D.; Manning, M.; Chen, Z.; Marquis, M.; Averyt, K.B.; Tignor, M.; Miller, H.L., eds. Climate change 2007: the physical science basis. Contribution of working group I to the fourth assessment report of the Intergovernmental Panel on Climate Change. Cambridge, United Kingdom and New York: Cambridge University Press: 433–497.

Jeschke, J.M.; Strayer, D.L. 2008. Usefulness of bioclimatic models for studying climate change and invasive species. Annals of the New York Academy of Sciences. 1134: 1–24.

Jessop, B.D.; Anderson, V.J. 2007. Cheatgrass invasion in salt desert shrublands: benefits of postfire reclamation. Rangeland Ecology and Management. 60: 235–243.

Johnson, D.M.; Germino, M.J.; Smith, W.K. 2004. Abiotic factors limiting photosynthesis in *Abies lasiocarpa* and *Picea engelmannii* seedlings below and above alpine timberline. Tree Physiology. 24: 377–386.

Johnson, K.N.; Bettinger, P.; Kline, J.D.; Spies, T.A.; Lennette, M.; Lettman, G.; Garber-Yonts, B.; Larsen, T. 2007. Simulating forest structure, timber production, and socioeconomic effects in a multi-owner province. Ecological Applications. 17: 34–47.

Joyce, L.A.; Blate, G.M.; McNulty, S.G.; Millar, C.I.; Moser, S.; Neilson, R.P.; Peterson, D.L. 2009. Managing for multiple resources under climate change: National Forests. Environmental Management. 44: 1022–1032.

Jump, A.S.; Matyas, C.; Peñuelas, J. 2009. The altitude-for-latitude disparity in the range retractions of woody species. Trends in Ecology and Evolution. 24: 694–701.

Jump, A.S.; Peñuelas, J. 2005. Running to stand still: adaptation and the response of plants to rapid climate change. Ecology Letters. 8: 1010–1020.

Jumpponen, A.; Brown, S.P.; Trappe, J.M.; Cázares, E.; Strömmer, R. 2012. Twenty years of research on fungal-plant interactions on Lyman Glacier forefront —lessons learned and questions yet unanswered. Fungal Ecology. 5: 430–442.

Kashian, D.M.; Romme, W.H.; Tinker, D.B.; Turner, M.G.; Ryan, M.G. 2006. Carbon storage on landscapes with stand-replacing fires. Bioscience. 56: 598–606.

Keane, R.E.; Arno, S.F.; Brown, J.K. 1990. Simulating cumulative fire effects in ponderosa pine/Douglas-fir forests. Ecology. 71: 189–203.

Keane, R.E.; Cary, G.J.; Davies, I.D.; Flannigan, M.D.; Gardner, R.H.; Lavorel, S.; Lenihan, J.M.; Li, C.; Rupp, T.S. 2004. A classification of landscape fire succession models: spatial simulations of fire and vegetation dynamics. Ecological Modelling. 179: 3–27.

Keane, R.E.; Holsinger, L.M.; Parsons, R.A.; Gray, K. 2008. Climate change effects on historical range and variability of two large landscapes in western Montana, USA. Forest Ecology and Management. 254: 375–389.

Keane, R.E.; Morgan, P.; Running, S.W. 1996. FIRE-BGC—A mechanistic ecological process model for simulating fire succession on coniferous forest landscapes of the northern Rocky Mountains. Res. Pap. INT-RP-484. Ogden, UT: U.S. Department of Agriculture, Forest Service, Intermountain Research Station. 122 p.

Kearney, M.; Porter, W. 2009. Mechanistic niche modelling: combining physiological and spatial data to predict species ranges. Ecology Letters. 12: 334–350.

Keeley, J.E.; McGinnis, T.W. 2007. Impact of prescribed fire and other factors on cheatgrass persistence in a Sierra Nevada ponderosa pine forest. International Journal of Wildland Fire. 16: 96–106.

Keeling, C.D.; Bacastow, R.B.; Bainbridge, A.E.; Ekdahl, C.A.; Guenther, P.R.; Waterman, L.S.; Chin, J.F.S. 1976. Atmospheric carbon dioxide variations at Mauna Loa Observatory, Hawaii. Tellus. 28: 538–551.

Keller, E.A.; Anekonda, T.S.; Smith, B.N.; Hansen, L.D.; St. Clair, J.B.; Criddle, R.S. 2004. Stress and respiration traits differ among four geographically distinct *Pinus ponderosa* seed sources. Thermochimica Acta. 422: 69–74.

Kelly, A.E.; Goulden, M.L. 2008. Rapid shifts in plant distribution with recent climate change. Proceedings of the National Academy of Sciences of the United States of America. 105: 11823–11826.

Kercher, J.R.; Axelrod, M.C. 1984a. Analysis of SILVA: a model for forecasting the effects of SO_2 pollution and fire on western coniferous forests. Ecological Modelling. 23: 165–184.

Kercher, J.R.; Axelrod, M.C. 1984b. A process model of fire ecology and succession in a mixed-conifer forest. Ecology. 65: 1725–1742.

Kerns, B.K.; Hemstrom, M.A.; Conklin, D.; Yospin, G.; Johnson, B.; Bachelet, D.; Bridgham, S. 2012. Approaches to incorporating climate change effects in state and transition simulation models of vegetation. In: Kerns, B.K.; Shlisky, A.J.; Daniel, C.J., tech. eds. Proceedings of the First Landscape State-and-Transition Simulation Modeling conference. Gen. Tech. Rep. PNW-GTR-869. Portland, OR: U.S. Department of Agriculture, Forest Service, Pacific Northwest Research Station: 161–171.

Kerns, B.K.; Naylor, B.J.; Buonopane, M.; Parks, C.G.; Rogers, B. 2009. Modeling tamarisk (*Tamarisk* spp.) habitat and climate change effects in the northwestern United States. Invasive Plant Science and Management. 2: 200–215.

Kerns, B.K.; Ohmann, J.L. 2004. Evaluation and prediction of shrub cover in coastal Oregon forests (USA). Ecological Indicators. 4: 83–98.

Kerns, B.K.; Thies, W.G.; Niwa, C.G. 2006. Season and severity of prescribed burn in ponderosa pine forests: implications for understory native and exotic plants. Ecoscience. 13: 44–55.

Kiehl, J.T.; Trenberth, K.E. 1997. Earth's annual global mean energy budget. Bulletin of the American Meteorological Society. 78: 197–208.

Kilham, K. 1994. Soil ecology. Cambridge, United Kingdom: Cambridge University Press. 242 p.

Klanderud, K. 2010. Species recruitment in alpine plant communities: the role of species interactions and productivity. Journal of Ecology. 98: 1128–1133.

Klemmedson, J.O.; Tiedemann, A.R. 2000. Influence of western juniper development on distribution of soil and organic layer nutrients. Northwest Science. 74: 1–11.

Klenner, W.; Arsenault, A. 2009. Ponderosa pine mortality during a severe bark beetle (Coleoptera: Curculionidae, Scolytinae) outbreak in southern British Columbia and implications for wildlife habitat management. Forest Ecology and Management. 258S: S5–S14.

Kliejunas, J.T.; Geils, B.W.; Glaeser, J.M.; Goheen, E.M.; Hennon, P.; Kim, M.-S.; Kope, H.; Stone, J.; Sturrock, R.; Frankel, S.J. 2009. Review of literature on climate change and forest diseases of western North America. Gen. Tech. Rep. PSW-GTR-225. Albany, CA: U.S. Department of Agriculture, Forest Service, Pacific Southwest Research Station. 54 p.

Knapp, P.A.; Soulé, P.T. 2005. Impacts of an extreme early-season freeze event in the interior Pacific Northwest (30 October–3 November 2002) on western juniper woodlands. Journal of Applied Meteorology. 44: 1152–1158.

Knapp, P.A.; Soulé, P.T.; Grissino-Mayer, H.D. 2001. Detecting potential regional effects of increased atmospheric CO_2 on growth rates of western juniper. Global Change Biology. 7: 903–917.

Knapp, P.A.; Soulé, P.T.; Grissino-Mayer, H.D. 2004. Occurrence of sustained droughts in the interior Pacific Northwest (AD 1733–1980) inferred from tree-ring data. Journal of Climate. 17: 140–150.

Knowles, N.; Dettinger, M.D.; Cayan, D.R. 2006. Trends in snowfall versus rainfall in the western United States. Journal of Climate. 19: 4545–4559.

Knutson, K.C. 2006. Climate-growth relationships of western juniper and ponderosa pine at the pine-woodland ecotone in southern Oregon. Corvallis, OR: Oregon State University. 55 p. M.S. thesis.

Knutson, K.C.; Pyke, D.A. 2008. Western juniper and ponderosa pine ecotonal climate-growth relationships across landscape gradients in southern Oregon. Canadian Journal of Forest Research. 38: 3021–3032.

Knutti, R. 2010. The end of model democracy? An editorial comment. Climatic Change. 102: 395–404.

Knutti, R.; Furrer, R.; Tebaldi, C.; Cermak, J.; Meehl, G.A. 2010. Challenges in combining projections from multiple climate models. Journal of Climate. 23: 2739–2758.

Koepke, D.F.; Kolb, T.E.; Adams, H.D. 2010. Variation in woody plant mortality and dieback from severe drought among soils, plant groups, and species within a northern Arizona ecotone. Oecologia. 163: 1079–1090.

Körner, C.; Basler, D. 2010. Phenology under global warming. Science. 327: 1461–1462.

Kowalchuk, G.A. 2012. Bad news for soil carbon sequestration? Science. 337: 1049–1050.

Kozlowski, T.T.; Pallardy, S.G. 2002. Acclimation and adaptive responses of woody plants to environmental stresses. Botanical Review. 68: 270–334.

Kramer, K.; Leinonen, I.; Loustau, D. 2000. The importance of phenology for the evaluation of impact of climate change on growth of boreal, temperate and Mediterranean forests ecosystems: an overview. International Journal of Biometeorology. 44: 67–75.

Krawchuk, M.A.; Moritz, M.A.; Parisien, M.A.; Van Dorn, J.; Hayhoe, K. 2009. Global pyrogeography: the current and future distribution of wildfire. PLoS ONE 4(4): e5102. doi:10.1371/journal.pone.0005102.

Kremer, A.; Ronce, O.; Robledo-Arnuncio, J.J.; Guillaume, F.; Bohrer, G.; Nathan, R.; Bridle, J.R.; Gomulkiewicz, R.; Klein, E.K.; Ritland, K.; Kuparinen, A.; Gerber, S.; Schueler, S. 2012. Long-distance gene flow and adaptation of forest trees to rapid climate change. Ecology Letters. 15: 378–392.

Kreyling, J.; Wenigmann, M.; Beierkuhnlein, C.; Jentsch, A. 2008. Effects of extreme weather events on plant productivity and tissue die-back are modified by community composition. Ecosystems. 11: 752–763.

Kuparinen, A.; Katul, G.; Nathan, R.; Schurr, F.M. 2009. Increases in air temperature can promote wind-driven dispersal and spread of plants. Proceedings of the Royal Society—Biological Sciences. 276: 3081–3087.

Kuramoto, R.T.; Bliss, L.C. 1970. Ecology of subalpine meadows in the Olympic Mountains, Washington. Ecological Monographs. 40: 317–347.

Kurz, W.A.; Beukema, S.J.; Klenner, W.; Greenough. J.A.; Robinson D.C.E.; Sharpe, A.D.; Webb, T.M. 2000. TELSA: the Tool for Exploratory Landscape Scenario Analyses. Computers and Electronics in Agriculture. 27: 227–242.

Kurz, W.A.; Dymond, C.C.; Stinson, G.; Rampley, G.J.; Neilson, E.T.; Carroll, A.L.; Ebata, T.; Safranyik, L. 2008. Mountain pine beetle and forest carbon feedback to climate change. Nature. 452: 987–990.

Kusnierczyk, E.R.; Ettl, G.J. 2002. Growth response of ponderosa pine (*Pinus ponderosa*) to climate in the eastern Cascade Mountains, Washington, USA: implications for climatic change. Ecoscience. 9: 544–551.

LaDeau, S.L.; Clark, J.S. 2001. Rising CO_2 levels and the fecundity of forest trees. Science. 292: 95–98.

LaDeau, S.L.; Clark, J.S. 2006. Elevated CO_2 and tree fecundity: the role of tree size, interannual variability, and population heterogeneity. Global Change Biology. 12: 822–833.

Lambers, H.; Chapin, F.S.; Pons, T.L. 1998. Plant physiological ecology. New York: Springer-Verlag. 540 p.

Lambrecht, S.C.; Loik, M.E.; Inouye, D.W.; Harte, J. 2007. Reproductive and physiological responses to simulated climate warming for four subalpine species. New Phytologist. 173: 121–134.

Landres, P.B.; Morgan, P.; Swanson, F.J. 1999. Overview of the use of natural variability concepts in managing ecological systems. Ecological Applications. 9: 1179–1188.

Lapenis, A.; Shvidenko, A.; Shepaschenko, D.; Nilsson, S.; Aiyyer, A. 2005. Acclimation of Russian forests to recent changes in climate. Global Change Biology. 11: 2090–2102.

Larson, A.J.; Franklin, J.F. 2005. Patterns of conifer tree regeneration following an autumn wildfire event in the western Oregon Cascade Range, USA. Forest Ecology and Management. 218: 25–36.

Larson, D.L.; Anderson, P.J.; Newton, W. 2001. Alien plant invasion in mixed-grass prairie: effects of vegetation type and anthropogenic disturbance. Ecological Applications. 11: 128–141.

Latta, G.; Temesgen, H.; Adams, D.; Barrett, T. 2010. Analysis of potential impacts of climate change on forests of the United States Pacific Northwest. Forest Ecology and Management. 259: 720–729.

League, K.; Veblen, T. 2006. Climatic variability and episodic *Pinus ponderosa* establishment along the forest-grassland ecotones of Colorado. Forest Ecology and Management. 228: 98–107.

Leakey, A.D.; Ainsworth, E.A.; Bernacchi, C.J.; Rogers, A.; Long, S.P.; Ort, D.R. 2009. Elevated CO_2 effects on plant carbon, nitrogen, and water relations: six important lessons from FACE. Journal of Experimental Botany. 60: 2859–2876.

Lee, T.D.; Tjoelker, M.G.; Reich, P.B.; Russelle, M.P. 2003. Contrasting growth response of an N_2-fixing and non-fixing forb to elevated CO_2: dependence on soil N supply. Plant and Soil. 255: 475–486.

Lenihan, J.M.; Daly, C.; Bachelet, D.; Neilson, R.P. 1998. Simulating broad-scale fire severity in a dynamic global vegetation model. Northwest Science. 72 (Special Issue): 91–103.

Le Treut, H.; Somerville, R.; Cubasch, U.; Ding, Y.; Mauritzen, C.; Mokssit, A.; Peterson, T.; Prather, M. 2007. Historical overview of climate change science. In: Solomon, S.; Qin, D.; Manning, M.; Chen, Z.; Marquis, M.; Averyt, K.B.; Tignor, M.; Miller, H.L., eds. Climate change 2007: the physical science basis. Contribution of working group I to the fourth assessment report of the Intergovernmental Panel on Climate Change. Cambridge, United Kingdom and New York: Cambridge University Press: 93–127. Chapter 1.

Leuzinger, S.; Bigler, C.; Wolf, A.; Körner, C. 2009. Poor methodology for predicting large-scale tree die-off. Proceedings of the National Academy of Sciences of the United States of America. 106(38): E106. doi:10.1073/pnas.0908053106.

Lewis, J.D.; Lucash, M.; Olszyk, D.M.; Tingey, D.T. 2004. Relationships between needle nitrogen concentration and photosynthetic responses of Douglas-fir seedlings to elevated CO_2 and temperature. New Phytologist. 162: 355–364.

Lincoln, D.E.; Fajer, E.D.; Johnson, R.H. 1993. Plant-insect herbivore interactions in elevated CO_2 environments. Trends in Ecology and Evolution. 8: 64–68.

Lindroth, R.L. 2010. Impacts of elevated atmospheric CO_2 and O_3 on forests: phytochemistry, trophic interactions, and ecosystem dynamics. Journal of Chemical Ecology. 36: 2–21.

Link, S.O.; Keeler, C.W.; Hill, R.W.; Hagen, E. 2006. *Bromus tectorum* cover mapping and fire risk. International Journal of Wildland Fire. 15: 113–119.

Littell, J.S.; McKenzie, D.; Kerns, B.K.; Cushman, S.; Shaw, C.G. 2011. Managing uncertainty in climate-driven ecological models to inform adaptation to climate change. Ecosphere. 2(9): 102. doi:10.1890/ES11-00114.1.

Littell, J.S.; McKenzie, D.; Peterson, D.L.; Westerling, A.L. 2009. Climate and wildfire area burned in western U. S. ecoprovinces, 1916-2003. Ecological Applications. 19: 1003–1021.

Littell, J.S.; Oneil, E.E.; McKenzie, D.; Hicke, J.A.; Lutz, J.A.; Norheim, R.A.; Elsner, M.M. 2010. Forest ecosystems, disturbance, and climatic change in Washington State, USA. Climatic Change. 102: 129–158.

Littell, J.S.; Peterson, D.L.; Millar, C.I.; O'Halloran, K.A. 2012. U.S. National Forests adapt to climate change through science-management partnerships. Climatic Change. 110: 269–296.

Littell, J.S.; Peterson, D.L.; Tjoelker, M. 2008. Douglas-fir growth in mountain ecosystems: water limits tree growth from stand to region. Ecological Monographs. 78: 349–368.

Little, R.L.; Peterson, D.L.; Conquest, L.L. 1994. Regeneration of subalpine fir (*Abies lasiocarpa*) following fire: effects of climate and other factors. Canadian Journal of Forest Research. 24: 934–944.

Little, R.L.; Peterson, D.L.; Silsbee, D.G.; Shainsky, L.J.; Bednar, L.F. 1995. Radial growth patterns and the effects of climate on second-growth Douglas-fir (*Pseudotsuga menziesii*) in the Siskiyou Mountains, Oregon. Canadian Journal of Forest Research. 25: 724–735.

Liu, Y.; Reich, P.B.; Li, G.; Sun, S. 2011. Shifting phenology and abundance under experimental warming alters trophic relationships and plant reproductive capacity. Ecology. 92: 1201–1207.

Lloret, F.; Escudero, A.; Iriondo, J.M.; Martínez-Vilalta, J.; Valladares, F. 2012. Extreme climatic events and vegetation: the role of stabilizing processes. Global Change Biology. 18: 797–805.

Loarie, S.R.; Duffy, P.B.; Hamilton, H.; Asner, G.P.; Field, C.B.; Ackerly, D.D. 2009. The velocity of climate change. Nature. 462: 1052–1055.

Lodge, D.M.; Williams, S.; MacIsaac, H.J.; Hayes, K.R.; Leung, B.; Reichard, S.; Mack, R.N.; Moyle, P.B.; Smith, M.; Andow, D.A.; Carlton, J.T.; McMichael, A. 2006. Biological invasions: recommendations for U.S. policy and management. Ecological Applications. 16: 2035–2054.

Logan, J.A.; Regniere, J.; Powell, J.A. 2003. Assessing the impacts of global warming on forest pest dynamics. Frontiers in Ecology and the Environment. 1: 130–137.

Long, S.P. 1991. Modification of the response of photosynthetic productivity to rising temperature by atmospheric CO_2 concentrations. Has its importance been underestimated? Plant Cell Environment. 14: 729–739.

Long, S.P.; Ainsworth, E.A.; Rogers, A.; Ort, D.R. 2004. Rising atmospheric carbon dioxide: plants FACE the future. Annual Review of Plant Biology. 55: 591–628.

Long, S.P.; Humphries, S.; Falkowski, P.G. 1994. Photoinhibition of photosynthesis in nature. Annual Review of Plant Physiology and Plant Molecular Biology. 45: 633–662.

Lonsdale, W.M. 1999. Global patterns of plant invasions and the concept of invasibility. Ecology. 80: 1522–1536.

Lopushinsky, W.; Max, T.A. 1990. Effect of soil temperature on root and shoot growth and on budburst timing in conifer seedling transplants. New Forests. 4: 107–124.

Lucash, M.S.; Farnsworth, B.; Winner, W.E. 2005. Response of sagebrush steppe species to elevated CO_2 and soil temperature. Western North American Naturalist. 65: 80–86.

Luo, Y.; Su, B.; Currie, W.S.; Dukes, J.S.; Finzi, A.C.; Hartwig, U.; Hungate, B.; McMurtrie, R.E.; Oren, R.; Parton, W.J.; Pataki, D.E.; Shaw, M.R.; Zak, D.R.; Field, C.B. 2004. Progressive nitrogen limitation of ecosystem responses to rising atmospheric carbon dioxide. Bioscience. 54: 731–739.

Luoto, M.; Pöyry, J.; Heikkinen, R.K.; Saarinen, K. 2005. Uncertainty of bioclimatic envelope models based on the geographical distribution of species. Global Ecology and Biogeography. 14: 575–584.

Lynn, B.H.; Healy, R.; Druyan, L.M. 2009. Quantifying the sensitivity of simulated climate change to model configuration. Climatic Change. 92: 275–298.

MacArthur, R.H. 1972. Geographical ecology: patterns in the distribution of species. Princeton, NJ: Princeton University Press. 269 p.

Mack, R.N. 1981. Invasion of *Bromus tectorum* L. into western North America: an ecological chronicle. Agro-Ecosystems. 7: 145–165.

Mack, R.N.; Rutter, N.W.; Valastro, S.; Bryant, V.M. 1978. Late Quaternary vegetation history at Waits Lake, Colville River Valley, Washington. Botanical Gazette. 139: 499–506.

Maestre, F.T.; Callaway, R.M.; Valladares, F.; Lortie, C.J. 2009. Refining the stress-gradient hypothesis for competition and facilitation in plant communities. Journal of Ecology. 97: 199–205.

Maherali, H.; DeLucia, E.H. 2000. Interactive effects of elevated CO_2 and temperature on water transport in ponderosa pine. American Journal of Botany. 87: 243–249.

Maherali, H.; DeLucia, E.H. 2001. Influence of climate-driven shifts in biomass allocation on water transport and storage in ponderosa pine. Oecologia. 129: 481–491.

Maherali, H.; Williams, B.L.; Paige, K.N.; Delucia, E.H. 2002. Hydraulic differentiation of ponderosa pine populations along a climate gradient is not associated with ecotypic divergence. Functional Ecology. 16: 510–521.

Malmsheimer, R.W.; Heffernan, P.; Brink, S.; Crandall, D.; Dencke, F.; Galik, C.; Gee, E.; Helms, J.A.; McClure, N.; Mortimer, M.; Ruddell, S.; Smith, M.; Stewart, J. 2008. Forest management solutions for mitigating climate change in the United States. Journal of Forestry. 106: 115–117.

Markesteijn, L.; Poorter, L. 2009. Seedling root morphology and biomass allocation of 62 tropical tree species in relation to drought- and shade-tolerance. Journal of Ecology. 97: 311–325.

Martin, M.; Gavazov, K.; Körner, C.; Hättenschwiler, S.; Rixen, C. 2010. Reduced early growing season freezing resistance in alpine treeline plants under elevated atmospheric CO_2. Global Change Biology. 16: 1057–1070.

Maseyk, K.; Grünzweig, J.M.; Rotenberg, E.; Yakir, D. 2008. Respiration acclimation contributes to high carbon-use efficiency in a seasonally dry pine forest. Global Change Biology. 14: 1553–1567.

Maslin, M.; Austin, P. 2012. Climate models at their limit? Nature. 486: 183–184.

Matesanz, S.; Gianoli, E.; Valladares, F. 2010. Global change and the evolution of phenotypic plasticity in plants. Annals of the New York Academy of Sciences. 1206: 35–55.

McCarthy, H.R.; Oren, R.; Johnsen, K.H.; Gallet-Budynek, A.; Pritchard, S.G.; Cook, C.W.; Ladeau, S.L.; Jackson, R.B.; Finzi, A.C. 2010. Re-assessment of plant carbon dynamics at the Duke free-air CO_2 enrichment site: interactions of atmospheric $[CO_2]$ with nitrogen and water availability over stand development. New Phytologist. 185: 514–528.

McCormack, M.L.; Pritchard, S.G.; Breland, S.; Davis, M.A.; Prior, S.A.; Runion, G.B.; Mitchell, R.J.; Rogers, H.H. 2010. Soil fungi respond more strongly than fine roots to elevated CO_2 in a model regenerating longleaf pine-wiregrass ecosystem. Ecosystems. 13: 901–916.

McDowell, N.G.; Beerling, D.J.; Breshears, D.D.; Fisher, R.A.; Raffa, K.F.; Stitt, M. 2011. The interdependence of mechanisms underlying climate-driven vegetation mortality. Trends in Ecology and Evolution. 26: 523–532.

McDowell, N.; Pockman, W.T.; Allen, C.D.; Breshears, D.D.; Cobb, N.; Kolb, T.; Plaut, J.; Sperry, J.; West, A.; Williams, D.G.; Yepez, E.A. 2008. Mechanisms of plant survival and mortality during drought: Why do some plants survive while others succumb to drought? New Phytologist. 178: 719–739.

McFarlane, K.J.; Schoenholtz, S.H.; Powers, R.F.; Perakis, S.S. 2010. Soil organic matter stability in intensively managed ponderosa pine stands in California. Soil Science Society of America Journal. 74: 979–992.

McKenney, D.W.; Pedlar, J.H.; Lawrence, K.; Campbell, K.; Hutchinson, M.F. 2007. Potential impacts of climate change on the distribution of North American trees. Bioscience. 57: 939–948.

McKenney, D.W.; Pedlar, J.H.; Rood, R.B.; Price, D. 2011. Revisiting projected shifts in the climate envelopes of North American trees using updated general circulation models. Global Change Biology. 17: 2720–2730.

McKenzie, D.; Gedalof, Z.; Peterson, D.L.; Mote, P. 2004. Climatic change, wildfire, and conservation. Conservation Biology. 18: 890–902.

McKenzie, D.; Peterson, D.L.; Littell, J.J. 2009. Chapter 15. Global warming and stress complexes in forests of western North America. In: Bytnerowicz, A.; Arbaugh, M.; Riebau, A.; Andersen, C., eds. Developments in Environmental Science. 8: 319–337.

McKinley, D.C.; Ryan, M.G.; Birdsey, R.A.; Giardina, C.P.; Harmon, M.E.; Heath, L.S.; Houghton, R.A.; Jackson, R.B.; Morrison, J.F.; Murray, B.C.; Pataki, D.E.; Skog, K.E. 2011. A synthesis of current knowledge on forests and carbon storage in the United States. Ecological Applications. 21: 1902–1924.

McLachlan, J.S.; Clark, J.S.; Manos, P.S. 2005. Molecular indicators of tree migration capacity under rapid climate change. Ecology. 86: 2088–2098.

McMurtrie, R.E.; Norby, R.J.; Medlyn, B.E.; Dewar, R.C.; Pepper, D.A.; Reich, P.B.; Barton, C.V.M. 2008. Why is plant-growth response to elevated CO_2 amplified when water is limiting, but reduced when nitrogen is limiting? A growth-optimisation hypothesis. Functional Plant Biology. 35: 521–534.

McPherson, G.R. 1997. Ecology and management of North American savannas. Tucson, AZ: University of Arizona Press. 208 p.

Medlyn, B.E.; Barton, C.V.M.; Broadmeadow, M.S.J.; Ceulemans, R.; De Angelis, P.; Forstreuter, M.; Freeman, M.; Jackson, S.B.; Kellomäki, S.; Laitat, E.; Rey, A.; Roberntz, P.; Sigurdsson, B.D.; Strassemeyer, J.; Wang, K.; Curtis, P.S.; Jarvis, P.G. 2001. Stomatal conductance of forest species after long-term exposure to elevated CO_2 concentration: a synthesis. New Phytologist. 149: 247–264.

Meehl, G.A.; Hu, A.X.; Tebaldi, C. 2010. Decadal prediction in the Pacific Region. Journal of Climate. 23: 2959–2973.

Meehl, G.A.; Stocker, T.F.; Collins, W.D.; Friedlingstein, P.; Gaye, A.T.; Gregory, J.M.; Kitoh, A.; Knutti, R.; Murphy, J.M.; Noda, A.; Raper, S.C.B.; Watterson, I.G.; Weaver, A.J.; Zhao, Z.-C. 2007. Global climate projections. In: Solomon, S.; Qin, D.; Manning, M.; Chen, Z.; Marquis, M.; Averyt, K.B.; Tignor, M.; Miller, H.L., eds. Climate change 2007: the physical science basis. Contribution of working group I to the fourth assessment report of the Intergovernmental Panel on Climate Change. Cambridge, United Kingdom and New York: Cambridge University Press: 747–845. Chapter 10.

Meehl, G.A.; Tebaldi, C. 2004. More intense, more frequent, and longer lasting heat waves in the 21st century. Science. 305: 994–997.

Melillo, J.M.; Butler, S.; Johnson, J.; Mohan, J.; Steudler, P.; Lux, H.; Burrows, E.; Bowles, F.; Smith, R.; Scott, L.; Vario, C.; Hill, T.; Burton, A.; Zhou, Y.M.; Tang, J. 2011. Soil warming, carbon-nitrogen interactions, and forest carbon budgets. Proceedings of the National Academy of Sciences of the United States of America. 108: 9508–9512.

Memmott, J.; Craze, P.G.; Waser, N.M.; Price, M.V. 2007. Global warming and the disruption of plant-pollinator interactions. Ecology Letters. 10: 710–717.

Mensing, S.; Livingston, S.; Barker, P. 2006. Long-term fire history in Great Basin sagebrush reconstructed from macroscopic charcoal in spring sediments, Newark Valley, Nevada. Western North American Naturalist. 66: 64–77.

Menzel, A.; Sparks, T.H.; Estrella, N.; Koch, E.; Aasa, A.; Ahas, R.; Alm-Kübler, K.; Bissolli, P.; Braslavská, O.G.; Briede, A.; Chmielewski, F.M.; Crepinsek, Z.; Curnel, Y.; Dahl, Å.; Defila, C.; Donnelly, A.; Filella, Y.; Jatczak, K.; Máge, F.; Mestre, A.; Nordli, Ø.; Peñuelas, J.; Pirinen, P.; Remišová, V.; Scheifinger, H.; Striz, M.; Susnik, A.; Van Vliet, A.J.H.; Wielgolaski, F.-E.; Zach, S.; Zust, A. 2006. European phenological response to climate change matches the warming pattern. Global Change Biology. 12: 1969–1976.

Millar, C.I.; Stephenson, N.L.; Stephens, S.L. 2007. Climate change and forests of the future: managing in the face of uncertainty. Ecological Applications. 17: 2145–2151.

Miller, J.D.; Safford, H.D.; Crimmins, M.; Thode, A.E. 2009. Quantitative evidence for increasing forest fire severity in the Sierra Nevada and southern Cascade Mountains, California and Nevada, USA. Ecosystems. 12: 16–32.

Miller, R.F.; Bates, J.D.; Svejcar, T.J.; Pierson, F.B.; Eddleman, L.E. 2005. Biology, ecology, and management of western juniper (*Juniperus occidentalis*). Technical Bulletin 152. Corvallis, OR: Oregon State University, Agricultural Experiment Station. 82 p.

Miller, R.F.; Rose, J.A. 1999. Fire history and western juniper encroachment in sagebrush steppe. Journal of Range Management. 52: 550–559.

Miller, R.F.; Svejcar, T.J.; Rose, J.A. 2000. Impacts of western juniper on plant community composition and structure. Journal of Range Management. 53: 574–585.

Miller, R.F.; Wigand, P.E. 1994. Holocene changes in semi-arid pinyon-juniper woodlands. BioScience. 44: 465–474.

Mimura, M.; Aitken, S.N. 2007. Adaptive gradients and isolation-by-distance with postglacial migration in *Picea sitchensis*. Heredity. 99: 224–232.

Mimura, M.; Aitken, S.N. 2010. Local adaptation at the range peripheries of Sitka spruce. Journal of Evolutionary Biology. 23: 249–258.

Mitton, J.B.; Ferrenberg, S.M. 2012. Mountain pine beetle develops an unprecedented summer generation in response to climate warming. American Naturalist. 179: E163–E171. doi:10.1086/665007.

Mohan, J.E.; Clark, J.S.; Schlessinger, W.H. 2007. Long-term CO_2 enrichment of a forest ecosystem: implications for forest regeneration and succession. Ecological Applications. 17: 1198–1212.

Monserud, R.A.; Rehfeldt, G.E. 1990. Genetic and environmental components of variation of site index in inland Douglas-fir. Forest Science. 36: 1–9.

Moore, M.M.; Covington, W.W.; Fulé, P.Z. 1999. Reference conditions and ecological restoration: a southwestern ponderosa pine perspective. Ecological Applications. 9: 1266–1277.

Morgan, J.A.; LeCain, D.R.; Pendall, E.; Blumenthall, D.M.; Kimball, B.A.; Carrillo, Y.; Williams, D.G.; Heisler-White, J.; Dijkstra, F.A.; West, M. 2011. C_4 grasses prosper as carbon dioxide eliminates desiccation in warmed semi-arid grassland. Nature. 476: 202–206.

Morgan, J.A.; Milchunas, D.G.; LeCain, D.R.; West, M.; Mosier, A.R. 2007. Carbon dioxide enrichment alters plant community structure and accelerates shrub growth in the shortgrass steppe. Proceedings of the National Academy of Sciences of the United States of America. 104: 14724–14729.

Moss, R.H.; Edmonds, J.A.; Hibbard, K.A.; Manning, M.R.; Rose, S.K.; Vuuren, D.P.; Carter, T.R.; Emori, S.; Kainuma, M.; Kram, T.; Meehl, G.A.; Mitchell, J.F.B.; Nakićenović, N.; Riahl, K.; Smith, S.J.; Stouffer, R.J.; Thomson, A.M.; Weyant, J.P.; Wilbanks, T.J. 2010. The next generation of scenarios for climate change research and assessment. Nature. 463: 747–756.

Mote, P.W. 2003. Trends in temperature and precipitation in the Pacific Northwest during the twentieth century. Northwest Science. 77: 271–282.

Mote, P.W. 2006. Climate-driven variability and trends in mountain snowpack in western North America. Journal of Climate. 19: 6209–6220.

Mote, P.W.; Hamlet, A.F.; Clark, M.P.; Lettenmaier, D.P. 2005. Declining mountain snowpack in western North America. Bulletin of the American Meteorological Society. 86: 39–49.

Mote, P.W.; Salathé, E.P. 2010. Future climate in the Pacific Northwest. Climatic Change. 102: 29–50.

Mueller, R.C.; Scudder, C.M.; Porter, M.E.; Trotter, R.T.; Gehring, C.A.; Whitham, T.G. 2005. Differential tree mortality in response to severe drought: evidence for long-term vegetation shifts. Journal of Ecology. 93: 1085–1093.

Nakawatase, J.M.; Peterson, D.L. 2006. Spatial variability in forest growth—climate relationships in the Olympic Mountains, Washington. Canadian Journal of Forest Research. 36: 77–91.

Nakićenović, N. 2000. Greenhouse gas emissions scenarios. Technological Forecasting and Social Change. 65: 149–166.

Nakićenović, N.; Alcamo, J.; Davis, G.; de Vries, B.; Fenhann, J.; Gaffin, S.; Gregory, K.; Grübler, A.; Jung, T.Y.; Kram, T.; La Rovere, E.L.; Michaelis, L.; Mori, S.; Morita, T.; Papper, W.; Pitcher, H.; Price, L.; Riahi, K.; Roehrl, A.; Rogner, H-H.; Sankovski, A.; Schlesinger, M.; Shukla, P.; Smith, S.; Swart, R.; van Rooijen, S.; Victor, N.; Dadi, Z. 2000. Special report on emissions scenarios, working group III, Intergovernmental Panel on Climate Change. Cambridge, United Kingdom: Cambridge University Press. 595 p. http://www.grida.no/climate/ipcc/emission/index.htm. (April 2012).

Nathan, R.; Horvitz, N.; He, Y.; Kuparinen, A.; Schurr, F.M.; Katul, G.G. 2011. Spread of North American wind-dispersed trees in future environments. Ecology Letters. 14: 211–219.

Nathan, R.; Schurr, F.M.; Spiegel, O.; Steinitz, O.; Trakhtenbrot, A.; Tsoar, A. 2008. Mechanisms of long-distance seed dispersal. Trends in Ecology and Evolution. 23: 638–647.

Naumburg, E.; Housman, D.C.; Huxman, T.E.; Charlet, T.N.; Loik, M.E.; Smith, S.D. 2003. Photosynthetic responses of Mojave Desert shrubs to free air CO_2 enrichment are greatest during wet years. Global Change Biology. 9: 276–285.

Neilson, R.P. 1995. A model for predicting continental-scale vegetation distribution and water balance. Ecological Applications. 5: 362–385.

Neilson, R.P.; Pitelka, L.F.; Solomon, A.M.; Nathan, R.; Midgley, G.F.; Fragoso, J.M.V.; Lischke, H.; Thompson, K. 2005. Forecasting regional to global plant migration in response to climate change. Bioscience. 55: 749–759.

Nicotra, A.B.; Atkin, O.K.; Bonser, S.P.; Davidson, A.M.; Finnegan, E.J.; Mathesius, U.; Poot, P.; Purugganan, M.D.; Richards, C.L.; Valladares, F.; van Kleunen, M. 2010. Plant phenotypic plasticity in a changing climate. Trends in Plant Science. 15: 684–692.

Niinemets, Ü. 2010. A review of light interception in plant stands from leaf to canopy in different plant functional types and in species with varying shade tolerance. Ecological Research. 25: 693–714.

Niinemets, Ü.; Flexas, J.; Peñuelas, J. 2011. Evergreens favored by higher responsiveness to increased CO_2. Trends in Ecology and Evolution. 26: 136–142.

Niu, S.; Wan, S. 2008. Warming changes plant competitive hierarchy in a temperate steppe in northern China. Journal of Plant Ecology. 1: 103–110.

Norby, R.J.; Warren, J.M.; Iversen, C.M.; Medlyn, B.E.; McMurtrie, R.E. 2010. CO_2 enhancement of forest productivity constrained by limited nitrogen availability. Proceedings of the National Academy of Sciences of the United States of America. 107: 19368–19373.

Norby, R.J.; Zak, D.R. 2011. Ecological lessons from free-air CO_2 enrichment (FACE) experiments. Annual Review of Ecology Evolution and Systematics. 42: 181–203.

Norris, J.R.; Jackson, S.T.; Betancourt, J.L. 2006. Classification tree and minimum-volume ellipsoid analyses of the distribution of ponderosa pine in the western USA. Journal of Biogeography. 33: 342–360.

Norton, U.; Saetre, P.; Hooker, T.D.; Stark, J.M. 2011. Vegetation and moisture controls on soil carbon mineralization in semi-arid environments. Soil Science Society of America Journal. 76: 1038–1047.

Oren, R.; Ellsworth, D.S.; Johnsen, K.H.; Phillips, N.; Ewers, B.E.; Maier, C.; Schafer, K.V.R.; McCarthy, H.; Hendrey, G.; McNulty, S.G.; Katul, G.G. 2001. Soil fertility limits carbon sequestration by forest ecosystems in a CO_2-enriched atmosphere. Nature. 411: 469–472.

Ormrod, D.P.; Lesser, V.M.; Olszyk, D.M.; Tingey, D.T. 1999. Elevated temperature and carbon dioxide affect chlorophylls and carotenoids in Douglas-fir seedlings. International Journal of Plant Science. 160: 529–534.

Pabst , R.J.; Goslin, M.N.; Garman, S.L.; Spies, T.A. 2008. Calibrating and testing a gap model for simulating forest management in the Oregon Coast Range. Forest Ecology and Management. 256: 958–972.

Pacala, S.W.; Canham, C.D.; Silander, J.A. 1993. Forest models defined by field measurements: I. The design of a northeastern forest simulator. Canadian Journal of Forest Research. 23: 1980–1988.

Paine, R.T.; Tegner, M.J.; Johnson, E.A. 1998. Compounded perturbations yield ecological surprises. Ecosystems. 1: 535–545.

Pan, Y.; Melillo, J.M.; McGuire, A.D.; Kicklighter, D.W.; Pitelka, L.F.; Hibbard, K.; Pierce, L.L.; Running, S.W.; Ojima, D.S.; Parton, W.J.; Schimel, D.S.; other VEMAP members. 1998. Modeled responses of terrestrial ecosystems to elevated atmospheric CO_2: a comparison of simulations by the biogeochemistry models of the Vegetation/Ecosystem Modeling and Analysis Project (VEMAP). Oecologia. 114: 389–404.

Parmesan, C. 2006. Ecological and evolutionary responses to recent climate change. Annual Review of Ecology Evolution and Systematics. 37: 637–669.

Parmesan, C. 2007. Influences of species, latitudes and methodologies on estimates of phenological response to global warming. Global Change Biology. 13: 1860–1872.

Pastor, J.; Post, W.M. 1988. Response of northern forests to CO_2-induced climate change. Nature. 334: 55–58.

Pauchard, A.; Kueffer, C.; Dietz, H.; Daehler, C.C.; Alexander, J.; Edwards, P.J.; Arevalo, J.R.; Cavieres, L.A.; Guisan, A.; Haider, S.; Jakobs, G.; McDougall, K.; Millar, C.I.; Naylor, B.J.; Parks, C.G.; Rew, L.J.; Seipel, T. 2009. Ain't no mountain high enough: plant invasions reaching new elevations. Frontiers in Ecology and the Environment. 7: 479–486.

Pearson, R.G.; Dawson, T.P. 2003. Predicting the impacts of climate change on the distribution of species: are bioclimate envelope models useful? Global Ecology and Biogeography. 12: 361–371.

Pelto, M.S. 2006. The current disequilibrium of North Cascades glaciers. Hydrological Processes. 20: 769–779.

Peñuelas, J.; Estiarte, M. 1998. Can elevated CO_2 affect secondary metabolism and ecosystem function? Trends in Ecology and Evolution. 13: 20–24.

Perry, G.L.W.; Enright, N.J. 2006. Spatial modelling of vegetation change in dynamic landscapes: a review of methods and applications. Progress in Physical Geography. 30: 47–72.

Perry, D.A.; Hessburg, P.F.; Skinner, C.N.; Spies, T.A.; Stephens, S.L.; Taylor, A.H.; Franklin, J.F.; McComb, B.; Riegel, G. 2011. The ecology of mixed severity fire regimes in Washington, Oregon, and northern California. Forest Ecology and Management. 262: 703–717.

Peterson, D.L.; Millar, C.I.; Joyce, L.A.; Furniss, M.J.; Halofsky, J.E.; Neilson, R.P.; Morelli, T.L. 2011. Responding to climate change in national forests: a guidebook for developing adaptation options. Gen. Tech. Rep. PNW-GTR-855. Portland, OR: U.S. Department of Agriculture, Forest Service, Pacific Northwest Research Station. 109 p.

Peterson, D.W.; Peterson, D.L. 1994. Effects of climate on radial growth of subalpine conifers in the North Cascade Mountains. Canadian Journal of Forest Research. 24: 1921–1932.

Peterson, D.W.; Peterson, D.L. 2001. Mountain hemlock growth responds to climatic variability at annual and decadal time scales. Ecology. 82: 3330–3345.

Peterson, D.W.; Peterson, D.L.; Ettl, G.J. 2002. Growth responses of subalpine fir to climatic variability in the Pacific Northwest. Canadian Journal of Forest Research. 32: 1503–1517.

Petit, R.J.; Hampe, A. 2006. Some evolutionary consequences of being a tree. Annual Review of Ecology Evolution and Systematics. 37: 187–214.

Petit, R.J.; Hu, F.S.; Dick, C.W. 2008. Forests of the past: a window to future changes. Science. 320: 1450–1452.

Phillips, R.P.; Meier, I.C.; Bernhardt, E.S.; Grandy, A.S.; Wickings, K.; Finzi, A.C. 2012. Roots and fungi accelerate carbon and nitrogen cycling in forests exposed to elevated CO_2. Ecology Letters. 15: 1042–1049.

Pietsch, S.A.; Hasenauer, H.; Thornton, P.E. 2005. BGC-model parameters for tree species growing in central European forests. Forest Ecology and Management. 211: 264–295.

Plaut, J.A.; Yepez, E.A.; Hill, J.; Pangle, R.; Sperry, J.S.; Pockman, W.T.; McDowell, N.G. 2012. Hydraulic limits preceding mortality in a piñon-juniper woodland under experimental drought. Plant, Cell and Environment. 35: 1601–1617.

Polgar, C.A.; Primack, R.B. 2011. Leaf-out phenology of temperate woody plants: from trees to ecosystems. New Phytologist. 191: 926–941.

Raffa, K.F.; Aukema, B.H.; Bentz, B.J.; Carroll, A.L.; Hicke, J.A.; Turner, M.G.; Romme, W.H. 2008. Cross-scale drivers of natural disturbances prone to anthropogenic amplification: the dynamics of bark beetle eruptions. Bioscience. 58: 501–517.

Rahmstorf, S.; Schellnhuber, H.J. 2006. Der Klimawandel. Munich: Beck Verlag. 144 p.

Raich, J.W.; Potter, C.S.; Bhagwati, D. 2002. Interannual variability in global respiration, 1980–94. Global Change Biology. 8: 800–812.

Randall, D.A.; Wood, R.A.; Bony, S.; Colman, R.; Fichefet, T.; Fyfe, J.; Kattsov, V.; Pitman, A.; Shukla, J.; Srinivasan, J.; Stouffer, R.J.; Sumi, A.; Taylor, K.E. 2007. Climate models and their evaluation. In: Solomon, S.; Qin, D.; Manning, M.; Chen, Z.; Marquis, M.; Averyt, K.B.; Tignor, M.; Miller, H.L., eds. Climate change 2007: the physical science basis. Contribution of working group I to the fourth assessment report of the Intergovernmental Panel on Climate Change. Cambridge, United Kingdom and New York: Cambridge University Press. 589–662. Chapter 8.

Rathcke, B.; Lacey, E.P. 1985. Phenological patterns of terrestrial plants. Annual Review of Ecology and Systematics 16: 179–214.

Rau, B.M.; Johnson, D.W.; Blank, R.R.; Lucchesi, A.; Caldwell, T.G.; Schupp, E.W. 2011a. Transition from sagebrush steppe to annual grass (*Bromus tectorum*): influence on belowground carbon and nitrogen. Rangeland Ecology and Management. 64: 139–147.

Rau, B.M.; Johnson, D.W.; Blank, R.R.; Tausch, R.J.; Roundy, B.A.; Miller, R.F.; Caldwell, T.G.; Lucchesi, A. 2011b. Woodland expansion's influence on belowground carbon and nitrogen in the Great Basin U.S. Journal of Arid Environments. 75: 827–835.

Raupach, M.R.; Marland, G.; Ciais, P.; Le Quéré, C.; Canadell, J.G.; Klepper, G.; Field, C.B. 2007. Global and regional drivers of accelerating CO_2 emissions. Proceedings of the National Academy of Sciences of the United States of America. 104: 10288–10293.

Rehfeldt, G.E. 1988. Ecological genetics of *Pinus contorta* from the Rocky Mountains (USA)—a synthesis. Silvae Genetica. 37: 131–135.

Rehfeldt, G.E. 1989. Ecological adaptations in Douglas-fir (*Pseudotsuga menziesii* var. *glauca*)—a synthesis. Forest Ecology and Management. 28: 203–215.

Rehfeldt, G.E. 1994a. Adaptation of *Picea engelmannii* populations to the heterogeneous environments of the intermountain West. Canadian Journal of Botany. 72: 1197–1208.

Rehfeldt, G.E. 1994b. Genetic structure of western red cedar populations in the Interior West. Canadian Journal of Forest Research. 24: 670–680.

Rehfeldt, G.E. 1995. Genetic variation, climate models and the ecological genetics of *Larix occidentalis*. Forest Ecology and Management. 78: 21–37.

Rehfeldt, G.E.; Crookston, N.L.; Warwell, M.V.; Evans, J.S. 2006. Empirical analyses of plant-climate relationships for the western United States. International Journal of Plant Sciences. 167: 1123–1150.

Rehfeldt, G.E.; Ferguson, D.E.; Crookston, N.L. 2009. Aspen, climate, and sudden decline in western USA. Forest Ecology and Management. 258: 2353–2364.

Rehfeldt, G.E.; Hoff, R.J.; Steinhoff, R.J. 1984. Geographic patterns of genetic variation in *Pinus monticola*. Botanical Gazette. 145: 229–239.

Rehfeldt, G.E.; Wykoff, W.R.; Ying, C.C. 2001. Physiologic plasticity, evolution, and impacts of a changing climate on *Pinus contorta*. Climatic Change. 50: 355–376.

Reich, P.B.; Hobbie, S.E.; Lee, T.; Ellsworth, D.S.; West, J.B.; Tilman, D.; Knops, J.M.H.; Naeem, S.; Trost, J. 2006a. Nitrogen limitation constrains sustainability of ecosystem response to CO_2. Nature. 440: 922–925.

Reich, P.B.; Hungate, B.A.; Luo, Y. 2006b. Carbon-nitrogen interactions in terrestrial ecosystems in response to rising atmospheric carbon dioxide. Annual Review of Ecology Evolution and Systematics. 37: 611–636.

Reich, P.B.; Tilman, D.; Craine, J.; Ellsworth, D.; Tjoelker, M.G.; Knops, J.; Wedin, D.; Naeem, S.; Bahaudden, D.; Goth, J.; Bengtson, W.; Lee, T.D. 2001. Do species and functional groups differ in acquisition and use of C, N and water under varying atmospheric CO_2 and N availability regimes? A field test with 16 grassland species. New Phytologist. 150: 435–448.

Ribbens, E.; Silander, J.A.; Pacala, S.W. 1994. Seedling recruitment in forests: calibrating models to predict patterns of tree seedling dispersion. Ecology. 75: 1794–1806.

Rice, J.; Tredennick, A.; Joyce, L.A. 2012. Climate change on the Shoshone National Forest, Wyoming: a synthesis of past climate, climate projections, and ecosystem implications. Gen. Tech. Rep. RMRS-GTR-264. Fort Collins, CO: U.S. Department of Agriculture, Forest Service, Rocky Mountain Research Station. 60 p.

Rich, P.M.; Breshears, D.D.; White, A.B. 2008. Phenology of mixed wood-herbaceous ecosystems following extreme events: net and differential responses. Ecology. 89: 342–352.

Richards, J.H.; Caldwell, M.M. 1987. Hydraulic lift: substantial nocturnal water transport between soil layers by *Artemisia tridentatea* roots. Oecologia. 73: 486–489.

Richardson, S.J.; Allen, R.B.; Whitehead, D.; Carswell, F.E.; Ruscoe, W.A.; Platt, K.H. 2005. Climate and net carbon availability determine temporal patterns of seed production by *Nathofagus*. Ecology. 86: 972–981.

Ritchie, M.E.; Tilman, D.; Knops, J.M.H. 1998. Herbivore effects on plant and nitrogen dynamics in oak savanna. Ecology. 79: 165–177.

Robinson, D.C.E.; Beukema, S.J.; Greig, L.A. 2008. Vegetation models and climate change: workshop results. 50 p. Unpublished report by ESSA Technologies Ltd. On file with: U.S. Department of Agriculture, Forest Service, Western Wildland Environmental Threat Center, 3160 NE Third St., Prineville, OR 97754.

Robinson, E.A.; Ryan, G.D.; Newman, J.A. 2012. A meta-analytical review of the effects of elevated CO_2 on plant-arthropod interactions highlights the importance of interacting environmental and biological variables. New Phytologist. 194: 321–336.

Rogers, B.M. 2009. Potential impacts of climate change on vegetation distributions, carbon stocks and fire regimes in the U.S. Pacific Northwest. Corvallis, OR: Oregon State University. 89 p. M.S. thesis.

Rogers, B.M.; Neilson, R.P.; Drapek, R.; Lenihan, J.M.; Wells, J.R.; Bachelet, D.; Law, B.E. 2011. Impacts of climate change on fire regimes and carbon stocks of the U.S. Pacific Northwest. Journal of Geophysical Research. 116: G03037. doi:10.1029/2011JG001695.

Running, S.W.; Nemani, R.R. 1991. Regional hydrologic and carbon balance responses of forests resulting from potential climate change. Climatic Change. 19: 349–368.

Runyon, J.; Waring, R.H.; Goward, S.N.; Welles, J.M. 1994. Environmental limits on net primary production and light-use efficiency across the Oregon transect. Ecological Applications. 4: 226–237.

Rustad, L.E.; Campbell, J.L.; Marion, G.M.; Norby, R.J.; Mitchell, M.J.; Hartley, A.E.; Cornelissen, J.H.C.; Gurevitch, J. 2001. A meta-analysis of the response of soil respiration, net nitrogen mineralization, and aboveground plant growth to experimental ecosystem warming. Oecologia. 126: 543–562.

Ryan, M.G. 1991. Effects of climate change on plant respiration. Ecological Applications. 1: 157–167.

Salathé, E.P.; Mote, P.W.; Wiley, M.W. 2007. Review of scenario selection and downscaling methods for the assessment of climate change impacts on hydrology in the United States pacific northwest. International Journal of Climatology. 27: 1611–1621.

Saxe, H.; Cannell, M.G.R.; Johnsen, B.; Ryan, M.G.; Vourlitis, G. 2001. Tree and forest functioning in response to global warming. New Phytologist. 149: 369–399.

Scheller, R.M.; Mladenoff, D.J. 2007. An ecological classification of forest landscape simulation models: tools and strategies for understanding broad-scale forested ecosystems. Landscape Ecology. 22: 491–505.

Scheller, R.M.; Mladenoff, D.J. 2008. Simulated effects of climate change, fragmentation, and inter-specific competition on tree species migration in northern Wisconsin, USA. Climate Research. 36: 191–202.

Schimel, D.S.; Braswell, B.H.; Parton, W.J. 1997a. Equilibration of the terrestrial water, nitrogen, and carbon cycles. Proceedings of the National Academy of Sciences of the United States of America. 94: 8280–8283.

Schimel, D.S.; VEMAP participants; Braswell, B.H. 1997b. Continental scale variability in ecosystem processes: models, data, and the role of disturbance. Ecological Monographs. 67: 251–271.

Schlaepfer, D.R.; Lauenroth, W.K.; Bradford, J.B. 2011. Ecohydrological niche of sagebrush ecosystems. Ecohydrology. 5: 453–466.

Schlaepfer, D.R.; Lauenroth, W.K.; Bradford, J.B. 2012. Consequences of declining snow accumulation for water balance of mid-latitude dry regions. Global Change Biology. 18: 1988–1997.

Schleppi, P.; Bucher-Wallin, I.; Hagedorn, F.; Körner, C. 2012. Increased nitrate availability in the soil of a mixed mature temperate forest subjected to elevated CO_2 concentration (canopy FACE). Global Change Biology. 18: 757–768.

Scholes, R.J.; Archer, S.R. 1997. Tree-grass interactions in savannas. Annual Review of Ecology and Systematics. 28: 517–544.

Schreiner, E.G.; Krueger, K.A.; Houston, D.B.; Happe, P.J. 1996. Understory patch dynamics and ungulate herbivory in old-growth forests of Olympic National Park, Washington. Canadian Journal of Forest Research. 26: 255–265.

Schwinning, S.; Starr, B.I.; Ehleringer, J.R. 2003. Dominant cold desert plants do not partition warm season precipitation by event size. Oecologia. 136: 252–260.

Segurado, P.; Araújo, M.B. 2004. An evaluation of methods for modelling species distributions. Journal of Biogeography. 31: 1555–1568.

Seidl, R.; Spies, T.A.; Rammer, W.E.; Steel, A.; Pabst, R.J.; Olsen, K. 2012. Multi-scale drivers of spatial variation in old-growth forest carbon density disentangled with lidar and an individual-based landscape model. Ecosystems. 15: 1321–1335.

Selås, V.; Piovesan, G.; Adams, J.M.; Bernabei, M. 2002. Climatic factors controlling reproduction and growth of Norway spruce in southern Norway. Canadian Journal of Forest Research. 32: 217–225.

Shafer, S.L.; Bartlein, P.J.; Thompson, R.S. 2001. Potential changes in the distributions of western North America tree and shrub taxa under future climate scenarios. Ecosystems. 4: 200–215.

Shugart, H.H.; West, D.C. 1977. Development of an Appalachian deciduous forest succession model and its application to assessment of the impact of the chestnut blight. Journal of Environmental Management. 5: 161–179.

Simard, M.; Romme, W.H.; Griffin, J.M.; Turner, M.G. 2011. Do mountain pine beetle outbreaks change the probability of active crown fire in lodgepole pine forests? Ecological Monographs. 81: 3–24.

Sinclair, S.J.; White, M.D.; Newell, G.R. 2010. How useful are species distribution models for managing biodiversity under future climates? Ecology and Society. 15(1): 8. http://www.ecology andsociety.org/vol15/iss1/art8/.

Skelly, D.K.; Joseph, L.N.; Possingham, H.P.; Freidenburg, L.K.; Farrugia, T.J.; Kinnison, M.T.; Hendry, A.P. 2007. Evolutionary responses to climate change. Conservation Biology. 21: 1353–1355.

Sklar, F.H.; Hunsaker, C.T. 2001. The use and uncertainties of spatial data for landscape models: an overview with examples from the Florida Everglades. In: Hunsaker, C.T.; Goodchild, M.F.; Friedl, M.A.; Case, T.J., eds. Spatial uncertainty in ecology: implications for remote sensing and GIS applications. New York, NY: Springer-Verlag: 15–46. Chapter 2.

Smith, B.; Prentice, I.C.; Sykes, M.T. 2001. Representation of vegetation dynamics in the modelling of terrestrial ecosystems: comparing two contrasting approaches within European climate space. Global Ecology and Biogeography. 10: 621–637.

Smith, S.D.; Huxman, T.E.; Zitzer, S.F.; Charlet, T.N.; Houseman, D.C.; Coleman, J.S.; Fenstermaker, L.K.; Seeman, J.R.; Nowak, R.S. 2000. Elevated CO_2 increases productivity and invasive species success in an arid ecosystem. Nature. 408: 79–82.

Smith, W.K.; Germino, M.J.; Hancock, T.E.; Johnson, D.M. 2003. Another perspective on altitudinal limits of alpine timberlines. Tree Physiology. 23: 1101–1112.

Solomon, A.M. 1986. Transient response of forests to CO_2-induced climatic change: simulation modeling experiments in eastern North America. Oecologia. 68: 567–580.

Soulé, P.T.; Knapp, P.A. 2007. Topoedaphic and morphological complexity of foliar damage and mortality within western juniper (*Juniperus occidentalis* var. *occidentalis*) woodlands following an extreme meteorological event. Journal of Biogeography. 34: 1927–1937.

Spies, T.A.; Giesen, T.W.; Swanson, F.J.; Franklin, J.F.; Lach, D.; Johnson, K.N. 2010. Climate change adaptation strategies for federal forests of the Pacific Northwest, USA: ecological, policy, and socio-economic perspectives. Landscape Ecology. 25: 1185–1199.

Sprugel, D.G.; Brooks, J.R.; Hinckley, T.M. 1996. Effects of light on shoot geometry and needle morphology in *Abies amabilis*. Tree Physiology. 16: 91–98.

Stephens, S.L.; Millar, C.I.; Collins, B.M. 2010. Operational approaches to managing forests of the future in Mediterranean regions within a context of changing climates. Environmental Research Letters. 5: 024003. doi:10.1088/1748-9326/5/2/024003.

Stewart, I.T. 2009. Changes in snowpack and snowmelt runoff for key mountain regions. Hydrological Processes. 23: 78–94.

Stewart, I.T.; Cayan, D.R.; Dettinger, M.D. 2004. Changes in snowmelt runoff timing in western North America under a 'business as usual' climate change scenario. Climatic Change. 62: 217–232.

Stiling, P.; Cornelissen, T. 2007. How does elevated carbon dioxide (CO_2) affect plant-herbivore interactions? A field experiment and meta-analysis of CO_2-mediated changes on plant chemistry and herbivore performance. Global Change Biology. 13: 1823–1842.

Stueve, K.M.; Cerney, D.L.; Rochefort, R.M.; Kurth, L.L. 2009. Post-fire tree establishment patterns at the alpine treeline ecotone: Mount Rainier National Park, Washington, USA. Journal of Vegetation Science. 20: 107–120.

Sturrock, R.N.; Frankel, S.J.; Brown, A.V.; Hennon, P.E.; Kliejunas, J.T.; Lewis, K.J.; Worrall, J.J.; Woods, A.J. 2011. Climate change and forest diseases. Plant Pathology. 60: 133–149.

Sultan, S.E. 2000. Phenotypic plasticity for plant development, function and life history. Trends in Plant Science. 5: 537–542.

Suttle, K.B.; Thomsen, M.A.; Power, M.E. 2007. Species interactions reverse grassland responses to changing climate. Science. 315: 640–642.

Svenning, J.C.; Skov, F. 2004. Limited filling of the potential range in European tree species. Ecology Letters. 7: 565–573.

Swanston, C.; Janowiak, M., eds. 2012. Forest adaptation resources: climate change tools and approaches for land managers. Gen. Tech. Rep. NRS-GTR-87. Newtown Square, PA: U.S. Department of Agriculture, Forest Service, Northern Research Station. 121 p.

Swetnam, T.W.; Allen, C.D.; Betancourt, J.L. 1999. Applied historical ecology: using the past to manage for the future. Ecological Applications. 9: 1189–1206.

Tans, P.; Keeling, R. 2013. Data from U.S. Department of Commerce, National Oceanic and Atmospheric Administration. http://www.esrl.noaa.gov/gmd/ccgg/trends/. (February 2013).

Taylor, A.H. 1995. Forest expansion and climate change in the mountain hemlock (*Tsuga mertensiana*) zone, Lassen Volcanic National Park, California, U.S.A. Arctic and Alpine Research. 27: 207–216.

Taylor, A.H.; Trouet, V.; Skinner, C.N. 2008. Climatic influences on fire regimes in montane forests of the southern Cascades, California, USA. International Journal of Wildland Fire. 17: 60–71.

Teskey, R.O.; Hinckley, T.M.; Grier, C.C. 1984. Temperature-induced change in the water relations of *Abies amabilis* (Dougl.) Forbes. Plant Physiology. 74: 77–80.

Thonicke, K.; Venevsky, S.; Sitch, S.; Cramer, W. 2001. The role of fire disturbance for global vegetation dynamics: coupling fire into a Dynamic Global Vegetation Model. Global Ecology and Biogeography. 10: 661–677.

Thuiller, W.; Albert, C.; Araújo, M.B.; Berry, P.M.; Cabeza, M.; Guisan, A.; Hickler, T.; Midgely, G.F.; Paterson, J.; Schurr, F.M.; Sykes, M.T.; Zimmermann, N.E. 2008. Predicting global change impacts on plant species' distributions: future challenges. Perspectives in Plant Ecology Evolution and Systematics. 9: 137–152.

Thuiller, W.; Brotons, L.; Araújo, M.B.; Lavorel, S. 2004. Effects of restricting environmental range of data to project current and future species distributions. Ecography. 27: 165–172.

Tiedemann, A.R.; Klemmedson, J.O. 1986a. Long-term effects of mesquite removal on soil characteristics: I. Nutrients and bulk density. Soil Science Society of America Journal. 50: 472–475.

Tiedemann, A.R.; Klemmedson, J.O. 1986b. Long-term effects of mesquite removal on soil characteristics: II. Nutrient availability. Soil Science Society of America Journal. 50: 476–480.

Tilman, D. 1982. Resource competition and community structure. Monographs in Population Biology 17. Princeton, NJ: Princeton University Press. 296 p.

Tilman, D. 2004. Niche tradeoffs, neutrality, and community structure: a stochastic theory of resource competition, invasion, and community assembly. Proceedings of the National Academy of Sciences of the United States of America. 101: 10854–10861.

Tomback, D.F.; Arno, S.F.; Keane, R.E. 2001. Whitebark pine communities: ecology and communities. Washington, DC: Island Press. 328 p.

Tranquillini, W. 1979. Physiological ecology of the alpine timberline: tree existence at high altitudes with species reference to the European Alps (Ecological Studies 31). Berlin: Springer-Verlag. 137 p.

Trenberth, K.E.; Jones, P.D.; Ambenje, P.; Bojariu, R.; Easterling, D.; Klein Tank, A.; Parker, D.; Rahimzadeh, F.; Renwick, J.A.; Rusticucci, M.; Soden, B.; Zhai, P. 2007. Observations: surface and atmospheric climatic change. In: Solomon, S.; Qin, D.; Manning, M.; Chen, Z.; Marquis, M.; Averyt, K.B.; Tignor, M.; Miller, H.L., eds. Climate change 2007: the physical science basis. Contribution of working group I to the fourth assessment report of the Intergovernmental Panel on Climate Change. Cambridge, United Kingdom and New York: Cambridge University Press: SM. 3–1–3–11.

Trouet, V.; Taylor, A.H.; Wahl, E.R.; Skinner, C.N.; Stephens, S.L. 2010. Fire-climate interactions in the American West since 1400 CE. Geophysical Research Letters. 37: L04702. doi:10.1029/2009GL041695.

Tylianakis, J.M.; Didham, R.K.; Bascompte, J.; Wardle, D.A. 2008. Global change and species interactions in terrestrial ecosystems. Ecology Letters. 11: 1351–1363.

U.S. Department of Agriculture. 2010. Strategic plan, FY 2010–2015. 21 p. http://www.ocfo.usda.gov/usdasp/sp2010/sp2010.pdf. (April 2012).

U.S. Department of Agriculture, Forest Service [USDA FS]. 2010. National roadmap for responding to climate change. http://www.fs.fed.us/climatechange/pdf/roadmap.pdf. (April 2012).

U.S. Department of the Interior [USDI]. 2009. Addressing the impacts of climate change on America's water, land, and other natural and cultural resources. Secretarial Order No. 3289. September 19, 2009.

Valladares, F.; Gianoli, E.; Gomez, J.M. 2007. Ecological limits to plant phenotypic plasticity. New Phytologist. 176: 749–763.

Van Cleve, K.; Oechel, W.C.; Hom, J.L. 1990. Response of black spruce (*Picea mariana*) ecosystems to soil temperature modification in interior Alaska. Canadian Journal of Forest Research. 20: 1530–1535.

van Mantgem, P.J.; Stephenson, N.L. 2007. Apparent climatically induced increase of tree mortality rates in a temperate forest. Ecology Letters. 10: 909–916.

van Mantgem, P.J.; Stephenson, N.L.; Byrne, J.C.; Daniels, L.D.; Franklin, J.F.; Fulé, P.Z.; Harmon, M.E.; Larson, A.J.; Smith, J.M.; Taylor, A.H.; Veblen, T.T. 2009. Widespread increase of tree mortality rates in the western United States. Science. 323: 521–524.

Verboom, J.; Wamelink, G.W.W. 2005. Spatial modelling in landscape ecology. In: Wiens, J.A.; Moss, M.R., eds. Issues and perspectives in landscape ecology. Greeley, CO: International Association for Landscape Ecology, Pioneer Press: 79–89.

Vitousek, P.M.; Aber, J.D.; Howarth, R.W.; Likens, G.E.; Matson, P.A.; Schindler, D.W.; Schlesinger, W.H.; Tilman, D.G. 1997. Human alteration of the global nitrogen cycle: sources and consequences. Ecological Applications. 7: 737–750.

Vose, J.M.; Peterson, D.L.; Patel-Weynand, T., eds. 2012. Effects of climatic variability and change on forest ecosystems: a comprehensive science synthesis for the U.S. forest sector. Gen. Tech. Rep. PNW-GTR-870. Portland, OR: U.S. Department of Agriculture, Forest Service, Pacific Northwest Research Station. 265 p.

Walck, J.L.; Hidayati, S.N.; Dixon, K.W.; Thompson, K.; Poschlod, P. 2011. Climate change and plant regeneration from seed. Global Change Biology. 17: 2145–2161.

Walther, G.R. 2010. Community and ecosystem responses to recent climate change. Philosophical Transactions of the Royal Society B Biological Sciences. 365: 2019–2024.

Walther, G.R.; Beissner, S.; Burga, C.A. 2005. Trends in the upward shift of alpine plants. Journal of Vegetation Science. 16: 541–548.

Waring, R.H.; Franklin, J.F. 1979. Evergreen coniferous forests of the Pacific Northwest. Science. 204: 1380–1386.

Waring, R.H.; Running, S.W. 1998. Forest ecosystems: analysis at multiple scales. 2nd edition. San Diego, CA: Academic Press. 370 p.

Way, D.A.; LaDeau, S.L.; McCarthy, H.R.; Clark, J.S.; Oren, R.; Finzi, A.C.; Jackson, R.B. 2010. Greater seed production in elevated CO_2 is not accompanied by reduced seed quality in *Pinus taeda* L. Global Change Biology.

Pacific Northwest Research Station	
Web site	http://www.fs.fed.us/pnw
Telephone	(503) 808-2592
Publication requests	(503) 808-2138
FAX	(503) 808-2130
E-mail	pnw_pnwpubs@fs.fed.us
Mailing address	Publications Distribution Pacific Northwest Research Station P.O. Box 3890 Portland, OR 97208-3890

U.S. Department of Agriculture
Pacific Northwest Research Station
1220 SW 3rd Avenue.
P.O. Box 3890
Portland, OR 97204

Official Business
Penalty for Private Use, $300

www.ingramcontent.com/pod-product-compliance
Lightning Source LLC
Chambersburg PA
CBHW080247290526
45790CB00005B/1728